P9-ELR-506

# THE FICTIONS OF ANITA BROOKNER

# The Fictions of Anita Brookner

## Illusions of Romance

JOHN SKINNER

*Senior Lecturer in English*
*University of Turku, Finland*

St. Martin's Press   New York

First published in the United States of America in 1992

Printed in Hong Kong

ISBN 0–312–06862–X

Library of Congress Cataloging-in-Publication Data
Skinner, John, 1945–
The fictions of Anita Brookner : illusions of romance / John
Skinner.
p.   cm.
Includes bibliographical references and index.
ISBN 0–312–06862–X
1. Brookner, Anita—Criticism and interpretation.   I. Title.
PR6052.R5816Z88   1992
823'.914—dc20                                          91–4989
                                                         CIP

for Carla

# Contents

# List of Abbreviations

The titles of Anita Brookner's novels in the index are abbreviated as follows:

SL      *A Start in Life*
P       *Providence*
LM     *Look at Me*
HL     *Hotel du Lac*
FF     *Family and Friends*
M      *A Misalliance*
FFE    *A Friend from England*
L       *Latecomers*
LP     *Lewis Percy*

# Acknowledgements

The author and publisher are grateful to Dr Brookner, Jonathan Cape Ltd and Pantheon Books for permission to quote from the novels discussed. The present study is unauthorized.

# 1

# Introduction

Among recent or contemporary novelists writing in English, Brookner is arguably one of the most significant not yet to be the subject of a full-length study; the present account is obviously an attempt to fill this gap. The word 'arguably' in this context is no mere rhetorical filler, since reactions to Brookner – positive or negative – have often been outspoken. There are even signs of a growing polarization among critics: whilst some voices continue to make impressive claims for her strength and originality, others have become increasingly hostile or dismissive. Such trends are most obvious in literary reviews, which make inevitably subjective but frequently arbitrary evaluations of her novels, even as they wilfully attempt to relate the novelist to other writers past and present.

In the most negative judgements, Brookner's nine novels of the eighties have been castigated (and only occasionally commended) for their 'minimalism'; they have also been more unreservedly attacked for their formulaic quality, their weak sentimentality and – more ominously – their close proximity to the conventions of Harlequin romance. Scathing opinions have been delivered on both sides of the Atlantic, although two of the most notorious attacks on Brookner have been British and (predictably) male.

In a BBC radio discussion between Anthony Burgess and Gore Vidal (*Horizon*, 9 November 1989), Burgess characterized the ideal candidate for Britain's Booker Prize as being a 'minimalist' novel dealing with 'menstrual cramps in a hotel in Switzerland', an obvious reference to Brookner's *Hotel du Lac*. Such comments do not perhaps qualify as literary criticism proper – their author seemed unduly tired and emotional – but they nevertheless suggest an emphatic male hostility towards a certain kind of 'woman's novel'.

An equally crude reaction to Brookner appeared in Peter Kemp's hostile review of *Lewis Percy* under the heading, 'The mouse that whinged' (*Sunday Times*, 27 August 1989). More detailed discussion of Kemp's critical naivety is deferred to the appropriate place;

1

although, at a glance, the article might not seem worthy of such attention, inviting dismissal as a hack contribution of column inches to a Sunday newspaper. But Kemp's strangely aggressive tone, with his absurd characterization of Brookner as the novelist of 'migraines, flushes and female malaises', or his curious desire to 'stamp out' *Lewis Percy*, constitutes a kind of 'verbal harassment' masking who knows what feelings of male insecurity: one may only wonder which *inches* of whose *column* are in jeopardy. More speculatively, one might also suggest that no novelist able to provoke such an intemperate outburst could be entirely unworthy of serious critical attention.

Positive reactions to Brookner happily remain in a clear majority, but most of these do not go far to explain her significance and appeal. The only extensive attention the novelist has received to date occurs in Manini Samarth's unpublished doctoral dissertation, and in isolated chapters of books by Olga Kenyon and Patricia Waugh.

Thus, in her account of 'the internalized narrative' in Brookner and Desai (1987), Samarth examines contrasting examples of a novelist's evolving sense of selfhood as reflected in the persona of her female protagonist. If Desai's lyricism celebrates an ultimate fusion of self with society through a process of 'epiphanic insight', Brookner's ironic novels reflect precisely the failure to achieve this form of synthesis. Samarth's categorization of both kinds of novel as female existentialist fiction suggests a critical respect not conspicuous in either Burgess or Kemp; her conclusion that existentialism, like every socio-political tradition, includes its gender prerogatives obviously relates her thesis to the two earlier essays on Brookner.

The first of these appears in Olga Kenyon's *Women Novelists Today* (1988), with its attempt to define a 'tradition' of women's writing in Britain that has emerged since the 1960's: the short account of Brookner follows chapters on such representative figures as Murdoch, Byatt, Drabble, Weldon and Figes.

Kenyon sees Brookner as a novelist skilfully able to represent 'the social frustrations and intimate thought processes of gifted undervalued women' (149), illustrating her thesis with readings of *Hotel du Lac* and *Family and Friends*. Particularly suggestive is Kenyon's attempt to regard Brookner's relation to the popular romance as one of self-conscious adaptation rather than slavish imitation; and her perhaps tendentious, but well-argued, conclusion that Brookner is feminist for 'viewing her protagonists' nineteenth-century predicaments with twentieth-century awareness' (162).

The most rigorous analysis of Brookner to date, however, appears in Patricia Waugh's ambitious and stimulating study, *Feminine Fictions: revisiting the postmodern* (1989). After examining the postmodern tendency to deconstruct the subject, even as contemporary femininism is attempting to construct one, Waugh goes on to discuss the implications of feminist psychoanalysis for theories of modern fiction. She situates Brookner convincingly within a group of post-war women writers (including Drabble, Plath, Tyler and Paley), whom she sees as offering 'significant, though often unobtrusive, formal innovations', and challenging the restrictive definitions of 'realist', 'modernist', 'postmodernist' etc. presupposed by the 'Liberal Tradition'.

Waugh concentrates on Brookner's first four novels, and her sensitive reading of *Hotel du Lac* stresses Edith's 'unresolved need of fear and connection' together with her 'obsession with denial and control of emotional need' (142). Waugh's thematic approach may occasionally seem reductive ('all of Brookner's novels explore the infantilizing effects of family life on women', 145), but her thesis is generally convincing.

In the absence of further critical accounts, the serious student of Brookner is particularly grateful for three substantial and rewarding personal interviews: with John Haffenden in *The Literary Review* (September 1984), Shusha Guppy in *The Paris Review* (Autumn, 1987) and Olga Kenyon in an anthology entitled *Women Writers Talk* (1989) – the latter a companion volume to the critical study mentioned briefly above. All three interviews are frequently quoted in the present study, but acquire particular prominence with the discussion of fiction and autobiography in Chapter 5.

          *                    *                    *

No attempt is made to mediate between the sharply conflicting responses to Brookner outlined here, although even such a brief account suggests a marked ambivalence regarding her significance as a writer. The same kind of uncertainty is also apparent, moreover, in attempts to relate Brookner to other writers – or to place her within a literary tradition – although critical opinion on this point is not so blatantly (or distressingly) gender bound.

The wide range of comparisons and analogies on offer may be conveniently reduced to four broad groupings: the French literary classics – particularly the eighteenth century moral tale, certain major English classics from each side of the Atlantic, a number of contemporary women's writers, and the literary underworld of the popular romance. I shall briefly consider each of these categories.

Critics answering the call of duty have, among conventional regurgitations of plot, related Brookner's first two books to French literary models. Some exceeding this call have reinforced their insights with Brookner's own comments to Haffenden: the novelist accepted this interviewer's characterization of *A Start in Life* and *Providence* as 'critiques of other fictions' – Balzac's *Eugénie Grandet* and Constant's *Adolphe*, respectively (Haffenden, 27). Brookner also reveals a familiarity with Voltaire, Diderot, Flaubert, Zola and Colette, although her greatest admiration seems reserved for Proust (as a writer) and Stendhal (as a man). In a later interview (Kenyon, 1989, 22), Brookner quotes the remark 'You write French books don't you?' as '[t]he most pertinent criticism I've had from a male reader'.

A fuller account of French models and influences is deferred to Chapter 1 ('The French Connection'), although two comments may be offered at once. Firstly, Brookner's detractors have sometimes claimed that parallels of this kind are merely evidence of a pseudo-profundity; they represent a strategy by the author to suggest connections between her own writing and 'the French classic tradition of finespun psychological and emotional analysis' (Kemp, 1989). In a broader perspective, however, it is ironic that French critics generally make no mention of a French tradition, and typically identify Brookner as solidly English: a reviewer of *Look at Me*, for example, related its author to 'la belle lignée de ces chères romancières anglaises: Charlotte Brontë, Katherine Mansfield, Virginia Woolf' (Bott, 1986); even more strikingly, *Latecomers* was regarded as belonging to 'la plus pure tradition du roman psychologique anglais' (Jordis, 1989).[1]

Among English reviewers, however, other classic authors are mentioned far more frequently than any of the above: two of these are English – Austen and Dickens – and two American – Wharton and James. Austen's novels are sometimes taken to exemplify the finely wrought but restricted writing against which Brookner's fiction may be measured. More originally, the American novelist David Leavitt seemed to define Brookner by contrast: without explicitly naming Austen, he evoked the figure of a 'lady-like chronicler of provincial mores and petite social interactions' (1989, 3), warning us that Brookner – with her 'insistent, even brutal explorations of power and inequity' – is quite a different proposition (Leavitt, 1989). But so, in fact, is Austen, and for much the same kinds of reason.

Dickens, on the other hand, has a deeper personal significance for Brookner. She makes a number of passing references to Trollope, but it is Dickens who is virtually enshrined in her own childhood mythology. All three major interviews contain the anecdote of the novelist's emigré father insisting on an extensive reading of Dickens, so that his daughter could learn what the English were really like; all three sources also pay tribute to Dickens's anger and 'indignation' at the 'unfairness of things'.

Links with Wharton and James have been more frequently proposed by American reviewers: the analogies between *Lewis Percy* and *Ethan Frome* or *The Age of Innocence* are clearly encouraged by the fact that Brookner's protagonist actually reads these novels. Comparisons with James are invited by several obvious textual parallels, in addition to more diffuse thematic or stylistic echoes. Thus, the cultural ambivalence of Kitty Maule in *Providence* may be compared to that of Hyacinth Robinson in *The Princess Casamassima*; Edith Hope's process of speculation about fellow guests in *Hotel du Lac* recalls similar operations in *What Maisie Knew* or *The Sacred Fount*. Brookner herself, moreover, has discussed Wharton and James at some length, referring to the theme of innocence in *Portrait of a Lady* and *The House of Mirth* (Guppy, 159).

The English and American traditions are neatly conflated (as they often were by James himself) in a generous review of *Latecomers* by John Updike. Within the same paragraph, Updike praises the 'lucid, balanced sentences that owe something to the scrupulous qualifications and dry moral vigilance of Henry James' but also comments wryly on Brookner's Englishness:

> She is, in the English tradition, a thoroughly social novelist, for whom there lies beyond the human spectacle nothing but death and scenery, . . . . (Updike, 1989)

I have found the combined influence of Austen, Dickens and James particularly noticeable in *A Friend from England*, and have attempted to develop these parallels in Chapter 3.

Contemporary novelists compared with Brookner include Margaret Drabble, Jean Rhys and – most insistently – Barbara Pym. The first two analogies are based on vague or tenuous thematic links: like Drabble, Brookner is seen as exploring how the 'modern woman' can reconcile 'emotional freedom with existential need'; like Rhys, she is found to portray the 'extreme isolation of a type of heroine one might describe as a female dandy, a deracinated woman' (Eberstadt, 1987). The comparison with Pym is a more complicated issue, not least for the relative frequency with which it is advanced.

One American reviewer thus writes of Brookner achieving the 'subtlety and breadth of the best novels of manners', a genre which she has inherited from Jane Austen and Barbara Pym (James, 1985); another suggests that the 'wit, detachment and gentle spinsters' of *Providence* seem drawn from Barbara Pym territory. Even Ann Tyler – sometimes regarded as a rough American equivalent of Brookner – develops the analogy with Pym ('less because of style, one supposes, than because of her cast of players') in a review of *Hotel du Lac* (Tyler, 1985). The tendency to equate Brookner with Pym may be exaggerated, and seems roughly proportionate to the critical emphasis placed on *Providence*. The relation between the two authors is therefore discussed more fully with reference to this novel.

I limit myself at this point, however, to questioning attempts to endow Brookner with the same quintessentially English insider status as Pym. Referring to her family's central European origins, Brookner has repeatedly emphasized her sense of marginality and alienation in England. Her predominantly female protagonists, too, are mentally, if not also ethnically, outsiders. It goes without saying that the major 'foreign writers' of the early twentieth century – one need look no further than Conrad or Joyce – did not attempt to write domestic novels of (English) manners. The activity is not an appropriate one for Brookner either. It may be admitted, however, that the novelist occasionally seems uncertain in her aims: stylistically, she will try to write like an insider – and comparisons with Pym or Austen are thus not entirely unfounded – but in effect she remains an alien. One reviewer stumbled on a shrewd insight, with a passing suggestion that Frances Hinton (*Look at Me*) rather than her creator would become 'a novelist like Barbara Pym' (Talafiero, 1984).

Brookner's ambivalent status may incidentally provide some justification for the American tendency to identify her with Wharton and James, although American critics understandably remain less aware of the writer's sense of alienation in England. The difficulty of 'defining' Brookner might also go some way to explaining the aggression of a critic like Kemp; could it be an expression of his uncertainty in his own attempts to place her?

Kemp has also drawn unflattering comparisons between Brookner and the popular romance. Such suggestions are by no means original, and two reviews of *Hotel du Lac* treated the novel as an example of the kind of fiction it might be thought of as subverting. Robert Jones (1985) thus developed analogies with Victoria Holt, Mary Stuart and Barbara Cartland, exculpating all of these writers, but castigating Brookner, who 'mask[ed] our most sentimental instincts in an aura of seriousness'. The novel 'pander[ed] to the sentimentality of every undergraduate majoring in English literature: to find a Leonard to play to one's Virginia'. For another reviewer, *Hotel du Lac* was merely a 'Harlequin Romance for highbrows' (Bayles, 1985).

The question of Brookner's links with the romance novel is discussed in greater detail with reference to *Hotel du Lac* and *Lewis Percy*. It may be emphasized here, however, that the nine novels may neither be crudely equated, nor yet totally divorced, from this kind of fiction. Brookner herself admits some familiarity with the genre, but makes a careful distinction between 'Romance novels' and 'Romantic novels':

> Romance novels are formula novels. I have read some and they seem to be writing about a different species. The true Romantic novel is about delayed happiness, and the pilgrimage you go through to get that imagined happiness. In the genuine Romantic novel there is confrontation with truth and in the 'romance' novel a similar confrontation with a surrogate, plastic version of the truth. (Guppy, 161)

The distinction may not be so simple, and one would wish to point out, for example, that 'plastic imitations' – not least in modern and sophisticated technologies of the word – are often extremely convincing. One might also question the implication that the literary authenticity of a narrative precludes a happy resolution, a position that reflects all too clearly Brookner's personal brand of determinism.

If the difference between Brookner and Mills-and-Boon cannot be satisfactorily explained in terms of a dualism confronting 'genuine articles' and 'plastic imitations', there are fortunately more subtle forms of relationship. Brookner's relation with Harlequin romance is a parodic one, and the precise nature of this connection is reflected in current theoretical discussion of literary parody.

Linda Hutcheon has argued in her *Theory of Parody* (1985) for a definition of the latter term which moves beyond the conventional mockery or ridicule of the 'target text'. Returning to the etymological root of *parodia* – 'counter-song' – she points out that the Greek prefix *para* not only means 'counter' or 'against' but also 'beside', and 'therefore there is a suggestion of an accord or intimacy instead of a contrast' (32).

Hutcheon's suggestion bears an interesting similarity to a concept previously discussed by Wolfgang Iser. Iser writes discerningly in *The Act of Reading* (1978) of some literary works being situated 'on the edge or just beyond a prevalent thought system' (73), rather than in any fundamental opposition to it. This is, for example, the position of such a 'classic parody' as *Tristram Shandy* in relation to the mainstream novel, or even *Don Quixote* to the novel of chivalry. If the concept of a 'thought system' may seem excessive in the context of Barbara Cartland or Georgette Heyer, with the substitution of some less intellectually loaded term – 'sexual ideology' perhaps – the analogy with Brookner nonetheless remains valid.

But even such tangential associations with romance may do Brookner little service. 'Novel' and 'romance' are not simply neutral poles on some mythical fictional continuum: if novel – in common critical coinage – will cover many things, romance – in most literary courts – is in need of special pleading. I shall avoid such procedures here, however, by refusing to regard Brookner's links with popular romance – any more than I would those of Lawrence or James – as reducing her value and interest as a writer.

*          *          *

I turn instead to Brookner's impressive intellectual background. Before writing her first novel, she already enjoyed an international reputation as an art critic, and was the author of four full-length studies: three on individual artists – Watteau, Greuze and Jacques-Louis David – and the fourth consisting of a series of essays in French art criticism, published under the title *The Genius of the Future*. Brookner's characteristic fictional technique of iconographic allusion demands some brief reference to this earlier scholarly activity.

Of the four monographs, the first and last are the most interesting in the present context. *Greuze* (1972), subtitled 'The rise and fall of an eighteenth-century phenomenon' is significant for its comments on *sensibilité*, particularly in its literary manifestations. The author discusses both the French novel and the 'conte moral', the traditions underpinning *A Start in Life* and *Providence*, respectively, and concludes with the summary judgement:

> The embryo of the eighteenth-century novel in France was the high-flown and idealized love story; in England it was the edifying religious tract. (Greuze, 21)

It is a view which privileges Richardson over Fielding, although in one aspect – woman's situation through marriage – Richardson and the French tradition are close. Thus, of Julie in Rousseau's *La Nouvelle Héloïse*, Brookner remarks:

> Marriage, in addition to providing her with her full stature as a woman, has brought her new moral distinction (fundamentally the same sentiment as that which clogs the second part of *Pamela*). (22)

Brookner might actually be considered a specialist of the modern 'idealized love story' (albeit one-sided and unhappy), whilst *Hotel du Lac* – of all the novels – is the most thoroughgoing study of woman's relative status before and after marriage.

*Greuze* began, incidentally, as a doctoral dissertation ('I lived very happily in Paris on $5 a week – for three years while writing my thesis on Greuze'; Kenyon, 10); and Brookner's reminiscences inevitably recall the situation of Ruth Weiss in *A Start in Life*.

*The Genius of the Future*, in turn, is based on a course in French art criticism first given at London's Courtauld Institute, and later 'escalated' into six of the Slade lectures in Cambridge, where Brookner was Visiting Professor in 1967–8. The essays in the book discuss Diderot, Stendhal, Baudelaire, Zola, the brothers Goncourt and Huysmans. Both Zola in *L'Oeuvre* (1886), and the brothers Goncourt in *Manette Salomon* (1867), incorporated their criticism in novels about artists; and in Brookner's fiction, too, artistic criteria play a significant role, culminating in the dominant structuring principle accorded to iconography in *A Misalliance* and *Family and Friends*.

\*　　　　　\*　　　　　\*

In the early eighties Brookner also wrote extensively for the *Times*

*Literary Supplement* on topics directly related to her fiction:[2] from the period immediately preceding *A Start in Life* and *Providence* there is, for example, a long and informative review essay on *Deliberate Regression* – Robert Harbison's indictment of Romantic mythologies. Her quotation from Madame de Stael's *Delphine*: 'Il ne faut à une femme, pour être heureuse, que la certitude d'être aimée' (*TLS*, 14 March 1980) is a sentiment echoed by romantic novelist Edith Hope in *Hotel du Lac*, and reiterated by the author herself in a revealing comment to Olga Kenyon:

> Romanticism is not just a mode; it literally eats into every life. Women will never get rid of just waiting for the right man. (Kenyon 1989, 15)

The operative words are probably 'eats into', with their connotations of blight or cancer, and Brookner refers elsewhere to the common cliché of the 'incurable romantic', an etiology that will invariably underly her fiction.

Elsewhere, Brookner discusses at length two of the great French romantic heroes: Stendhal and Berlioz. Reviewing Robert Alter's biography of the former (*TLS*, 30 May 1980), she comments on various social, economic and even physical disadvantages which conspired against the novelist from his early years:

> He was an unlikely candidate for the pursuit of happiness. *A narrow and confined childhood*, the eternal need to earn money and position and favour, a stocky and graceless body (even in his twenties), . . . no home but a chosen place of exile, and *a lack of true worldliness* for which he strove furiously to compensate by measuring up to the rules of the game, even when no game was being played. (my emphasis)

Read together with certain references to Stendhal in her sometimes disarmingly candid interviews, Brookner's comments suggest unusually powerful sympathies and affinities. Such sentiments would go some way towards explaining the author's simultaneous admiration for Stendhal and reservations towards most other Romantics:

> If Stendhal joins up at all with the more standard Romantic dreamers it is because he shares with them the fantasy of the

supreme emotional adventure. If he surpasses them, it is because
he knows how to convince us, by extraordinary means, that this
is actually taking place. (*TLS*, 30 May 1980)

In his apparently successful negotiation of the 'supreme emotional
adventure', Stendhal, the great illusionist, perhaps achieves what
Brookner heroines can never attain, and what their creator could not
even aspire to.

In 1982, Brookner reviewed Peter Raby's *Fair Ophelia: A Life
of Harriet Smithson Berlioz*. The composer himself is an almost
archetypal Romantic hero; so much so, that when Kitty Maule
has misgivings about teaching Constant's *Adolphe*, she momentarily considers replacing this text with Berlioz's *Memoirs*. The
most revealing part of Brookner's review, however, is her theory
of Berlioz, the creative artist:

> His 'prodigieuse aptitude au bonheur', unexpectedly frustrated
> of fulfilment in love, or perhaps bored with the littleness of
> fulfilment, went instead into the creation of great works. (*TLS*,
> 12 December 1982)

She refers to this process as a kind of conversion hysteria, the very
phrase she had used with Haffenden (26) to describe the 'perverse
energy' that produced her own novels.

But if Brookner's scholarly and critical activity left various traces
on her new career as a novelist, many years of practical involvement
with art may in turn be responsible for a characteristic emphasis on plastic form. Brookner's plots – formulaic or not – often
seem less indebted to any deep metaphoric structures, than to
quasi-schematic patterns of repetition, replication, proportion or
symmetry. Such tendencies are illustrated in the context of individual novels, although I have generally concentrated my arguments to
the structural analysis proper at the beginning of the last chapter.

Less space has been given to character and characterization. In
spite of her vaunted ties with the nineteenth-century 'classic realist'
tradition, Brookner cannot be regarded as having 'created' many
quaint or memorable characters in a traditional manner. She is no
female Angus Wilson. If indeed, Dickens's characters are commonly regarded as larger than life, most of Brookner's are probably
smaller. James Phelan's excellent rhetorical theory of characterization – *Reading People, Reading Plots* (1989) – distinguishes between

three components in fictional characters. These may be briefly summarized as the synthetic dimension (or 'knowing that he/she/(it?) is a construct'); the mimetic dimension ('the concept implied in the phrase "this person"'); and a thematic dimension (character 'taken as a representative figure, as standing for a class') (Phelan, 2–3). It is the third of these aspects that usually predominates in Brookner, reflecting the novelist's general emphasis on thematic elements.

Those familiar with Brookner more by hearsay will be ready to extrapolate whole series of alienated academic heroines, with their bold, provocative rivals, unsuitable establishment lovers, selfish irresponsible parents . . . etc.: like emblematic figures from some cautionary tale, returning the reader once more to Phelan's thematic dimension.

There is always, however, at least one 'memorable' character in a Brookner novel: the hapless protagonist, whether in pristine form (the first four books), doubled (*A Misalliance, A Friend from England*), redoubled (*Family and Friends, Latecomers*), or – most recently – regendered as in *Lewis Percy*. The emphasis on a single character is also the most obvious characteristic of autobiographical writing; and however vulgar or specious many attempts to identify the 'work' with the 'life' have often proved, it is a dimension of Brookner's fiction which can hardly be ignored. I therefore briefly consider the question of autobiography in formal, generic and rhetorical (or deconstructive) terms.

Autobiography is defined by its most eminent French theorist as:

> Retrospective prose narrative written by a real person concerning his own existence, where the focus is his individual life, in particular the story of his personality. (Lejeune, 1989, 4)

For Lejeune, a Brookner novel would thus only be distinguished formally from autobiography by the difference in the author's and protagonist's names, the absence of the 'autobiographical pact' hypothesized in Lejeune's most famous essay. Lejeune, it must be said, seems to accept quite uncritically the problematic concept of a 'real person', and also fails to consider texts which do not adhere to the autobiographical pact, but which are arguably more autobiographical than other texts which do. And he obviously provides no indication of how these tendencies might be quantified. Brookner might be presumed to share Lejeune's assumptions about the status of the autobiographical subject; at the same time, however, one can only suspect that certain intimate fictional portraits (neurasthenic Frances or ideologically ambivalent Edith) are indirectly more revealing than the generally well-crafted comments of the polished interview subject.

In generic terms, modern feminist theory is surprisingly close to traditional patriarchal practice in stressing the autobiographical element of contemporary women's writing; or, to modify the perspective, James Olney – in the introduction to his seminal *Autobiography: Essays Theoretical and Critical* (1980) – has stressed the importance of the subject as a focal point for courses and programmes in Women's Studies. Chapter 5 is more indebted to the generic than to the formal approach.

Brookner herself has clear ideas about which elements of her novels may be regarded as autobiographical. There are also interesting verbal slips in the interviews, suggesting forms of unconscious identification with fictional characters. Finally, at a more subliminal level still, the novels themselves raise certain repeated motifs to the level of virtual obsession. I have tried to document all three tendencies.

My aim is not, however, to locate Brookner generically within the category of the 'autobiographical novel', any more than it is to isolate formally the autobiographical element in her fiction. For if fiction may be 'autobiographical', then autobiography may be 'fictional' and the final chapter pursues this rhetorical – if not indeed ontological – conflation. My argument draws on Paul de Man's essay, 'Autobiography as Defacement', reinforced by a fruitful analogy from another literary medium, the poetry of Philip Larkin. Both novels and interviews – by analogy with the celebrated example of Barthesian anti-biography – might in fact be regarded as a single indivisible text: *Anita Brookner by Anita Brookner*.

In the main body of the study I have also occasionally borrowed concepts from structuralist narratology, although on these occasions I have kept formal terminology to a minimum. From Genette I have taken the distinction of *intradiegetic* and *extradiegetic* narrators as more precise than the familiar labels 'internal' or 'external'. For the traditional term 'point of view', I have substituted *focalization* in respect of its ability to distinguish between 'perspective' and 'narration'.[3] As Rimmon-Kenan has pointed out:

> . . . it is almost impossible to speak without betraying some personal 'point of view', if only through the very language used.

But a person (and, by analogy, a narrative agent) is also capable of undertaking to tell us what another person sees or has seen. Thus, speaking and seeing, narration and focalization, may, but need not be attributed to the same agent. (1983, 72)

Brookner's external narrators characteristically and conspicuously 'betray' points of view: 'negative capability' is not their strongest asset!

One of Rimmon-Kenan's examples illustrating her theoretical distinction is drawn from *Great Expectations,* where the narrator is Pip, the adult, while the focalizer is Pip the child. The same double dimension emerges immediately in *A Start in Life* and remains an important element of Brookner's technique.

I have reinforced these distinctions by occasionally borrowing the terminology of Dorrit Cohn's *Transparent Minds* (1978). Cohn's classic study of 'narrative modes for presenting consciousness in fiction' follows the broad division between consciousness in third person contexts and that in first person texts. In the former category, Cohn introduces the useful neologism, *psycho-narration,* to replace such terms as 'omniscient description' or 'internal analysis', which she regards as outmoded and imprecise. This technique in turn is distinguished from *quoted monologue* (to denote the 'traditional monologue' or 'silent soliloquy' found in pre-Joycean novels); and from *narrated monologue* (an English suggestion for the French *style indirect libre* or the German *erlebte rede*).[4]

Such distinctions are important in the context of Brookner's third-person narrators, although it must be said immediately that clear demarcations between the first and last of these forms are more a property of Cohn's theoretical model than Brookner's fictional practice. Ambiguities of focalization and narration are commonplace in Brookner, but in no way imply derogatory value judgements; in a reading of the technically conservative *A Friend from England,* I have in fact drawn a brief analogy with the narrator of *Mansfield Park.*

*             *             *

The present study, then, is essentially a chronological account of Brookner's nine novels to date, with particular emphasis on structural and thematic questions, and occasional narratological excursions.

The novels may be divided without undue distortion into equal sets of three. The first group – gathered here under the heading 'The French Connection' – are all closely modelled on previous literary texts: Balzac's *Eugénie Grandet* (*A Start in Life*), Constant's *Adolphe* (*Providence*), and – less explicitly – Proust's *À la Recherche du Temps perdu* (*Look at Me*).

Not even *A Start in Life* (1981), however, should be regarded as a simple critique of Balzac. It also has significant links with Dickens, reflected not simply in a shared indebtedness to the tradition of the *Bildungsroman*, but in a common use of the *leitmotiv* of food. *A Start in Life* announces, moreover, what will become Brookner's running engagement with the themes and conventions of popular romance. The major emphasis of the present reading nevertheless remains the 'French Connection'.

From the moment when the adolescent Ruth discovers her talent for French, the narrative offers a metacommentary on her progress thorough a web of literary allusion; Brookner will later complement, and sometimes virtually replace, this procedure with the related technique of iconographical reference. The major literary source for *A Start in Life* is however *Eugénie Grandet*, and a detailed comparative analysis of the two novels is provided.

The same kind of procedure is also applied in the reading of *Providence* (1982). A brief recapitulation of Constant's *Adolphe* proves extremely revealing, both in terms of what Brookner's narrative has omitted, and how much it has modified what remains. With the completion of a second novel so similar in structure to the first, moreover, it becomes possible to identify the thematic concerns which will predominate in Brookner's fiction: an insistent dualism – whether ethical (Pagan or Christian), physical (plain or beautiful), social (insider or outsider), or even existential (participant or observer) – any or all of which may be combined with a determinism generating its endemic cycles of expectation and delusion.

One is also aware, in retrospect, of how another of Brookner's major sources of metonymic detail from *A Start in Life* – clothes – joins food in the drive towards full metaphoric status. If food (in terms of the shared meal) becomes the major figure for *communion*, then clothing – seen literally by the self-conscious narrator as the social fabric – comes to symbolize *communication*. The heroine's departure in her finest dress for the novel's grandest ceremonial meal only reaffirms the absence of an elusive third term, a term which Brookner – in subsequent novels and interviews – does not hesitate to identify. Asked if *love* was her subject, she replied disarmingly. 'What else is there? Everything else is literature' (Kenyon, 15).

Such assertions might appear to pull Brookner unambiguously towards the abyss of sentimentality. But a more careful reading of the novel will show how the interest of *Providence* lies precisely in its juxtaposition of Romantic longing with the detached analysis of such feelings; the novel's lasting achievement is to unite convincingly a sense of deep vulnerability with a capacity for dipassionate inquiry, and these within the same actor/observer figure.

The French connection is more diffuse in *Look at Me* (1983). If *A Start in Life* and *Providence* were close thematic critiques of earlier novels, *Look at Me* is a formal parody – without connotations of ridicule – in respect to its fictional model. Frances Hinton's final decision to make a novel of her experiences ('I pick up my pen. I start writing.') inevitably recalls the structure of *À la Recherche du Temps perdu*; whilst her frequent references to, and quotations from, a private journal during the course of her narrative are also reminiscent of *Les Faux-Monnayeurs*. The analogies with Proust and Gide are both carefully considered in the present reading of *Providence*.

But Brookner's third novel also introduces the major technical innovation of a first person intradiegetic narrator. The experiment cannot be regarded as an unqualified success, and some reference is made to inconsistencies in narrative voice. The role of Olivia as a virtual *alter ego* for Frances – allowing regular (third person) commentary on the events of the narrative – may even conceal authorial nostalgia for the earlier method of external presentation.

If *Providence* has thematic and structural links with its predecessors, however, it also hints at what is to come. The novel's interior duplication or *mise en abyme*, no less than its periodical vacillations in point of view, prefigures the polyfocalism of *Hotel du Lac*; the harrowing climax of the narrative – with its archetypal associations of night journey and rebirth – anticipates the final chapters of *A Misalliance*; Frances's barely suppressed memories of earlier erotic experience are paralleled in *A Friend from England*. All of these elements – it is suggested – are an implicit warning against too rigid an adherence to the 'rule of three' adopted by the present study.

The second group of narratives – as indicated by the heading 'Novel Departures' – are marked by a greater interest in technical experiment: this appears most obviously in the now more extensive application of *mise en abyme* in *Hotel du Lac* (1984), widespread 'literary framing' in *Family and Friends* (1985), and a new comprehensive iconography in *A Misalliance* (1986).

It now seems increasingly clear that the award of Britain's Booker Prize to *Hotel du Lac* was a heartening example of public recognition coinciding with genuine literary merit. As my own reading suggests, this is the Brookner novel which offers the greatest textual resistance, a narrative which – in de Man's celebrated phrase – simultaneously asserts and denies the authority of its own rhetorical mode.

Although *Hotel du Lac* is shown to reflect once again the uneasy balance between romantic sensibility and intellectual detachment, I also extend discussion of the novel by considering it in broader terms of 'authority' and 'anxiety', and as a point of convergence for two contrasting texts. One of these, a traditional script generated by what Brookner has referred to as her 'grounding in nineteenth-century novels and nineteenth-century behaviour', reveals significant analogies with Eliot and James. This dimension is generally explicable in terms of traditional thematics, and such formal concepts as focalization and *mise en abyme*. The novel then emerges as a critique of discursive practices institutionalizeded by the etymologically related concepts of author and authority.

But *Hotel du Lac* is also the site of a second enigmatic script, requiring a more radical theoretical approach. Using Shoshana Felman's neo-Lacanian concept of a textual unconscious, I have tried to locate points in the text which literally resist interpretation: certain rapid shifts of focalization in the opening chapter, Edith's anxiety and silence, in addition to her obsessive concern with Jennifer's physical appearance.

With the help of various gynocritical insights, I have suggested that these symptoms literally enact female resistance to *man-made language*, thus claiming a new ideological significance for the novel.

In its pervasive dualism and pronounced determinism familiar from previous novels, *Family and Friends* (1985) is not conspicuous for thematic innovation. In technical terms, however, it is notable for its ingenious avoidance of the exhaustive referentiality conventionally associated with the family chronicle. Brookner's solution is to allow her anonymous narrator to proceed from a series of wedding photographs (and several analogous *tableaux*), preserving the context – and even occasionally the discursive syntax – of an excursion through a family album. My discussion of this technique draws on the most comprehensive account of 'literary framing', Mary Ann Caws' *Reading Frames in Modern Fiction.*

Caws has particularly emphasized how the framing process often entails an appropriation of the text by other extra-literary impulses: the structures of music, the perceptions of visual art, or the dialogue and gestures of dramatic form. The mere use of the term *tableau* in the present context clearly reflects the narrative's reliance on two of these supplementary modes.

Technical and thematic concerns converge in the formal experiment that underpins *A Misalliance* (1986), as Brookner develops a comprehensive iconography to emphasize a by-now familiar dualism within the novel. The regular visits of the lonely narrator-protagonist to the galleries of London produce a detailed series of references to the classical and biblical mythology inspiring medieval and renaissance art.

On the one hand, *A Misalliance* rearticulates Brookner's characteristic division of universal womanhood, repeated with growing insistency in each successive novel and articulated with particular succinctness in *Hotel du Lac* during Edith's memorable disquisition on 'hares and tortoises'. On the other hand, it produces the apparently original manifestation of the silent, unspeaking child, Elinor, as the infantile counterpart to the exploited and neglected Blanche Vernon. But Elinor also echoes the more explicit orphan motif of *Providence* and *Look at Me*, even as she helps to achieve the kind of structural parallelism prominent in both *Family and Friends* and *Latecomers*, and – through her silence – recalls a fleeting subtext (also involving a silent child) introduced by *Hotel du Lac*. All of these dimensions – I have argued – nonetheless remain subordinate to Brookner's coherent and consistent central ideology of Christians and Pagans, exhaustively figured in iconographic terms.

The admittedly less homogeneous third group of novels – gathered under the heading 'Creative Returns' – draws on divergent meanings of the word return: the sense of 'profit' or 'gain' as much as 'regression' or 'reversal'. All three novels show Brookner capitalizing on her previous exercises in formal experiment, even as she falls back on earlier narrative patterns: the bifurcation or splitting of the characteristic Brookner heroine (*A Friend from England*), new thematic emphasis on otherwise familiar male voices (*Latecomers*), or the knightly quest and hitherto most explicit parody of Romance (*Lewis Percy*).

*A Friend from England* (1987) might seem, on initial reading, a virtual compendium of Brookner motifs – the literal or figurative orphan, the solitary and alien heroine, the dualism of observer and participant – all ultimately invested in a characteristically ambivalent critique of Romantic myth. Brookner herself has also referred elsewhere to the novel's important theme of female friendship; although the relationship of narrator-protagonist Rachel Kennedy with the shadowy Heather Livingstone is ultimately less reminiscent of the friendship portrayed in *Providence* than of the sibling rivalry of *Family and Friends*. It may also anticipate the splitting process which characterizes the portrayal of Hartmann and Fibich in *Latecomers*.

I have also regarded *A Friend from England* as the novel where the literary influences of classic English novelists – essentially Austen, Dickens and James – are particulary noticeable. The analogies with Austen appear at both the thematic and the structural levels. If sibling rivalry and the possible bifurcation of the heroine recall prominent features of *Mansfield Park*, then the ambivalent divisions between external narration, quoted or narrated monologue and psycho-narrative imitate a kind of narrative ambiguity that is widespread in Austen.

The parallels with Dickens, on the other hand – involving Rachel Kennedy's symbolic orphan status and her relations to surrogate parents – are equally apparent in several other novels (cf. *A Start in Life* and *Providence*), whilst the elevation to metaphorical status of food as communion-and-ceremony also repeats an earlier strategy.

Points of contact with James are likewise familiar from *Providence* or *Hotel du Lac*, but the insistent use in *A Friend from England* of the characteristically Jamesian 'expanded' or 'extended' metaphor – (here the raw material is water) – probably represents the most striking trace of James in all of Brookner's fiction.

*Latecomers* (1988) also justifies its inclusion under the rubric of 'Creative Returns', although it has arguably not 'returned' as far as *A Friend from England*. The perennial themes of parental inadequacy, personal alienation and feminine rivalry point once again to the most central impulses of Brookner's fiction; but the use of four leading characters and the quasi-mechanical symmetry of the novel's structure have their immediate predecessor in *Family and Friends*, again recalling Brookner's comments to Kenyon on composition ('A chapter to each one is almost the easiest form').

I have also emphasized *Latecomers* as being the novel where –

intentionally or unintentionally – very little happens. The most intriguing formal property of the narrative, in fact, may be precisely this 'refusal of emplotment', studied here in relation to three specific examples. I have then speculated briefly whether this 'refusal' may be explained reductively in terms of Brookner's method of composition, or whether it is authentic evidence of suppressed material in the mind of the narrator or the consciousness of the implied author.

*Lewis Percy* (1989) was characterized by its author as a complete departure from her earlier fiction, but such claims should not be exaggerated. It is of course marginally longer than its predecessors, and focalization is limited almost exclusively to a single male protagonist; seen from another perspective, however, the novel repeats familiar dualistic patterns: predominantly sexual (the bold versus the timid woman) or existential (the academic versus the active life).

Like earlier novels, *Lewis Percy* makes wide use of literary reference; but it is the first novel since the 'French' group to develop its web of literary cross-reference into a comprehensive and structurally integrated device, much as *A Misalliance* had done for iconography.

The novel is also original in its exploitation of Mock Epic techniques, as Brookner reverts to more historically proven methods for undermining the Romantic myths. Lewis is thus often regarded as an absurd or pathetic figure involved in a pseudo-knightly quest. The novel's ending is also significant, in that it provides Brookner's second major example of narrative ambiguity. If the main generative power of Brookner's fiction does indeed lie in a tension between intellectual detachment and emotional susceptibility in relation to the Romantic myths, then *Lewis Percy* – together with *Hotel du Lac* – is the novel which most clearly rejects simple resolutions of this thematic conflict.

The concluding chapter – entitled 'Fictions of the Self' – echoes the suggestive title of Arnold Weinstein's fine study of the autobiographical novel from *Lazarillo de Tormes* to Rousseau's *Confessions*. Behind Weinstein's deceptively innocent descriptive title, is a full awareness that 'the very notion of an integral, unenmeshed being is – psychically and socially – something of a fiction' (vii). Weinstein's subtly ambiguous title stops short of more radical post-modernist hypotheses on the disappearance of the self; but both its explicit and its implicit senses are exploited in the argument of Chapter 5.

The latter thus begins by considering to what extent all nine of the novels might be regarded as analogous versions of a single fiction. I begin with a brief structural analysis of Brookner's plots, and the striking resemblances that emerge are then related more explicitly to a putative autobiographical dimension of the novels. In the process, however, I do not seek to unveil hitherto disregarded or unimagined elements of autobiography in the fiction, but rather question – on rhetorical grounds – certain formal and ontological distinctions between the two.

*       *       *

Having laid such emphasis on formal patterns in Brookner's fiction, I would be extremely naive to remain unaware of my own narrative plot. The present study has followed its own archetypal tripartite pattern, beginning with an awareness of stasis and origin ('The French Connection') existing concurrently with an emphasis on recapitulation or moving back, as Brookner relies on earlier established novels.

The grouping together of three more innovatory texts ('Novel Departures') would then correspond to that classic middle ground of narrative, with its digressions, divagations and experimental space.

The three 'last' novels ('Fictional Returns') are then seen as a process of consolidation, reflecting another universal narrative pattern: 'after the digression, the return'.

If the form of my narrative is timeless, however, its contents are threatened by rapid obsolescence. What aims at being a comprehensive survey is – with the arrival of the autumn booklists – to some extent transformed into an interim report. Brookner has completed a tenth novel, *Brief Lives,* and confirmed that she has begun work on an eleventh. The present study is therefore expressly confined to Brookner's novels of the eighties. If it thus loses any claim to completeness as a survey of Brookner's fiction to date, it nevertheless suggests that we may look forward happily to what is to come.

# 2

# The French Connection

Brookner's first novel, published in 1981, was to prove a kind of literary prototype for her entire production, anticipating themes and structures repeated insistently – if not sometimes obsessively – in all of her subsequent books, as they appeared with annual regularity throughout the eighties.

Together with its two immediate successors, *Providence* and *Look at Me*, *A Start in Life* is generally regarded as explicitly autobiographical; and it is not difficult to find common links between all of these, particularly on the basis of Brookner's comments in her three major interviews. But one might equally suggest that the other six novels are also autobiographical, or that all nine together actually constitute some kind of monolithic and continuously expanding psychobiography. And thus, even without reference to generic or ontological distinctions between 'fiction' and 'autobiography', the question soon becomes complex. I therefore leave broader discussion of the issue – with all its theoretical implications – until Chapter 5, by which point all of the novels to date will have been presented.

Brookner's career as a writer of fiction opens with the prophetic words: 'Dr Weiss, at forty, knew that her life had been ruined by literature'; and relations between 'literature' and 'reality' – or, more specifically, the tension between a passive studiousness and active involvement – will achieve thematic prominence in all the subsequent novels.

*     *     *

*A Start in Life* describes the childhood and adolescence of Ruth ('a pale, neat child, with extraordinary hair that made her head ache', 11); and her ill-acquired belief, derived from Grimm, Andersen and

Dickens, that 'virtue would surely triumph, patience would surely be rewarded'. Her parents – emigré antiquarian bookseller George ('with a desperately assumed English nonchalance', 11) and comic actress Helen ('beautiful and successful, her thin cheeks and jaw still unmodified by advancing years', 13) – remain eternal children. The household is therefore run by George's mother, with her 'sad European past', perpetuated in the décor of the family's large and gloomy Oakwood Court apartment; and, on the death of Mrs Weiss, by 'our darling Maggie' Cutler ('a wry, spry widow, quick to take offence', 19).

Ruth's escape from neglect and indifference lies in books: a burgeoning talent for French in her early teens, followed by studies at London University. Here she makes friends with her spiritual counterpart, Anthea ('sharp-witted, lightweight and beautiful', 31), and falls in love with the god-like Richard Hirst (with the 'unblemished blonde good looks of his Scandinavian mother' plus Christian convictions and an ulcer). The portrait is drawn with an ominous acerbity:

> Richard, a psychologist, by training, was a student counsellor, and would devote three days a week to answering the telephone and persuading anxious undergraduates that it was all right to enjoy sex with every partner, or alternatively, that it was all right if you didn't. Then Richard would wing home to his parish and stay up for two whole nights answering the telephone to teenage dropouts, battered wives, recidivists, and alcoholics. There seemed to be no end to the amount of bad news he could absorb. (37–8)

Here, in fact, together with the first hints of authorial alienation from late twentieth century mores, is the incarnation of the 'staunch Christian' Brookner hero, neatly identified by Haffenden ('they wear their hearts or hurts on their sleeves, and they are egotistical and uninvolved while apparently being disinterested', 27).

The deftly ironic treatment of this relationship must incidentally undermine any attempt literally to equate, rather than more legitimately relate, Brookner with the the world of Mills & Boon: Ruth leaves home and finds a flat of her own, virtually in order to be able to cook a dinner for Richard (a meal bland enough, moreover, not to aggravate his ulcer). Preparations for this event cover several chapters, require the advice of Ruth's mother, the housekeeper

Mrs Cutler, and a fellow student; prompt a lengthy search for out of season ingredients (including a trip to Harrods), and end – appropriately enough for the bookish Ruth – with a close reading of the *Larousse gastronomique* in the public library.

On the evening appointed for dinner, Richard arrives hours late and the food is ruined. The mild exasperation displayed by Ruth at Richard's interminable litany of needy social cases earns immediate reproach: ('"Sometimes Ruth," he murmured, letting his golden-lashed eyelids slowly fall, "I wonder if you're really a caring person."' 59). Ruth is fortunately able to prove otherwise, by a charitable loan to Richard of a hundred pounds, which forces her to move home to her parents again.

There is further subversion of romance conventions by a virtual repetition of Ruth's frustrating emotional experiences – now on a more elaborate scale – in the second half of the novel. She wins a British Council scholarship which enables her to work on her dissertation for a year in Paris. Here she lodges with her parents' friends, the Wilcoxes ('severe and owlish enough to inspire a certain discomfort', 89), under conditions quite as inhospitable as those existing at Oakwood Court. The Dickensian foster-parent figures are here no more caring than the actual biological parents.

But Ruth now blossoms on an even grander scale, thanks to a chance encounter in the Louvre with Jill and Hugh Dixon, a young English couple living in Paris. Their influence is more substantial than Anthea's: Ruth cuts her hair, revamps her wardrobe and submits to Hugh's sexual advances. The whole episode places a temporary check on the ruinous effects of literature: her visits to the *Bibliothèque Nationale* become less regular, her explorations of Paris more extensive, and the general effect is beneficial: 'There was no doubt that her looks improved. She put on weight and brushed her hair and learnt the difficult Parisian art of being immaculately turned out' (99).

As Ruth warms to her new image and grows in self-assurance, she also wins the attention of the distinguished Professor Duplessis. Hugh and Jill Dixon now also become the concrete agents of her escape, as she is able to take over their Paris flat, a practical necessity if she is to invite the professor for tea.

The prospective idyll is quickly terminated by Mrs Cutler's news of a crisis at home, where Helen has in fact just discovered her husband's infidelity. The housekeeper leaves shortly afterwards to get married, and Ruth's parents depart for another holiday by the sea, on the return from which, Helen dies and George suffers a stroke. Ruth is never able to go back to Paris, but accepts the offer of an assistant lectureship in London, dividing her time between academic work and care of her invalid father. She eventually marries Roddy, the hypochondriac son of her father's ex-mistress, but her husband is killed in a motor accident after only six months of marriage.

The apparent banality of Ruth's story, in bare outline, cannot possibly reflect the skill and wit with which it is presented. Brookner establishes, for example, a neat correlative for the lack of care and affection felt by Ruth and, to some extent, her father: it is expressed in terms of food. Domestic precariousness at Oakwood Court is reflected in the disillusionment of old Mrs Weiss, who shares breakfast with George, lunch and tea with Ruth and her nurse, and never a meal with Helen. Ruth realizes at an early age that, without her grandmother, 'there might be no more food' (16). There is a touching scene on the death of the grandmother, as Ruth retires to the kitchen and tries to prepare the evening meal by herself ('Why not?' her mother wonders as she comes home later, 'at her usual time', 18). Under the régime of Mrs Cutler, neglect at home continues to be indexed by a lack of meals: Ruth occasionally penetrates the smoke of her mother's room to ask if there is anything for supper (19). Food is now eaten on trays, and only at school can Ruth be sure where the next meal will come from.

It is perhaps understandable, therefore, that her whole life at a later point comes to be absorbed by the preparations for cooking Richard a meal. Even the successful consummation of this relationship is fantasized in gastronomic rather than erotic terms:

> Ruth saw herself, in a long skirt and her Victorian blouse and cameo, casually taking the complete dish from the oven when Richard arrived. (43)

For George, too, affection is closely associated with food: there is a memorable scene when he arrives home and mediates in a half-drunken quarrel between his wife and Mrs Cutler with an offer (Brookner should normally be allowed the credit for puns) of *tongue* sandwiches. Hands reach out to the plate without a break in the conversation, and Ruth, returning home later, finds her father alone in the kitchen eating artichokes from a tin. Even George's infidelities are comically presented as a quest for home-cooking rather than sexual diversion. His assistant Miss Moss 'cooked him a snack in the evenings, took him seriously and thereby proved herself invaluable' (14). Intimacy with Mrs Jacobs likewise begins over a shared meal of ryebread and liver sausage in the back of the shop (47). Sally's farewell, as she escapes to her sister in Manchester, is a meat loaf and an almond pudding (delivered with her voice shaking, 168).

Even Ruth's dreams are concerned with food: bolting down coffee and rolls in Brussels (89), or sitting for a meal in the dining car of a luxurious intercontinental train – just as she is about to order *Contrefilet à la sauce ravigote* (144), she catches sight of her mother in a siding, looking 'thin, sardonic and helpless'. Food has explicitly erotic associations for the Brookner narrator: Ruth's adolescent diet of eggs, boiled potatoes and salads is referred to as 'spinsterish fare'; the blandness of the meal cooked for Richard echoes Anthea's crude warning ('[d]on't expect him to be any good in bed', 38); the ironic choice of cake prepared by the revamped Ruth in Paris is 'la Reine de Saba' – the queen of Sheba.

Another obvious form of compensation for missing affection (sometimes simultaneously viewed in simple terms of food) lies in the world of books. Ruth has a literal 'greed' for books, taking them to the table with her and reading through meals (28). In the library, 'she came as close to a sense of belonging as she was ever likely to encounter' (28–9). Her work is generally promising, certainly a necessary situation for one who approaches her essays 'as many women approach a meeting with a potential lover'.

The replacement or compensation of the erotic by the gastronomic has interesting echoes in Dickens, an author regularly cited by Brookner as a formative influence, ever since she was made to read him as a child to gain a 'true picture of England' (Guppy, 149; cf. Haffenden, 28). On the very first page of of the novel, moreover, Ruth refers to a childhood spent emulating David Copperfield and Little Dorrit (the incarnations, presumably, of unwanted child and self-denying daughter). In the following chapter, the narrator provides another Dickensian reference ('It was the best of times, it was the worst of times', 16), perhaps an ironic allusion to the fact that Ruth's story, too, will also effectively become a 'tale of two cities'. And at the virtual midpoint of the novel, Ruth signals her newly assumed selfishness by a casting-off of Dickens and a

taking-on of Balzac. But the significance of food as fellowship –
almost a form of secular communion in *A Start in Life* – suggests
more specific Dickensian parallels, recalling the shared meals in,
for example, *Great Expectations*: the adult tyranny at the Christmas
table in the forge, the relaxed warmth of Pip's London feast with
Matthew Pocket, the coldness and restraint of dinner with the
impassive Jaggers.[1] Food and meals in Brookner in fact transcend
their purely metonymic context – where they may already receive
undue prominence for texts often regarded by critics and author
alike as minimalist – to become mythologized through elevation to
metaphor.

          \*                   \*                 \*

The regular debunking of the kind of yearning associated with
'romance' novels might suggest a simultaneous process of demys-
tification, if some critics did not regard Brookner's relationship to
the novelette as a more ambivalent and less flattering one. Certainly,
*A Start in Life* wittily demonstrates considerable familiarity with the
genre: Helen has a collection of historical romances (predominantly
Georgette Heyer) and clear preferences with regard to the six nearly
identical stories she borrows from the library each week:

> These had to do with maidens in the nineteenth century, taking
> posts as governesses and losing their hearts to the rakish son who
> was also the black sheep of the family. (111)

Mrs Cutler's tastes are equally specific ('Nothing with an unhappy
ending. And nothing set in the colonies. And preferably with
nobody called Douglas in it' 41–2). The name of Mrs Cutler's
husband had been Douglas.
    In her interview with Shusha Guppy, Brookner made an extensive
comment on the contrast between the 'romance' novel and what she
unequivocally described as the 'genuine article':

> Romance novels are formula novels. I have read some and they
> seem to be writing about a different species. The true Romantic
> novel is about delayed happiness, and the pilgrimage you go
> through to get that imagined happiness. In the genuine Romantic
> novel there is confrontation with truth and in the 'romance' novel
> a similar confrontation with a surrogate, plastic version of the
> truth. (Guppy, 161)

Guppy had shrewdly asked whether the real difference between the two was in 'the quality of writing and the mind behind [them]', or only in the 'invariably happy ending'; but Brookner significantly confines her answer to the second of these aspects.

The sharpness of the author's satirical edge is obvious enough in *A Start in Life* (and elsewhere), but the invariably unhappy ending does not in itself automatically distinguish these books from the 'romance' novel. In any attempt to separate the two types, various dimensions of literary and intellectual complexity are clearly quite as important as the nature of the endings. But final judgement on Brookner's precise relation to the 'popular romance' must await discussion of the subsequent novels – together with an inquiry (conducted with reference to *Lewis Percy*) into the nature of parody. In the meantime, however, it might be remembered that the far more vigorous satire of *Don Quixote*, in relation to an earlier form of romance, has not precluded that novel from sometimes being regarded simultaneously as satire, or as the last and greatest example of a romantic genre.[2]

*          *          *

But *A Start in Life* draws explicitly on another tradition, that of French realism exemplified by the novels of Balzac. If the more solidly respectable achievement of the *Comédie humaine* offers intellectual escape or domestic release for Ruth, it also provides the major structuring principle of the novel. For like *Providence* – and also less conspicuously, *Look at Me* – *A Start in Life* is closely linked to a single earlier fictional text. I therefore turn to a question quite as important as autobiography or parody in the early novels, the role of direct literary models.

In an interview with John Haffenden in 1984, Anita Brookner accepted that *A Start in Life* was a 'critique' of Balzac's *Eugénie Grandet*. But the analogues between the two novels are, in fact, merely the most prominent of the many literary references in *A Start in Life*: thus, on the very first page, it will be remembered, we are told more specifically of how a life can be ruined by literature. Ruth's 'faulty moral education' – the legacy of irresponsible parents – dictates that she 'ponders the careers of Anna Karenina and Emma Bovary, but that she emulate those of David Copperfield and Little Dorrit' (7).

Dr Weiss's major academic achievement is a study entitled *Women in Balzac's Novels*, one volume of which has already been published and two more of which are to follow. Among these novels, *Eugénie Grandet* naturally occupies a special place, and the helpless cry of Balzac's heroine 'Je ne suis pas assez belle pour lui' explicitly anticipates the story of Ruth's own life, now reproduced in a lengthy retrospective.

Ruth is the first in a succession of Brookner females with a special relationship to France and French culture. At school, her initial academic success comes in her early teens when she begins to study French: she starts with Hugo and Vigny, before moving on to Zola and Balzac at the age of fourteen or fifteen. The Balzac connection will remain and develop. At London University, Ruth studies French literature and completes a doctoral dissertation on 'Vice and Virtue in Balzac's Novels', identifying one of the master's lessons as 'the supreme effectiveness of bad behaviour', (33). It is impossible, incidentally, to ignore the striking biographical parallels with an author who also studied French literature at London University and could remark to an interviewer: ' . . . I think it's better to be a bad winner than a good loser. I don't think the meek inherit the earth' (Kenyon, 1989, 22).

The literary references reflect a number of motifs which will recur in the narratives of other Brookner heroines: two of these are the 'waiting woman' and the romantic interest (barely reciprocated) in a self-absorbed man. Ruth's regular reading of Balzac now provides (by a characteristic Brookner technique of literary, and even verbal, association) a kind of metacommentary on her own progress: as she painstakingly prepares dinner for Richard, she meditates on manipulative powers and the 'plain woman's revenge' (44), exemplified in *La Cousine Bette* (Lisbeth Fischer, jealous of her beautiful cousin Adeline Hulot and unable ever to possess the man she loves, plots the downfall of the entire Hulot family); but as the hours pass by, without a sign of her guest, Ruth appropriately begins Balzac's story 'Un Début dans la Vie' (the American edition of *A Start in Life* was actually called *Debut*). Later, as she is about to depart for Paris to continue her research, she dreams of taking the city by storm like a Balzac hero – but is wryly presented as in the process of reading *Modeste Mignon* (84). When the Romantic cycle begins again on a grander scale in Paris, Ruth listens to the advice of her new easy-going English friends, becoming ready to accept everything that was offered, and even to take by force when necessary. It is here that she momentarily abandons Dickensian values:

Ruth, who knew most of this by instinct, began to think of the world in terms of Balzacian opportunism. Her insights improved. She perceived that most tales of morality were wrong, that even Charles Dickens was wrong, and that the world is not won by virtue. (99)

In the January of the following year, she leaves Paris for a tour of the Balzac country, a trip ironically accompanied by a reading of *La Muse du Département*.

Allusions to the French classics frequently range beyond Balzac, as in the reference to student essays on Molière's *Le Misanthrope*, or the comparison between Richard and Hippolyte in Racine's *Phèdre*: if Hippolyte is Richard, 'la jeune Arricie' is a reference to any unknown rival (or later, perhaps, Richard's wife Joanna), whilst Ruth herself identifies rather improbably with Phèdre. Three distinct references to Racine's play (46, 58, 131) suggest that a point is reached where mere *diegesis* (the analogy elaborated in the account given by the external narrator) merges imperceptibly with *mimesis* (the characterization of Ruth by this rather inflated analogy focused through her).[3]

It is Balzac, however, who remains a kind of literary touchstone throughout the novel. As she absorbs the lessons of the master in Paris, Ruth decides that she does not wish to live virtuously like Henriette de Mortsauf or Eugénie Grandet; she does not wish to be courageous or ridiculous like Dinah de la Baudraye; or have many lovers but end in a nunnery like the Duchesse de Langeais. She would prefer to be the lady who 'spells death to Eugénie Grandet's hopes', the beauty glimpsed at a ball in Paris: '[b]etter a bad winner than a good loser' (136).

Following the death of Helen, and during George's convalescence after hospitalisation, Ruth's life returns to some semblance of order, through the offer of an assistant lectureship and marriage to Roddy. The narrator remarks ironically at this point that '[h]er work on Balzac, after hanging fire for a year or two, eventually picked up again and she was able to plan the second volume' (174). But Ruth herself, perhaps closer to the author than any other Brookner protagonist, writes to her editor to express satisfaction with a study of Diane de Maufrigneuse and offers the final narrative joke: 'The section on Eugénie Grandet has turned out rather longer than expected. Do you think anyone will notice?' (176).

Literary (and later iconographical) cross-reference will later emerge as a characteristic Brookner technique, a device – it must be added – which occasionally risks degenerating into pure mannerism. After so many and such elaborate allusions to French classics, however, one inevitably remembers what Brookner has described as 'the most pertinent criticism' she has had from a male reader: 'You write French books, don't you?' (Kenyon, 1989, 22).

Of at least equal comparable interest to the network of literary citations, however, is the author's own highly personal reading of *Eugénie Grandet* itself. A glance at the elements she has chosen to emphasize, and those she has repressed or consciously omitted proves an instructive exercise. Ruth actually provides her own extended gloss of Balzac's novel at a point in the narrative which will later become a virtual Brookner *topos*: the cautious, diffident heroine believes she has found love and some kind of spiritual rebirth, just before the final ironic reversal (the closest parallel is the dinner party after Kitty Maule's guest lecture in *Providence*).

After a lifetime of self-effacement, Ruth finally attempts to disassociate herself from Balzac's heroine:

She could no longer identify with her favourite heroine, Eugénie Grandet. She felt she was in control of her life, that it was no longer at the mercy of others, that she could not be disposed of against her will or in ignorance of her fate. Eugénie, waiting for her handsome cousin Charles to come home to Saumur and marry her, sits dreamily in her garden, on a wormeaten bench, under a walnut tree. For relief and diversion, she looks at the miniature of her aunt, his mother, that he has given her and sees his features there. She herself, she thinks, has little to offer for she is not beautiful, although Balzac stoutly defends what looks she has and compares her kind face and large brow to those of a Madonna. But Eugénie humbly recognizes her lack of beauty as an almost fatal flaw. *'Je suis trop laide; il ne fera pas attention à moi'*. Eugénie's mother learns with dismay of her attachment; her nurse tries to inject some character into her; but her obdurate and miserly father is quite content to have her at home for that way he can control her fortune. Grandet is a byword in Saumur for cunning and cheek. Eugénie is a good catch, but she is so listless, so absent, so mild. Her cousin Charles, of whom someone reports that fateful glimpse at a ball in Paris when Eugénie supposes him to be on the high seas, never returns to claim her. Eugénie, her parents dead, makes a loveless match which is never consummated. She, in her turn, becomes a byword in Saumur. (*A Start in Life*, 139–40)

If we disregard the reference to Grandet's Amazonian housekeeper as Eugénie's nurse (a curious lapse for a Balzac scholar!), the most striking textual revision centres on Eugénie's physical appearance. Unlike Ruth (and every subsequent Brookner heroine), Balzac's Eugénie is 'robust and strongly made', and if her face is compared to that of a Madonna, her figure resembles that of the Venus de Milo (94). The general impression, moreover, is of a kind of innocent sensuality:

> Her throat was round and flawless. The curve of her breast in a dress modestly buttoned to the throat caught the eye and stirred the imagination. No doubt she possessed little of the grace which is lent by well-made and fashionable clothes, put on with an eye to their effect, but to judges of beauty the firmness of her tall well-knit figure must constitute a charm. (*Eugénie Grandet*, 94)[4]

In relation to *Eugénie Grandet*, therefore, there is a significant reversal of physical types in *A Start in Life* (and, incidentally, other Brookner novels), where the 'robust' and full-figured woman (Jennifer in *Hotel du Lac*, Maria in *Look at Me*) normally poses a threat to the thin, frail protagonist. But Eugénie's cousin Charles, far from choosing a sultry temptress, marries for social cachet – accepting a skinny wife whose physically grotesque appearance puts her into contention with Grandet himself:

> Mademoiselle d'Aubrion was a damsel as long of body, as thin and slender, as the insect, her namesake. She had a disdainful mouth, over which hung a nose which was too long, thick at the tip, pasty in its normal state, but blossoming out into a display of red immediately after meals, a kind of botanical phenomenon peculiarly disagreeable when appearing in the middle of a pale, bored face. (228)

But Brookner virtually supplements this aesthetic reversal with a new moral polarity, so that if in *Eugénie Grandet* 'plump' is 'desirable', in *A Start in Life* 'slim' is 'good'.

In one important structural aspect, however, the two novels are quite distinct. If Balzac's novel is dominated by the grasping cooper and winegrower of Saumur ('not a miser but Avarice', 43), the book is actually named for the daughter. This creates an impressive textual antithesis: Grandet himself is given a full physical description in the opening pages (44), whereas his ironically inappropriate first name (Felix) occurs only once, towards the end of the novel; his daughter, on the other hand, is immediately identified as Eugénie (55), but the details of her physical appearance are strategically delayed until much later, after the arrival of her cousin Charles from Paris. It is when she is already struck by love for this 'paragon of beauty' (73) and laments 'I am not good-looking enough for him!' (94), that we receive the first extended physical description, thus dramatically emphasizing the instrumentality of Eugénie's self-perceived appearance for the story itself.

Ruth, however, is insistently portrayed from the beginning as a plain, dull (but quite serious) child, in contrast with her beautiful, vivacious (but utterly frivolous) mother.

Other structural parallels between *A Start in Life* and *Eugénie Grandet* are also apparent. The gloom and heaviness of the Weiss appartment in Oakwood Court – minutely described in the opening chapters – reproduce something of the oppressive quality of Grandet's house in Saumur. Each home provides the sole environment for the long and lonely adolescence of an only child. The arrival of Eugénie's cousin Charles from Paris and the revelation of Richard to Ruth have similar associations:

> It seemed to Eugénie, who had never in her life seen such a paragon of beauty, so wonderfully dressed, that her cousin was a seraph come from heaven. She breathed the perfume of that shining head of hair, so gracefully curled, with delight. (*Eugénie Grandet*, 73)

In *A Start in Life*, Richard – 'a prize beyond the expectations of most women and certainly beyond those of Ruth' – is also portrayed as a kind of demi-god:

> He was one of those exceptionally beautiful men whose violent presence makes other men, however superior, look makeshift. . . . He had the unblemished blond good looks of his Scandinavian mother; (*A Start in Life*, 37)

Although neither female protagonist would consider an open erotic initiative, each is described dressing with particular care to impress the virtual stranger with whom she has fallen in love. Each heroine turns to the most obvious compensatory activity of eating: Eugénie prepares the most luxurious clandestine breakfasts she can manage in her miserly father's house, whilst Ruth virtually moves into a flat of her own so that she can invite Richard for what proves to be an abortive dinner.

After their respective crises of confidence ('Je ne suis pas assez belle pour lui'), each heroine lends to her divine apparition something as crass and concrete as a large sum of money. Each man later returns the money in a letter announcing his marriage to another woman: Charles in a long pathetic missive composed with total cynicism, and Richard in a casually thoughtless letter ('he was blissfully happy and he hoped that she was too', 131). The receipt of the respective letters is one of the closest textual parallels between the two novels: 'Eugénie opened the envelope with fingers that shook' (232), and later 'jumped up . . . and went to find a seat on one of the courtyard steps' (233); '[Ruth] sat down on the edge of the bath, trembling. Could this still happen?' (131).

Both men remain quite unaware of the emotional suffering they have inflicted, and the two women each later accept loveless marriages of convenience, long after their romantic dreams have faded. Both marriages are equally short-lived: Eugénie's with Monsieur de Bonfons, who dies a week after he has been appointed deputy for Saumur, and Ruth's with Roddy (son of her father's ex-mistress), who is killed six months later in a crash on the Kingston bypass. Dr Weiss's narrative ends with the portrait of a neurotic academic of forty, whilst Eugénie is an unhappy widow of 'nearly forty'.

No other Brookner fiction has such an intimate relation with another text. Constant's *Adolphe* certainly receives considerable exposure in *Providence*, whilst *Look at Me* – I shall argue – has a close structural analogy with Proust; but neither of these novels contains such a wide range of thematic and structural parallels as those between *A Start in Life* and *Eugénie Grandet*. One is immediately tempted to think in terms of *Urtext* and literary *palimpsest*, although parody – in its technical sense – is perhaps a more suitable name. Applied to a musical composition, the word is still used to describe close thematic or stylistic links with an earlier work, but without current cultural associations of caricature or ridicule. Linda Hutcheon (*A*

*Theory of Parody*, 1985) has – not least on etymological grounds – also attempted to restore this sense of the term to literary discussion.[5]

A remarkably close analogy to the relationship of Brookner's first novels to *Eugénie Grandet* and *Adolphe*, respectively, is offered by Golding's rather laboured parables of the fifties: if *The Lord of the Flies* represented a disillusioned and post-nuclear *Coral Island*, *The Inheritors* glossed Wells's *Outline of History*. The analogy ultimately falls short in the light of Golding's ideological hostility – as opposed to Brookner's more ambivalent feelings – with regard to the 'target' texts, but in terms of literary stimulus or structural and thematic similarities, it is nonetheless suggestive.

\*       \*       \*

*A Start in Life* is also the novel which the reader may instinctively experience as being the most 'autobiographical'. At this point of the study, there is clearly little basis for comparison, and the whole subject of autobiography – as I have already indicated – is deferred until the final chapter. Even there, however, I have refrained from rash judgements, preferring to use Brookner as a basis for discussing the nature of autobiography itself; and the inevitable result of these reflections is a growing awareness – in a post-structuralist context – that the issue of fiction as autobiography must with any author (and not least Brookner) be related to that of autobiography as fiction.

Traditionally, however, first novels (and even their immediate successors) are regarded as showing a greater propensity for the autobiographical, and Brookner herself is certainly aware of this distinction. Asked by Haffenden whether her (first three) novels spoke of her own condition, she replied that, although the particulars were 'all invented', they did 'speak of states of mind which forced me to do something about those states of mind', (25). They were thus 'impure novels', as opposed to *Hotel du Lac*, which was the 'least impure', a matter of 'invention pure and simple'. The implication, of course, is that the earlier novels were not merely invention, but consciously mediated autobiography.

One may postpone judgements at this point by pointing out that Brookner's comments, together with the themes and structure of the novel itself, place *A Start in Life* firmly within the realist tradition of reflected or refracted biography that forms the classic European *Bildungsroman*. *Providence* and *Look at Me* move progressively away from this fictional genre.[6]

## PROVIDENCE

*Providence*, Brookner's second novel, has obvious analogies with *A Start in Life*, and establishes further structural and thematic patterns that will continue to occur in the later fiction.

The heroine, Thérèse (Kitty) Maule, resembles her predecessor, Ruth Weiss, in her foreign background, her (now literal) orphan status, and her combination of academic success with emotional failure. Less space is now devoted to childhood scenes, but the family's exotic origins are carefully established by an account of Kitty's French grandparents: Vadim, a circus acrobat of Russian extraction, and Louise, a seamstress from the Rue St Denis, move to London and eventually open a dressmaker's salon in Grosvenor Street. Their only child, Marie-Thérèse, married to an English army officer and almost immediately widowed, leaves a daughter – the novel's heroine – caught between two cultures, two languages and even two names.

As one of its major themes, therefore, the novel provides another study in alienation (Kitty is described as an 'island of remoteness', 7), and chronicles a similar process of emancipation achieved through academic talent: the heroine obtains a research appointment at a well-endowed provincial university, where her subject is the Romantic Tradition. As with Ruth, Kitty's emotional fate is also sealed when she predictably falls in love with an unsuitable and inaccessible man: Maurice Bishop, professor of Medieval History and a 'romantic and devout Christian', entrances large university audiences with his lectures on the cathedrals of England:

> Kitty Maule, dressed in her best, although Maurice could not see her, would watch the handsome smiling figure mounting the steps to the platform, and try not to sigh as he surveyed the image on the screen before turning to his audience, his hands on his hips, his legs and buttocks braced as if for sexual activity. He was a beautiful man and everyone was faintly in love with him. (20)

For habitual Brookner readers, the uncharacteristically explicit eroticism fails to hide a clear family resemblance. Maurice is perhaps the prime specimen of the men described by the novelist as 'conservative Establishment creations' (Haffenden, 27): his impeccable social background includes a large country home in Gloucestershire, a titled mother and a comfortable private income. He and Kitty have enjoyed a brief affair, which has now subsided – at least, in Maurice's mind – into a 'comradely routine'.

Kitty's teaching duties are apparently limited to a seminar with three students on one book, Constant's *Adolphe*, which also provides the paradigm for her own narrative. She moves methodically through her set text, guiding the discussions and correcting the essays of her pupils: brilliant John Larter ('painfully thin, excited and excitable', 44); the older Philip Mills ('[p]olite, cautious, bifocalled', 45); and, between them, beautiful Jane Fairchild ('full and rather low bosom' / 'pre-Raphaelite tendrils of beige hair', 46–7), so beautiful, in fact, that 'it seemed a concession for her to have written anything at all' (46).

A dinner with Maurice is followed by the crucial exchange over coffee, where 'providence' – the novel's complementary theme – is pitted against Kitty's implicit determinism:

> '. . . . You, dearest Kitty, live in a world of unbelief. It makes you tense. I can't tell you how simple life is when you know that you are being looked after. How can you survive one blow after another?'
>
>   'Does God organize the blows?' asked Kitty somewhat tartly?
>   'Who knows?'
>
>   'Then what exactly do you believe in?' asked Kitty.
> Maurice took his arms from behind his neck and sat forward, elbows on his knees, staring at the floor.
>   'I believe in Providence,' he said. (58)

Maurice's combination of bland sententiousness and utter insensitivity to Kitty's feelings recalls a similar after-dinner conversation in *A Start in Life*, where Richard Hirst – another self-absorbed Christian 'hero' – speculated on whether Ruth Weiss could really be a 'caring person'. Haffenden perceptively questioned Brookner on her 'grouse against Christianity', and was rewarded with one of her most candid responses: 'I would love to think that Jesus wants me for a sunbeam but he doesn't' (Haffenden, 27).

Kitty's encounters with her colourful divorcée neighbour, Caroline, are an opportunity to articulate a familiar, if unoriginal, Brookner insight (already exemplified by her student, Jane Fairfax): that there is one law for the beautiful and another for the plain:

Beauty, of course, offered its own dispensations: beautiful
women, by a rule she acknowledged but did not understand,
were somehow allowed to do nothing of worth and yet to
command the time and attention of others. Kitty preferred her
busy life, which she characterized as an easy life spent doing
difficult things. (31)

But it is also because of Caroline that Kitty later agrees to visit
a clairvoyant, doubtless in the hope of escaping her own rigidly
deterministic views. Here she is portrayed with fine irony, grasping
at any straw Madame Eva can offer ('Mother's watching . . . ', 'I
think he loves you', 'Try your luck abroad', 74–5), as she hands
over ten pounds in a 'daze of gratitude'. Kitty leaves, resolute
and determined, convinced that 'some shift in her consciousness'
has taken place. There is an inevitable echo of a previous message
of encouragement, discovered in her mother's Bible ('beauty for
ashes, the oil of joy for mourning, the garment of praise for the
spirit of heaviness', 29), with perhaps an ironic equation of Bible
and crystal ball for their common uselessness as viable sources of
hope.

Caroline is furthermore presented as a kind of counterpart to
Pauline, the teaching colleague ('gifted' but 'sarcastic [and] sentimental'), with whom Kitty spends the following weekend. The
two women epitomize to some extent the alternative destinies in
store for the solitary Brookner heroine: if Caroline waits in lonely
splendour for the right man to materialize, Pauline grows old faith-
fully nursing an invalid parent. Kitty sees the contrast explicitly, as
Brookner heroines invariably do:

> She felt an urgent need to put her own life into some sort of order,
> to ensure that she did not turn out like Caroline or like Pauline,
> the one so stupid, the other so intelligent, and both so bereft. (84)

The weekend in Gloucestershire with Pauline and her unusually
well-informed mother offers further barely digested discussion of
Romanticism, existentialism and the absurd, all perhaps less natural
outside the context of the university seminar. Kitty retires to bed
with renewed scepticism and despair:

> Oh, I am misbegotten, she thought. I am not anywhere at home.
> I believe in nothing. I am truly in an existentialist world. There
> are no valid prophecies. (91)

Redemption is nowhere to be found, 'not in the Bible nor Providence nor Madame Eva.'

The rest of the novel may be read as a countermovement to Kitty's now reinforced existential despair, and the return to fresh states of Romantic expectancy. It is also worth remembering Brookner's comments on significant form,[7] for – as in *A Start in Life* – the cycle of hope and illusion is again enacted twice: first with a fine comic irony, and subsequently in more tragic terms.

At the beginning of the first cycle, the tenacious quality of human hope is ironically suggested in Louise's spontaneous toast – when she senses that her granddaughter is in love – *Que tous vos rêves se réalisent* (102). And when Kitty goes to Paris in the summer vacation with the expectation of meeting Maurice, she experiences an improbable 'renewal of her powers' as soon as she reaches '[t]he wider shore, the wider sky' of France (108).

But the arrival of Maurice on an architectural field-trip is a profound anti-climax: his only contact with Kitty is on the day before he leaves France, when the couple visit the abbey church of Saint-Denis, and Maurice falls asleep on the train. On returning to Kitty's hotel, Maurice does no more than take a bath, after which the would-be lovers consume apple chaussons and croissants filled with almond paste: they eat 'ravenously'. Before Maurice leaves, the couple kiss – exchanging 'identical breaths' – and Kitty vows that she will 'never forget that particular taste as long as she live[s]' (126). The separation among fumes of almond paste exudes a kind of *bathos*, drawing on a mock-romantic typology discussed later in the present chapter.

On her return to England, however, Kitty begins to work in earnest on her public lecture, and a new cycle of hope begins, particularly after Maurice's promise of a celebratory dinner. The sense of anticipation is now stronger: Kitty appreciates the fine weather and dry sunny evenings, grows lyrical about the time of promise and fulfilment, and begins, for the first time, to feel a sense of her own worth. The long crescendo of hope portrayed here is a pattern closely paralleled in both *A Start in Life* and *Look at Me*. The relentlessness and enormity of the novel's ironic build-up is in fact quite worthy of the classic exponent of determinism in the English novel, Thomas Hardy.

Kitty returns to Madame Eva and gets 'the truth again'; recalls the marriage of her cousin Jean-Claude and the sly references of

aunts and uncles to her own wedding; experiences a new 'sense
of well-being' and 'almost of worth' (179), in the knowledge that
her apprenticeship has finally come to an end:

> For two days she had rested secure in this knowledge and also
> in anticipation of a pleasant future. Pleasant in the sense of
> corresponding to her modest worth; pleasant in the sense of its
> being the correct conclusion of her attempts to achieve a position
> that would somehow merge her anomalous beginnings into her
> stronger linguistic background; pleasant in the sense that at last
> she had a feeling of place and could connect herself with an
> institution in which her ambitions, which were as modest as her
> experience, could be and would be realized. (179)

The actual contents of the passage, no less than its careful rhetorical
articulation – with mounting emphasis achieved by verbal repetition – suggest that it is probably the novel's central formulation of
the simultaneous desire and need for social and cultural integration.
If an academic appointment resolves the problem of alienation
for Kitty, the aftermath of Maurice's (and her) dinner party will
presumably provide for her stronger emotions ('[f]or the first time
in her life she felt nothing but confidence in the future', 179).

Louise meticulously prepares what may be her last dress for her
granddaughter, and as Ruth leaves for the university, she feels
'quite equal to the brilliant day' (173).The account of the lecture
itself is limited to the opening words, but with their inevitable
application to Kitty herself, they provide one of the neatest ironic
touches in the entire novel:

> 'I should like to imagine, if I may, some aspects of the Romantic
> Tradition, a tradition which still affects us today, although we
> may not recognize it. For although we think we know what
> a Romantic is, Romantics do not always know it themselves.'
> (177)

We are once again witness to Kitty's characteristic combination of
intellectual insight and emotional ingenuousness.

The narrative ends with the celebratory dinner and Maurice's
emergence from the kitchen with Jane Fairfax (carrying a large
tureen of soup); at which point, it is easy to understand Brookner's

admiration for her beloved Stendhal's aphorism on the Romantic state: 'I walk along the street, marvelling at the stars, and all of a sudden I'm hit by a cab'.

*          *          *

Of the three first novels, *Providence* is in some ways the most impressive, with its intensified treatment of familiar themes, and its openness to new formal solutions. In retrospect, one is also aware of how two of Brookner's major sources of metonymic detail – clothes and food – move closer to full metaphorical status. The two subjects appear to run like leitmotivs throughout the novel, the former inevitably associated with Louise, the latter with Vadim; and the link is explicitly established on one of Kitty's visits to her grandparents at the beginning of the novel:

> Vadim unpacked her basket, inhaling with ecstasy the freshly ground coffee that she bought for him. Louise was mostly interested in her clothes. 'Off the peg? *Mais tu es folle, ma fille.*' (14)

In a later reference to her grandparents' expectations, Kitty suggests amusingly that she 'could never eat enough or wear enough to conciliate them with her way of life' (54–5).

The preparation and eating of meals formed a substantial part of *A Start in Life*, but in *Providence*, these activities acquire a heightened relevance. For the culturally alienated Kitty, food is one of the strongest expressions of an irrecuperable, but never forgotten past:

> An air of dimness, of stuffy comfort, an emanation of ceremonial meals, long past, an airlessness, hours spent on the routine matters of rising and eating and drinking coffee; an insistence on food, the centrality of food. (6)

To emphasize Kitty's rootlessness, such moments are associated with Paris 'or perhaps further east'.

Kitty's mother had died at dinner, and the daughter still carries the 'faintly sour scent' of discarded fruit peel in her nostrils (18). When eating alone, she tries to dispatch meals as quickly as possible; sometimes she can eat with enjoyment, as when she prepares a meal for Maurice. In marked contrast to Ruth Weiss, Kitty can envisage food as a source of pleasure, and the meal itself – a ritual of fellowship – is part of her cultural heritage: her students

Larter and Mills (as she fancifully imagines) have 'grown pale on cheap food' (68), whereas – only pages later – an 'exquisite aromatic smell' (77) drifts under the door of her grandparents' living-room. Meals sketched with random metonymic detail – tea with the Bentleys (156), a 'substantial breakfast' in Paris (118) – are overshadowed by the deeper implications of food as ritual: there is again a Dickensian awareness of eating as a social act, even if it is only cake and 'sticky liqueur from small glasses' (101) after the impromptu taxi ride with Vadim and Louise. The archetypal meal with Kitty and her grandparents, with its subtle emphasis on bread and wine, may even hint at the celebration of a private eucharist:

> They ate together, since it was simpler that way, speaking French, the bottle of wine recorked at the end of the meal, salad eaten from the same plates as the meat; much bread. (13)

In this light, the purely metonymic meals fantasized by Kitty on her visit to the Bentleys produce a strangely incongruous effect. Thematically remote from the surrounding text, they even suggest a simple lapse into cultural snobbery:

> Disconsolate families ate baked beans on toast and wrapped handkerchiefs around the stinging handles of metal teapots, for this was tourist country. (82)

Not by chance are the novel's two scenes of emotional anti-climax both expressed in the context of eating: whilst Maurice and Kitty separate inconclusively in Paris – amid fumes of almond paste – the unfortunate dinner at Maurice's is the final example of *consumption* without *consummation*. But if food expresses a kind of secular communion, clothes represent another form of communication. Brookner is always precise about details and conventions of dress; Kitty's friend, Caroline, is realized almost exclusively in terms of what she wears, as in the trip to Madame Eva:

> For the visit to the clairvoyant Caroline wore violet trousers, a blue silk shirt, and several chains round her neck. Dressing the part, thought Kitty, watching her twine a blue trailing scarf round her hair. (67)

Most of the characters are carefully indexed by clothing, from Larter's 'filthy jeans and sweater' (45) to Jane's 'cotton skirt and dark blue jersey, borrowed from a brother' (47). Maurice's 'hand-made shirts without a tie, cashmere pullovers instead of jackets' are conspicuous in a Senior Common Room of 'grey flannel or beige tweed' or 'maroon socks and ginger suede shoes' (24).

Kitty herself ('Milady Maule') is a subject of great envy to the department secretary for her exquisite clothes. Brookner follows a long tradition of meticulous realism in details of dress, traceable in English literature as far back as Chaucer, in order to index status, profession and individual self-awareness. Not least, in the novelist's conventional middle-class settings, dress must be viewed – in more than one sense – as the very social *fabric*.

As elsewhere in the context of food, it is the ceremonial aspect of clothing which effectively grasps the reader's attention. The new dress for Kitty's public lecture, perhaps the last that Louise will ever make, is produced according to a familiar 'rite de passage' associated with every major transformation in Kitty's life. As she leaves in her finest dress for the novel's most important ceremonial meal, communion and communication seem to beg for union under the aegis of an elusive third term. It is a term which Brookner – repeatedly in novels and interviews – does not hesitate to identify: to the interviewer who suggested that love was her subject, she answered disarmingly: 'What else is there? Everything else is mere literature' (Kenyon, 15).

In comments such as these, a certain banality of expression cannot conceal the sublimity of what is expressed. The same contrast is of course apparent throughout Kitty's own emotional and intellectual progress in *Providence*. In spite of her considerable intelligence, together with more specific academic talents, the heroine sees her teaching duties as 'a temporary and rather pleasant way of filling in the time until her true occupation should be revealed to her' (32). This activity, she believes, will clearly involve great emotional intensity.

The interest of *Providence* in fact lies in its confrontation of Romantic longing with detached analysis of such feelings; its lasting achievement is to unite convincingly a sense of deep vulnerability with a capacity for dispassionate analysis in the same actor/observer figure. But the apparent reserve and discretion of the novel's narrator and heroine are surely misleading; not to *Adolphe* alone, might one apply Kitty's seminar comment:

the potency of this particular story comes from the juxtaposition of extremely dry language and extremely heated, almost uncontrollable sentiments. (135)

Occasionally, the text of *Providence* also clearly transcends the use of such 'extremely dry language', as in Kitty's momentous insight:

It had been revealed to her, this evening, this momentous evening that there was a safety beyond anything she had ever known, that the love of one person for another can confer such a charmed life that even the memory of it bestows immunity. (62)

By an ironic epistemological reversal, however, a certain nobility of expression now only refers to a relationship which is, in reality, futile and abortive. But such discrepancies between the purity of longing and the defilement of experience will be best illumined by the intertextual relations of the novel.

*　　　*　　　*

Like *A Start in Life*, *Providence* also has close ties with the French literary tradition, although in this case predominantly to a single text – Benjamin Constant's *Adolphe* (1806). In her interview with John Haffenden, Brookner comments at some length on *Adolphe;* she accepts the interviewer's suggestions that 'literature can damage life' and that 'fiction provide[s] role models'. Of related interest here, are the commonplace critical references to Brookner's links with the French *conte* or moral tale.

The *conte* evolved from its original seventeenth century sense of short allegory or fantasy – in the hands of La Fontaine or Perrault – to the social satire and greater psychological realism of the Crébillon *fils* (say *Les Égarements du coeur et de l'esprit*, 1736) and Duclos (*Histoire de Mme de Luz*, 1741). It is perhaps the dry, concise style of the latter that Kitty has in mind when she describes Adolphe as being written 'in the driest traditions of the eighteenth century moral tale' (51).

And yet there are even closer textual parallels in *Providence* to the philosophical tales of Voltaire, and in particular to the satire of *Candide* (1759). Vadim is portrayed as a latter-day Pangloss ('Vadim never told her exactly how things were. Everything was always for the best in the best of all possible worlds', 53). Perhaps even his dietary advice to Kitty ('Never neglect the vegetables, said Vadim passionately', 54) carries a faint echo of Candide's final words to Pangloss: 'il faut cultiver notre jardin'. Captain John Maule had shared Vadim's optimism, and thus – by heredity no less than environment – Kitty's life work consists of 'establishing the true and the good and perhaps the beautiful, of believing the best of everyone, of enjoying what life offered, not lamenting what it withheld' (6).

As far as Maurice is concerned, it might also be remembered how, in another of Voltaire's tales, *Zadig* (1748), the well-endowed and highly educated young hero achieves high office, but is unfortunate in love. After many vicissitudes, he is told by an angel that there is no evil in the world, but some good comes of it. Zadig is rescued from slavery in Egypt, marries the queen – whom he loves – and becomes king. Predictably, he worships Providence; as with Maurice himself, anything less might surely be seen as ingratitude!

Brookner herself has certain reservations about the closeness of the parallels to *Adolphe* that she has introduced in *Providence* ('It's a little bit mechanical I think, or forced: I wouldn't do that again', Haffenden, 27). But interviewer and subject then go on to discuss their reactions to Adolphe, with Haffenden remarking on the 'relentless and cold logic of the hero's career', and Brookner expressing full agreement:

> Yes, and he is quite unapologetic about the whole thing. He is serious and in fact extremely grave. It is a moral catastrophe. But he doesn't enjoy it. Ellénore is unsuitable, and it kills her; it ruins him, but of course we don't know for how long. (Haffenden, 27)

Since this summary implies a particularly personal account of Adolphe, I offer a brief recapitulation of the novel (attempting, nevertheless, to avoid another equally personal reading), in order once again to consider what Brookner has omitted, and how much she has modified what remains.

The young Adolphe, motherless and always remote and constrained with his father, describes his 'vague emotional torment' and sensation of 'wanting to be loved' (45).[8] He meets Ellénore, the mistress of a Polish count and – using his highly personal mixture of internal anguish and external strategem – succeeds in winning her love.

Almost immediately, he begins to feel resentment and frustration at his new emotional dependence, although he begs leave from his father to stay six more months in Poland, in order to be with Ellénore. The latter breaks with the Count, her protector, and eventually leaves Poland completely with Adolphe, after which the couple live for a year in Bohemia. A friend of Adolphe's father, the well-meaning but worldly Baron T——, tactfully attempts to separate Adolphe from Ellénore. Adolphe eventually assures Baron T—— that he will break completely with her within three days, although he is unable to keep his word. Ellénore comes into possession of the letter in which this promise is made, together with a second letter from Baron T—— himself. She is struck with a violent illness from which she never recovers.

On Ellénore's death, Adolphe reads her posthumous letter which he had actually promised to destroy. The letter contains a number of particularly sharp insights: it comments, amongst other things, on the imbalance of the union ('Love was my whole life, but it could not be yours', 115), and accuses Adolphe of lacking the moral courage to have broken a mutually destructive relationship ('What misguided pity makes you afraid to break a tie you find irksome', 121). Finally, it warns Adolphe of the solitude he will now experience. According to a common convention of early fiction, the volume contains an exchange of letters between publisher and the possessor of the manuscript, where it emerges that Ellenore's prediction is well founded.

*Adolphe*'s relation to *Providence* is obviously almost as close as that of *Eugénie Grandet* to *A Start in Life*: the heroine, Kitty – who is herself half French – is writing a thesis and preparing a public lecture on the Romantic Tradition, besides covering the topic in a seminar, where *Adolphe* is the principle, and to all appearances the only, text. Brookner herself is perhaps aware of this saturation process, for the narrator notes ironically on one occasion how Kitty – during a visit to her colleague, Pauline – was 'lost in the Romantic Tradition and the dog observed a suitable silence' (153).

We may begin a comparison with the obvious equation, according to which Constant's Adolphe would seem to correspond to Maurice, and Kitty to Ellénore; but even here, there are significant differences. Most obviously, the story of Kitty and Maurice is filtered through the woman's consciousness. Furthermore, Kitty exercises the dual function of commentator and protagonist, providing a shrewd and comprehensive analysis of *Adolphe* – in her seminar and research – but virtually reenacting the story of Ellénore and Adolphe in her own relationship with Maurice. She is never explicit about this link, but her hostility towards *Adolphe* ('a short novel about failure. She did not care for it much . . . ', 29), and a reference to its 'terribly enfeebling' lesson ('that a man gets tired of a woman if she sacrifices everything for him', 44) suggest a subliminal awareness of certain analogies, even if her own narrative represses them.

At her first seminar session, Kitty and her students translate a lengthy passage from the preface to the third edition of *Adolphe*, including the admonitory statement:

> It is felt that attachments which have been made without reflection can be broken without any harm being done. (*Providence*, 48)

This Kitty identifies approvingly as 'what the novel is all about', and it might equally well provide a suitable epigraph for *Providence*. Maurice clearly stands in the same relation to Kitty as does Adolphe to Ellénore, although it should be emphasized that this mature, established and professionally successful academic has little in common with Adolphe, other than his overwhelming self-absorption.

In view of Brookner's habitual reticence, moreover, the closeness of the analogy to Adolphe and Ellénore in purely erotic terms is also unclear: in the second chapter, it is true, Kitty refers to the enjoyment of eating 'when she prepared a meal for her lover, Maurice Bishop', and she later describes Maurice on the lecturing podium – with uncharacteristic candour – as 'hands on his hips, his legs and buttocks braced as if for sexual activity'. But even these comments suggest textual more than sexual diversion. The exact nature of the relationship is not clearly defined.

The obsessive quality of Adolphe's attachment, that curious mingling of 'selfishness and emotionalism' (124), is not visibly reproduced in Maurice. He does not seem the man to have seduced Kitty with any sense of ruthlessness, or even with any kind of enthusiasm at all; to the end of the novel, he remains apparently unaware of the effect he has produced on her; and as he moves to his post at Oxford, he may be expected to find some happiness – if little bliss – whether or not he shares this existence with Kitty's ex-student, Jane Fairfax.

Kitty's actual relation to Ellénore is even more attenuated. The

two women admittedly share a common background of displacement and alienation: Ellénore, child of an illustrious Polish family,
had lost her father to political exile, and been transplanted by her
mother to France; on her mother's death she had been left alone in
the world, before meeting Count P——. Kitty had never known her
father and, as a result of her mother's helplessness, had been raised
in London by her totally unassimilated French grandparents.

But depth of characterization in *Providence* has shifted – together
with narrative focus – from hero to heroine. Adolphe's compulsion
becomes Kitty's, and the final judgement on Adolphe by the severe
and uncompromising 'publisher' acquires a new application:

> Circumstances are quite unimportant, character is everything; in
> vain we break with outside things or people; we cannot break
> with ourselves. (*Adolphe*, 125)

This now seems the perfect expression of the novelist's own pronounced determinism and a fitting epitaph for the typical Brookner
heroine.

Kitty Maule does not seem, any more than Maurice, to live in the
throes of an overwhelming passion, remaining closer to the chaste
heroines of the romantic novels she occasionally borrowed from her
mother. She describes her own behaviour as 'discreet in a way that
would have been becoming in a nineteenth-century governess' (33)
– it will be remembered that Helen Weiss read six identical stories
a week about 'maidens in the nineteenth century, taking posts as
governesses and losing their hearts to the rakish son' (*A Start in Life*,
111).

Brookner clearly possesses sufficient familiarity with the genre to
pass on to her female characters. Unlike Ellénore, however, Kitty
would – in her own mind – place safety and security before passion.
But according to the more scathing external narrator, Kitty casts
Maurice more luridly as 'the unfettered man, the mythic hero, the
deliverer', and herself as 'the unclaimed woman' (94) – an example
of considerable romantic license in the shrewd young academic with
her otherwise disciplined weekly dissections of *Adolphe*. And yet
the ambivalence of Kitty's relationship to romance heroines merely
reflects and encapsulates the greater ambivalence of *Providence*'s
relation to the entire field of popular romance. Like the more
illustrious example of *Don Quixote* with respect to another form

of romance, *Providence* may well be both parody and apotheosis of the genre.

The portrayal of the relationship between Maurice and Kitty may owe as much, therefore, to another literary typology – founded on comic satire – as it does to the patterns of romance tragedy. This point is well illustrated as Kitty waits patiently for the planned meeting with Maurice in Paris. The latter's behaviour when he arrives in Kitty's hotel room (where his sole activity is to take a bath), or on the excursion to St Denis (where he rudely falls asleep on the train) hardly qualifies him for the role of Romantic hero; and – in another ironic comment – Brookner actually inserts a cruder pastiche of the Romantic hero in the person of Pascoe, the handsome schoolteacher, harassed by his group of infatuated schoolgirls: the new exemplar is even endowed with a Byronic limp.

The episode with Maurice in Paris may be read as a form of anti-romance. The discrepancy between Kitty's expectations and the banal reality of the celebration dinner (Maurice's unexpected appearance with Jane Fairfax) reaches almost quixotic proportions. The incongruity is emphasized by a genial choice of detail as Jane enters with Maurice, 'carrying a large tureen of soup' (188). The *bathos* of the scene may be increased by that most banal of figurative associations: Kitty herself is now, emotionally speaking, thoroughly *in the soup*.

*       *       *

The author's recourse, once again, to a French literary model may easily obscure the significant differences between *A Start in Life* and *Providence*. The latter novel is, for example, virtually devoid of childhood reminiscences, and – after a brief chapter on Kitty's exotic grandparents – the narrative plunges straight into a university environment. With its attempts at academic satire (faculty meetings, the dean's receptions) and scenes from provincial life (visits to a colleague's family home in Gloucestershire), *Providence* is clearly Brookner's most concerted attempt to write as an 'insider'. It is probably an over-familiarity with *Providence*, at the expense of the other novels, which has given rise to a critical *canard* whereby, Brookner is identified with Pym:

> Anita Brookner's novels have a great deal in common with Barbara Pym's: they tend to be about single women whose love

affairs don't conclude satisfactorily (though Brookner's affairs
are far sexier than Pym's); they focus closely on the daily details
of cooking, sewing and general household tasks; they contain
such fixtures of English country life as jumble sales, garden
parties, and vicars (though Pym is much heavier on the vicars
than Brookner); and they emphasize the value of wit, giving
great credit to characters for small amusing observations. The
humorous eye which Pym often turns upon the church, Brookner
reserves for academia. (Lessing, 1984)

Such an account would seem to fluctuate between wilful misreading
and woeful ignorance. Superficially, one might relate degrees of
sexiness in Pym and Brookner to Dr Johnson's celebrated comment
on settling the point of precedency between a louse and a flea; more
rigorously, one may insist on the difficulty of finding – in Brookner
– any suggestion of a vicar or a jumble sale. Most pertinently,
however, one must question the attempt to endow Brookner with
the insider status of Pym (or even Austen) in relation to English
society.

Referring to her family's central European origins, Brookner has
repeatedly emphasized her own sense of marginality and alienation
in England. Her predominantly female protagonists are also mentally, if not actually ethnically, outsiders. If, moreover, Brookner
has exhausted the potential of childhood reminiscence, even as she
remains excluded from the innermost sanctums of English life, the
undeniable sense of impasse which characterizes her third novel,
Look at Me, is not derived solely from the conditions of personal
crisis under which it was written.

Look at Me further curtails scenes of childhood or adolescence,
even as it excludes virtually any form of insider knowledge. Its
claustrophobic atmosphere is in fact well-suited to the organic
requirements of the novel. It was perhaps only after Look at
Me that Brookner faced the real threat of a creative impasse.

In a minor interview with Michael Barber in 1983, for example, she apparently assumed that there would be no more novels
('that particular vein is now exhausted', 27). The potential obstacle
was overcome, however, by a renewed receptivity towards formal
experimentation – and the unconditional surrender of Pym's terrain,
as she concentrated on a foreign setting. These two tendencies merge
most spectacularly in Hotel du Lac, but the first direction is already
evident in Look at Me.

## *LOOK AT ME*

Brookner's third novel, *Look at Me*, has various points of contact with its predecessors. It also has one major technical modification, distinguishing it from the rest of her fiction to date (with the single exception of *A Friend from England*): the consistent use of a first person intradiegetic narrator – a 'chronicler-protagonist', centrally involved in the events of which she provides an account.[9] The story of Frances Hinton – 'Little Orphan Fanny' – thus possesses an immediacy not present in the earlier novels; Fanny's Candide-like ingenuousness occasionally mellows into poignancy or pathos, without however excluding occasional touches of the grotesque and absurd.

The introduction of a self-conscious narrator, or the writer literally writing, also anticipates the more elaborate *mise en abyme* of *Hotel du Lac*. But the great potential of the new narrative model has its price: *Look at Me* has simultaneously lost the sharply discriminating external voice, with its almost infinite gradations of narratorial involvement or detachment. For a viable comparison, one might consider the effect of a *Mansfield Park* narrated by Fanny Price.

The limitations of the method are already apparent in the first chapter, where Frances describes her work in the reference library of a medical research institute. Here, in keeping with the occasionally morbid propensities of Brookner protagonists, she looks after the 'pictorial material', with its endless historical perspectives on melancholy, madness, death and dreams. Frances shares the responsibility with her friend Olivia, 'never less than totally composed' (15), but slightly more handicapped – following a car accident – than was Ruth Weiss (*A Start in Life*) after a childhood attack of meningitis. An air of calm detachment, together with the duplication of a mild physical handicap, are features suggesting their own affinities with earlier Brookner heroines, and suggest Olivia's role as virtual *alter ego* to Frances; her own comments, naturally presented in third person form, may also conceal an authorial hankering for earlier methods of external presentation.

The marginal figures studying in the library include the astrologer Mrs Halloran ('a wild-looking lady with a misleading air of authority') and Dr Simek ('an extremely reticent Czech or Pole', 10); but the stars are James Anstey and – in the familiar mould of Richard Hirst and Maurice Bishop – 'everybody's favourite', Nick Fraser:

> For as long as Olivia and I have known him he has been dis-
> tinguished by that grace and confidence of manner that ensure
> success. He is tall and fair, an athlete, a socialite, well-connected,
> good-looking, charming: everything you could wish for in a man.
> Our all-England hero, Olivia once called him, in those days when
> she was more than a little in love with him. (11)

The phrase 'all-England hero' might have sounded positively sardonic rather than just mildly ironic coming from Frances's own lips,
and the presence of Olivia as subsidiary focus is again useful.

Nick, with his 'hectic charm' and 'generally golden quality',
together with his beautiful but more menacing wife ('the careless
hair and the rapacious teeth' [!], 47) seems – in the opinion of Frances
– to vindicate nineteenth-century theories of natural selection. The
couple are also the cue for a familiar Brookner contrast between the
beautiful and the homely, now given fresh thematic impetus by a
parallel division into 'participants' and 'observers':

> I have noticed that extremely handsome men and extremely
> beautiful women exercise a power over others which they them-
> selves have no need, or indeed no time, to analyse. People like
> Nick attract admirers, adherents, followers. They also attract
> people like me: observers. One is never totally at ease with
> such people, for they are like sovereigns and one's duty is to
> divert them. (14)

Frances lives with Nancy, the Irish maid, in a large and lonely flat in
Maida Vale, where she attempts to take refuge each evening in her
writing. The sense of an 'intolerable life' and the resultant 'yearning
for freedom' are equally common Brookner motifs; the Frasers, in
accordance with another familiar pattern, will be the agents of her
rescue. As they lay the foundations for her 'new life' and 'further
education', Frances can even contemplate a symbolic move from
her ossified apartment ('zig-zag rugs and creaking hide chairs', 69),
acquired by her parents in wartime London.

As her relationship with the Frasers develops, however, the
reader may again be aware of tensions and inconsistencies produced by the author's choice of narrative model as much as by
the characters' incompatibility of temperament. In order to tell her
story, the otherwise ingenuous Frances has already had recourse to
recantation ('I exaggerate of course'), overheard conversations, and

inordinate insight into other people's reactions; it is, above all, her shrewd analysis of the Frasers' sexual exhibitionism (and her own vaguer sensations of voyeurism) which seem beyond the capacity of the chosen form of presentation:

> What interested me far more, although I also found it repellent, was their intimacy as a married couple. I sensed that it was in this respect that they found my company necessary: they exhibited their marriage to me, while sharing it only with each other. I soon learned to keep a pleasant non-committal smile on my face when they looked into each other's eyes, or even caressed each other; I felt lonely and excited. I was there because some element in that perfect marriage was deficient, because ritual demonstrations were needed to maintain a level of arousal which they were too complacent, perhaps too spoilt, even too lazy to supply for themselves, out of their own imagination. I was the beggar at their feast, . . . (57)

The alertness to sexual idiosyncracy – not conspicuous even in the otherwise sophisticated narrators of the previous novels – is now invested in the *credulous* protagonist of *Look at Me*. Or if Frances *is* considered capable of such insights, it is hard to imagine her simultaneously expressing herself so naively about 'those droll and piquant comic novels enjoyed by dons at Oxford and Cambridge colleges' (16), or ingenuously comparing the likes of the Frasers to 'some natural phenomenon: a rainbow, a mountain, a sunset' (15).

It is, however, for James Anstey – meticulous, military and 'just conceivably a leader of men' (73–4) – that Frances feels the greatest attraction. Her minutely recorded sensations in this respect – 'I felt strong, I felt energetic, I felt . . . young' [the dots are in the original] / 'life was opening up' / 'I was only just beginning my life' / 'he had given validity to my entire future' (86–91) – do indeed have the ring of the romantic novelette. And yet the wry comment a few pages previously again introduces a dubious element of inconsistency into the narrative voice:

> I sensed that Dr Anstey and I had a good deal in common in the way of good behaviour, moral stuffiness, and general lack of experience in the wilder and more interesting areas of human conduct . . . (75)

The same kind of polarization may also be present when Frances, the fulfilled romantic heroine, remarks pointedly after walking home with James: 'That night I did not bother to write' (83); whereas Frances, the self-conscious narrator thinking in more sophisticated terms, exclaims triumphantly that she is 'being written into the plot' (82).

Brookner novels characteristically exhibit shrewd, intelligent heroines who are nevertheless prey to Romantic mythology in its more banal incarnations; in fact, the tendency is not always absent from the author's own interviews. The formal contrast established in *A Start in Life* or *Providence* – detached extradiegetic narration, with frequent focalization through the susceptible heroine – is obviously forfeited in *Look at Me*. It is surely significant that only one subsequent Brookner novel has consistently used a first person intradiegetic narrator.

Frances's relationship with James effectively deteriorates from the moment the latter moves into the Frasers' spare room. Here, too, the novel suffers from the lack of Brookner's habitual clear-sighted external narrator, since Frances's version of events is necessarily confused. Thus, Alix is obviously a malevolent influence, although even the most careful reading fails to reveal whether she is merely obstructive or more explicitly seductive in her relations with James.

The same kind of unresolvable ambiguity characterizes the account of Frances's own dealings with James. Frances has a naive disregard for any erotic feelings that James may have for her; and yet the failure of the couple's only attempt at sexual consummation ('Not with you, Frances. Not with you', 127) seems rather to suggest James's inability to combine the physical and emotional dimensions in a single relationship. The reader obviously has no automatic right to reliable information, but the ambivalence here seems dictated by structural weakness rather than thematic motivation. Frances, in any case, feels a sense of defeat ('And then, I think, I knew that I had lost him long before the evening had ever started', 127).

The remainder of the novel (like *Latecomers* – if for different reasons) is striking for its paucity of action, reminding us that both *A Start in Life* and *Providence* had only maintained their dramatic impetus by duplicating a series of events. Ruth had *twice* found her own apartment and prepared food for the man she loved, Richard Hirst in London, Professor Duplessis in Paris; with Maurice

Bishop, on the other hand, Kitty Maule had undergone *two* cycles of expectation and delusion.

Frances, in turn, now anticipates a Christmas dinner with the Frasers, James and their friend, Maria. Brookner has few rivals in chronicling the hours of a waiting woman; and as Frances reviews the events of the year, studying her reflection in the mirror ('some beady Victorian child'), the long ironic crescendo presents a familiar pattern: it finds its closest parallel in Kitty's protracted anticipation of her public lecture. The denouement is swift and traumatic: Christmas dinner in a restaurant is fraught by the presence of two women of the type so threatening to the Brookner heroine: Alix ('opulent curves' increasingly evident), and the sauntering Maria (a 'low hoarse voice' /'haughty physical presence', 158).

Maria reveals by a crudely explicit remark that she is already James's lover, and Frances's sense of delusion is complete. She leaves the restaurant with the bitter insight that 'for love, a rampant egoism serves one better than an unsophisticated hope', together with an indelible set of images:

> I remembered the noise and heat of that restaurant, the intent and flushed faces, the oozing custard, the sucking inhalations of cigarettes, the raucous but sly excitement, the watchers. (163)

The repressed erotic associations of such details may remain beyond recovery, or – in terms of author *vs.* narrator – even beyond attribution.

Frances now struggles home through Hyde Park in darkness and rain, literally 'walking from memory' to sanctuary and sustenance with Nancy:

> I felt the cup guided towards my mouth and I drank steadily as Nancy held the cup to my mouth, lowering it when she thought I ought to take a breath, as she had when I was a child. (172)

The explicit process of regression resolves itself in sleep, effectively anticipating a spiritual rebirth even while it marks some form of emotional death, and on the following day, Frances's true career as a writer begins.

\*          \*          \*

There is an interesting postscript to the discussion of narrative

models. The choice of the first person intradiegetic narrator in
*Look at Me* might be easily defended on simple autobiographical
grounds. *Look at Me* inevitably impresses the reader as a painfully
intimate and personal document, and Brookner almost immediately
seeks a certain detachment from it:

> *Look at Me* is a very depressed and debilitated novel, and it's one
> I regret. When I published it, a very old friend of my mother's
> summoned me and said, 'You are getting yourself a bad reputa-
> tion as a lonely woman. Stop it at once.' (Haffenden, 25)

It is an amusingly ambivalent anecdote, but the clear implication
remains that the apparent contradictions and inconsistencies of
Frances are disconcertingly close to the contradictions and inconsistencies of the author herself. And yet Brookner, with her extreme
sensitivity to formal structure, would surely insist that artistic
form cannot always follow the divagations of human experience.
Her other novels, of course, will often display characteristic (and
occasionally unresolved) tensions between rigorous external narrators and vulnerable internal focalizers, masking the kind of inner
conflicts that modern criticism now even finds in Austen.[10]

In terms of the immense personal investment involved in these
narratives, the analogy with Austen seems additionally justified.
And yet the impression sometimes remains that *Look at Me* only
avoids the narrative discrepancies of an *Emma* or *Mansfield Park* for
the cruder ambiguities of a *Roxana* or *Moll Flanders*.

But Brookner's family anecdote has another dimension: very old
friends of one's mother are presumably oblivious of distinctions
between narrators and focalizers, and doubtless understandably
so; but writing interesting novels is not always consonant with
the conventions of South Kensington. It is difficult to imagine an
old family friend reproaching Beckett for being 'gloomy' – or trying
to remonstrate on any grounds at all with Philip Roth!

For *Look at Me* is, above all, an extremely brave novel; the shift to
intradiegetic narration is not all loss. The transparent ingenuousness
of the early chapters ('even for one as invulnerable as myself', 9 /
'[f]ortunately I'm not a hysterical person', 18 / 'We rationalists
must fly the flag together, you know', 51) has an impressive pathos.
The harrowing night-walk through a dark and rainy London – with
its archetypal hints of purification before rebirth – is worthy of the

very Romantic tradition which, in one form or another, has played such a prominent role in Brookner's fiction.

\* \* \*

There is one further dimension of *Look at Me* demanding close consideration: the novel's self-conscious narration. Of all Brookner's fiction, it is *Hotel du Lac* which most clearly proclaims its self-reflexivity, a condition reflected primarily in the novel's elaborate use of *mise en abyme*. But Brookner's development of this technique has its origins in *Look at Me*, and it is therefore necessary to transgress momentarily the tripartite divisions imposed on the present study, in order to discuss the two novels together. I begin with *Hotel du Lac*, in order to return to *Look at Me*.

If a major thematic concern of *Hotel du Lac* is (re)valuation, the predominant structural feature – as the external narrator presents Edith in the very process of transforming daily experience into romantic fiction – is that of *mise en abyme*. The device also has a prominent role in the novel's critique of authority (discussed in the following chapter) and thus makes double demands on our critical attention.

The device in itself is neither specifically traditional nor modern: if Jean Ricardou has suggested that 'most books of the *nouveau roman* contain, in one fashion or the other, one or more *mises en abyme*', Claude Ollier clamed that 'the renowned mise en abyme can be found more or less everywhere through the centuries' (quoted by Morrisette, 145, 152).

A most illuminating account of the technique may be found in Morrisette's own *Novel and Film: Essays in Two Genres*. The tenth essay in this collection, 'Interior Duplication' i.e. *mise en abyme* – first published in 1971 – is a useful survey of the device, taking Gide's discussion in his *Journal* of 1893 as a starting point, but ranging widely between fifteenth century Flemish painting and the French *nouveau roman*. The 1971 article should be supplemented by the 1975 essay on 'Post-modern Generative Fiction' (the opening essay in *Novel and Film*) where Morrisette also makes the important theoretical distinction between thematic and formal (or 'generative') *mise en abyme*.

In its thematic function, as exemplified in *Hamlet* or Gide's own *Les Faux-Monnayeurs*, the interior duplication may be regarded as a 'type of inner reflection of the main significance of a work in another work explicitly or implicitly present'.

In post-modernist theory, however, the concept of *mise en abyme*

58

is extended to include purely formal duplications; as Ricardou has suggested, the technique then has the function of 'emphasizing that the novel primarily relates only to itself. Instead of drawing attention to the daily world we are in, it seems that there is in this procedure a sort of extremely concerted will towards the secret corners of the book' (Morrisette, 152). *Mise en abyme* thus becomes a 'generative' practice concerned to contest, attack or destroy (Ricardou's word is 'abîmer') 'such traditional concerns as thematic causality, linear chronology, justified narrative view-point etc'; such an assault on referentiality ultimately works at the aesthetic level for the 'revolutionary overthrow of bourgeois values' (10).

On the basis of careful study, one would hesitate to suggest that such an attitude could provide an explicit model for Brookner's fictional practice. But before returning to a specific (and hardly revolutionary) example of a novelist writing a novel about a novelist who writes novels, it will helpful to consider one more perceptive comment by Morrisette.

In his discussion of the basic metaphor of *abyme* (or *abîme*) – drawn from heraldry, where it signifies the centre of the blason, or coat of arms – Morrisette notes that never, in all the works on heraldry he has consulted, has he found an inset miniature blason identical with the blason at large figured by the surface of the shield (143–4). The distinction is relevant to *Hotel du Lac*, where we are constantly aware of a distinction between the supposed authority of the assured frame narrator / 'implied author' / 'Anita Brookner' – the point is too essential to be allowed to founder on terminological wrangles – and the anxiety reflected in the various exhausting attempts of Edith to write.

But the observation is also significant for *Look at Me*, when due allowances have been made for its first person narrative model. For if Frances the diarist keeps an ingenuous account of her daily hopes and disappointments, Frances the retrospective narrator writes quite a different narrative from her perspective of disillusion. In a quite obvious way, the dual thrust of the narrative recalls the Dickens of *Great Expectations*, with Pip, the adult as narrator, and Pip, the child, as focalizer; in its broader implications – as I shall later suggest – the formal precursor is Proust.

Alternating between the intradiegetic account of Edith Hope, writer of popular novelettes, and a more or less detached external narrator,

*Hotel du Lac* manages – more than any other Brookner narrative – to incorporate within the text the very process of literary production. But *Look at Me*, its immediate predecessor, also introduces an intra-diegetic narrator who is a writer of fiction – admittedly not yet as established as Edith Hope, although she is literally responsible for the entire narrative in which she appears!

Frances's self-reflexivity is, moreover, no marginal phenomenon: the presence of some fifty references to the actual writing process give the latter a prominence that can hardly be ignored.

The narrator's comments on her own writing begin in the very first chapter and continue steadily throughout the novel. It is her friend Olivia who gives her the initial impulse to write:

> She encouraged me to write it all down, and so I bought the usual large exercise book and kept a sort of diary, and I like to think that one day I will use this material and write a comic novel, one of those droll and piquant chronicles enjoyed by dons at Oxford and Cambridge colleges. (16)

Her first fictional efforts are a substitute for the oral fantasies she once elaborated for her mother:

> Since my mother died, I have had no one to talk to about these things, no one who is so interested, who knows the characters, who wants to find out what happens next, who responds with such delight. (16)

She now writes on lonely evenings after work and 'struggle[s] to keep a note of despondency out of what gets put down' (16); certain subjects ('low spirited people' or 'unfortunate people') are at all costs to be avoided – 'I have put all that sort of thing behind me'). Frances has published one short story about the library in which she works ('heavily disguised, of course'), although, as she admits, 'I was not on the whole as pleased with it as everyone else seemed to be' (16).[11]

Such an apparently artless account actually recognizes several major aspects of the heroine's writing activity. Thus, if narrative discourse is accepted – according to critical consensus among more pragmatically minded readers – as 'someone telling someone else that something happened', Frances provides for her own case an unusually explicit account of these conditions: conditions which

Barbara Herrnstein Smith, for example, has defined as 'those circumstantial and psychological variables of which every utterance is a function' (Mitchell, 1981, 221).

The delights of literary invention – of which her mother is the first beneficiary – suggest, firstly, the importance for Frances of simple wish-fulfilment; the censorship of certain material ('the time of which I never speak', 121) then becomes an exercise in repression. In concrete terms, one might suggest that she is concerned with what didn't happen, although she would have *liked* it to; and what actually happened although she wished it *hadn't*.

Her subsequent dissatisfaction with the results ('I was not on the whole as pleased with it as everyone else seemed to be', 16) suggests a critical awareness of the gap between desire and performance. In fact, if Frances naively reveals the simple contingencies that shape representation, she also suggests the incommunicable residue left by the process. Frances's self-reflexivity in narrating a simple series of events thus becomes a paradigm for the autobiographical mode itself, and therefore anticipates the discussion of fiction and autobiography in the final chapter.

The 'circumstantial and psychological variables' of Frances's narrative – wish-fulfilment and repression, desire and performance – are prominently maintained for the reader throughout the novel. In another self-reflexive passage, the narrator sees writing as a way of 'reminding people that I am here' (19). But if she manages to write transparently enough, Frances will paradoxically conceal her first true motive for writing, the need to win attention:

> If my looks and my manner were of greater assistance to me I could deliver this message in person. 'Look at me,' I would say. 'Look at me.' (20)

The initial mode of Frances's writing is confessional, in the form of a quite concrete diary (cf. 54, 56) maintained with a view to her 'nebulous novel': this relation is an accurate, if obvious, *mise en abyme* of the composition of *Look at Me* itself. If the diary records the activities of Frances (the naive protagonist), Frances (the narrator of *Look at Me*) portrays – at a higher narrative level – the more self-conscious writer of the diary.[12]

Frances's authorial activity is also closely integrated to a major thematic concern of the novel (and indeed of all of Brookner's fiction), the polarity of observer and participant: 'I had long ago cast myself in the role of observer, always with my writing in mind' (59)/ 'One is, let it be remembered, an observer, an unblinking eye recording what is thought, at the time, to be unremarkable' (164). Only during her budding relationship with James is Frances aware of being herself 'written into the plot'; as Ruth Weiss had set aside her Balzac during a similar period of emotional fulfilment, so Frances does not write for many evenings (84). Like Kitty Maule's academic study, moreover, Frances's creative writing is more a question of passing time, before – as the workings of her self-delusion suggest to her – her true destiny is revealed.

Her dreams are not always devoid of a certain banality:

I sometimes have fantasies of a life in which I would spend evenings sitting on somebody's bed, exchanging confidences, keeping up with each other's love affairs, comparing clothes, trying out new hairstyles . . . (23)

This passage, too, has a distinctive Mills & Boon flavour, and is in fact immediately qualified ('Although all that is hardly to my taste'). In a more ambitious fantasy Frances sees herself as a successful writer ('I could already see the reviews . . . ', 132); in a more calculating one she sees an available husband in Olivia's brother ('David would wait for me to make up my mind', 151).

Frances is ostensibly happier in the active state: 'the thought of reverting to the role of observer rather than participant filled me with dread and sadness' (132); and the participatory role that she craves with James and the Frasers is always quite explicit:

I know that euphoria, that mania, that love and carelessness breed. And because I longed to experience it again on my own account, and not just to watch it, I had to trust them. (58)

And yet several important hints in the course of the narrative suggest that these are precisely the experiences that Frances would *not* wish to relive. Figures arise from 'some area which I cannot control and which I would dearly love to forget about' (44). Nick and Alix produce a particularly disturbing image from 'some basement area' (102) of her personality. The thought that Alix might have fallen in love with James also has its 'full accompaniment of ugly and erotic images' (119).

But the central act of repression in Frances's narrative ('that time of which I never speak') reproduces a virtual Brookner *topos* – the distressing memory of an earlier erotic experience. The most explicit account of this episode acquires (as the narrator herself is aware) a strangely archaic quality:

> That secrecy, that urgency, that bitterness, that lack of hope . . . . I had enjoyed the openness of consorting with an eligible man (how prehistoric that sounds!) in full view of others, after those strategems and those returns in the early hours of the morning, weeping, my coat huddled round me to conceal the clothes so hastily put on and now creased. The concealed pain, the lying morning face. I could not go through that again. (121–2)

Frances idealizes her relation to James as a 'renewal of innocence', but the desire for a full relationship and the awareness of the kind of erotic experience it would presumably involve are perhaps a source of unresolved conflict within her. It is unnecessary to point out that it is Frances who eventually takes the initiative and leads James to the bedroom; but the latter's despairing 'Not with you, Frances, not with you' (127) may suggest – if such unambiguous meaning is recoverable – that he has accurately read the signals emitted by Frances.

For all its agonized record of suffering, Frances's self-reflexive narrative sometimes produces insights quite as shrewd and suggestive as those advanced by the more dispassionate Edith Hope. On the conventional nature of any narrative mode and the inevitable 'falsification' of past experience, she thus remarks:

> I knew that they were all stored somewhere, and could, at some future date, be retrieved, intact. It would be my wearisome task to retrieve them with gusto, to make my readers smile wryly at the accuracy of my detail. (174–75)

The comment recognizes the disengagement of remote retrospective narrative (not unlike the Wordsworthian aesthetic of emotion recollected in tranquillity). But it may also anticipate Brookner's subsequent abandonment of the first person narrator and return to her earlier relatively controlled external voice.

Most significant of all, however, is a remark on the actual epistemology of fiction; Kitty refers here to a scene of a gift of chocolates to her mother:

I could not quite dismiss this image, although I had conjured it up. It did not strike me until much later that this scene, which was so vivid to me, had not yet taken place. I saw no significance in the fact that this episode, pieced together from elements observed at disparate moments (the box of chocolates from many occasions, the tears from yet another), seemed to be a memory but was in fact a conjuration. The fact that two sets of time had come together in this way I accepted as perfectly normal. (71)

The first of these comments suggests the author's sensitivity towards the entire question of narration and focalization, an awareness which will assume even greater significance in *Hotel du Lac*. The second reflects an even more fundamental question – considered in Chapter 5 – the relationship between Brookner's 'true' autobiography and her 'invented' fiction. In anticipation of this, one may also remember Brookner's throwaway remark in an interview that, in a certain sense, writers of fiction are the only ones who are telling the truth.

*              *              *

In *Look at Me*, the 'French Connection' is also important, if now less explicit, for the most striking literary analogy now appears solely in the overall structure of the novel, and not simultaneously in thematic terms.

As she goes to visit her retired predecessor from the reference library, Frances speaks of 'reverting to the role of observer rather than participant' (133), thus foregrounding her two complementary roles within the novel. The lonely, alienated figure of the first chapter muses on her own experiences: 'I like to think that one day I will use this material and write a comic novel' (16); this resolve is strengthened after getting to know the Frasers – she is 'going to write . . . ' (52), and is now recording the material in her diary for a 'nebulous novel' (53).

As her social group is extended by the addition of Dr Anstey, Frances responds accordingly ('[t]he novelist in me took over' 76) and notes with delight that she is 'being written into the plot' (82). In the 'new security' provided by the blossoming relationship with James, her role of observer is momentarily eclipsed by that of participant, and she can announce 'I did not write for many evenings that followed' (84).

Shortly after this, however, Fanny's world disintegrates as she learns – according to a classic Brookner pattern – that James has succumbed to the 'scornful temptress', Maria (158), and that the two are having an affair. Hereafter, Fanny withdraws into herself once again, but carefully stores the traumatic details which 'could, at some date, be retrieved, intact' 174):

> In future I would become subsumed into my head, and into my hand, my writing hand. (179)

In this painful state of emotional retreat or even psychological regression, Fanny begins 'working at it, with my pen and my notebook', 181), amassing her 'notes for a satirical novel'. The latter is suitably inspired – in view of Brookner's own literary and artistic formation – by an eighteenth-century French print on her wall (a skating scene with the admonishing title, *Glissez, mortels: n'appuyez pas*). Now she must go back and study the group afresh ('I must know them once again at first hand', 190); and the final sentences announce, with a dramatic shift to the present tense 'I pick up my pen. I start writing' (192). But Fanny's story is, of course, already written.

Of the major twentieth-century French novelists, the most important theorist and practitioner of *mise en abyme* is Gide; with her academic background in French literature, Brookner can hardly be unaware of the complexities of *Les Faux-Monnayeurs* [The Counterfeitors] (1926). The focal point of Gide's novel is the novelist Édouard, who is himself writing a novel to be called *Les Faux-Monnayeurs*; the journal recording this process forms a large part of the novel, and has its counterpart in Gide's own *Journal des Faux-Monnayeurs* (1926). Gide also discussed *mise en abyme* at some length in his *Journal* for 1893. His ideas have been usefully summarized in Bruce Morrisette's essay 'Interior Duplication' (*Novel and Film* 1985, 140ff), and will acquire greater relevance in the following chapter, in the context of *Hotel du Lac*.

In terms of narrative structure, however, there is another analogue to *Look at Me*, an even closer and more obvious parallel: it is, of course, Proust's *À la Recherche du Temps perdu*. Brookner made an extended comment on Proust in conversation with Shusha Guppy:

> He is an exceptional case and very precious to me. He kept himself in a state of mind so hypnotic and dangerous that one

approaches reading him almost with fear. He remained always marginal, observing. The cost was too high, when all is said and done. The periods of remaining in that childlike state of receptivity are terrifying. The awful thing is that he got it *right all the time*. It is all true! (Guppy, 157–8)

And Kenyon's interview reproduces this tribute in uncannily similar terms.

The connection between Proust and *Look at Me* is primarily structural, rather than thematic or stylistic. When Marcel attends the reception of the Duchesse de Guermantes in the second part of *Le Temps retrouvé*, he experiences a series of trivial incidents through the agency of 'involuntary memory'; this leads to the famous insight that 'reality' is no more or less than the spiritual significance of everything we experience in life. This reality both transcends time, and is universal. He will now recuperate the 'vraie verité' of his life by returning to some significant point in his childhood, in effect the 'drame du coucher' episode which had been described at the very beginning of *Du coté de chez Swann*. But the novel we are invited to read is of course already written.

*Look at Me*, with its closing image of Frances ('I pick up my pen. I start writing'), has an essentially analogous structure. In one sense, the narrative of *Look at Me* may be closer to *Les Faux-Monnayeurs* than to *À la Recherche du Temps perdu* – Frances, like Édouard, is explicitly writing throughout the novel; Marcel has only implicitly written. It may be fairest to suggest, however, that – by a reproductive feat that would surely have delighted the progenitors – *Look at Me* emerges by Gide out of Proust.

The more general and abstract reliance on the models of Proust and Gide marks the end of overt relations between Brookner's novels and French literary sources. The use of *mise en abyme* in *Look at Me* anticipates the growing interest in formal devices that characterizes the next group of three novels. In *Hotel du Lac*, this technique acquires even greater prominence; *Family and Friends*, on the other hand, is interesting – among other things – for its attempt to solve certain problems of the family chronicle novel by the extended use of 'literary frames'; *A Misalliance*, finally, develops the novelist's predilection for analogies from painting into a consistent and comprehensive iconography. It is now time to consider each of these novels in turn.

# 3
# Novel Departures

## HOTEL DU LAC

*Hotel du Lac* is the most original and innovative of Brookner's novels, even as it also remains the one most intimately linked to the world of popular romance. The latter is squarely confronted by the introduction of heroine Edith Hope, 'a writer of romantic fiction under a more thrusting name' (8).

The previous books all contained various indirect (and even more direct) allusions to the genre. In *A Start in Life*, for example, Helen and Mrs Cutler had both been avid readers of novelettes, and there is amusing satire of their tastes: Helen requiring six tales a week of governesses losing their hearts to the rakish son; Mrs Cutler – more flexible – but drawing the line at unhappy endings, colonial settings, or characters called Douglas like her late husband. Here at least is an awareness of what a true formula novel might involve.

Kitty Maule's grandmother, Louise, had been another great reader of popular romances, a entertainment which she alternated with television soap opera. Kitty herself, as a child, had sometimes borrowed her grandmother's books!

It is Edith Hope (or Vanessa Wilde), however, who is the ultimate authority: eloquently outspoken, but without ever losing a fundamental ambivalence towards the genre. She claims to believe every word she writes, although over lunch with her agent she also ridicules women's adherence to the 'old myths':

> They want to believe that they are going to be discovered, looking their best, behind closed doors, just when they thought all was lost, by a man who has battled across continents, abandoning whatever he may have had in his in-tray, to reclaim them. Ah! if only it were true,' she said, breathing hard, . . . (27)

Some of Brookner's remarks in interviews are undoubtedly close to the type of sentiment expressed in this quotation – or at least reflect the same kind of ingenuousness that is associated with such views. Twice she referred to her preference for the subject of 'love' ('What else is there? All the rest is mere literature!') – and in her acceptance of the Booker prize for *Hotel du Lac*, she explained:

> When I started the book, I simply wanted to write a love story in which something unexpected happened, and in which I think love really triumphed. (also quoted by Kenyon, 1989, 13)

The distinction between 'Romance novels' and 'Romantic novels' is still current in *Lewis Percy*, where the hero – like most Brookner protagonists – is fully conversant with both genres. Lewis's reading fluctuates between nineteenth-century French 'professional' reading, certain weightier British and American classics, and the lighter works exemplified by his mother's old library books.

It is *Hotel du Lac*, above all, that exemplifies the ambivalent relationship of 'parody' and 'target text' that I have discussed at greater length in the introduction. If Linda Hutcheon referred, on etymological grounds, to the 'suggestion of an accord or intimacy instead of a contrast' (1985, 32), Wolfgang Iser had spoken of literary works situated 'on the edge or just beyond a prevalent thought system'. Neither of these possible relations seems detrimental to the novel.

The effect of *Hotel du Lac* is to confirm an impression suggested by *Providence*, that the juxtaposition of Romantic longing with detached analysis of such feelings remains central to Brookner's fiction.

But *Hotel du Lac* is also more obviously different from its predecessors by virtue of its foreign setting: the main events of the narrative – or, more properly, the events of the main narrative – occur in a Swiss hotel, although a long series of flashbacks to London, and occasionally beyond, acquires increased significance as the story progresses. Narrative responsibilities are divided, moreover, between a characteristic third person external narrator (providing quoted monologue, related monologue and psycho-narration) and the first person narrative of Edith Hope.[1]

Two other innovations – the frequent recourse to analepsis, and the internal narrator's constant errors of judgement – are indirectly related to each other. For with the external narrator's skilful use of suspense and various false leads, it is hardly possible to read the novel without also oneself drawing hasty and erroneous conclusions – which are then corrected by flashback as much as by denouement. The reader thus duplicates the kind of error made by Edith, effectively a form of 'extradiegetic' *mise en abyme*, supplementing the more obvious internal variety (anticipated in *Look at Me*) of Edith's authorial activities.

It is an instructive example of the extreme sophistication of *Hotel du Lac*, and reason enough to proceed cautiously with attempts at synopsis. I therefore plunge directly to the thematic core of the novel – here identified in terms of *authority* and *anxiety*.

Not even the latter concepts, however, are limited to the connotations they may have acquired from previous Brookner novels. Textual authority is not confined to another rigorous critique of Romantic mythology; textual anxiety is not merely a further reflection of the uneasy ideological balance between intellectual detachment and romantic sensibility. *Hotel du Lac* may actually be seen as a point of convergence for two sometimes complementary, but often contradictory texts: a traditional script, generated by what Brookner has described elsewhere as her 'grounding in nineteenth-century novels and nineteenth-century behaviour' (Haffenden, 27), and generally explicable in terms of traditional thematics supplemented by such formal concepts as focalization and *mise en abyme*; and a second unconscious and therefore more enigmatic script, requiring more radical critical approaches.

At first glance, the story is distinctly Jamesian, with its focus on wealthy, leisured Anglo-Saxons in a continental setting. More specifically, Brookner at one point actually indexes male egoism in terms identical to those used in a novel of James: Gilbert Osmond (*Portrait of a Lady*) possesses a beautiful house in Florence, filled with *objets d'art* and his famous collection of *capo di monte* porcelain; whilst the hotel's only male guest – Philip Neville – is equally discriminating with 'a small estate and a very fine house, Regency Gothic', together with his 'rather well-known collection of *famille rose* dishes' (164). Each man is effectively in need of a wife to provide the final touch to an exquisite private collection.

In simple structural terms, moreover, it would also be easy to abstract analogous narrative sequences in the stories of Edith Hope and Isabel Archer. Just as Isabel's 'crazy aunt Lydia' is instrumental in introducing her neice to the English lord, Warburton, so Edith's friend Penelope tries to match her reluctant *protegée* with Geoffrey Long. At the corresponding point of bifurcation in the two narratives, each woman is offered the security and stability of marriage with a wealthy, established man, and each woman declines. The major structural contrast between the two plots emerges when marriage is next proposed: Isabel accepts Osmond, whilst Edith Hope bravely rejects Neville.

In a thematic context, however, one is reminded of the critical commonplace (among male readers at least) that the portrayal of the Jamesian heroine is evidence of some deep authorial empathy with the feminine mind; although it is equally clear that Jamesian sympathies only emerge at their finest as his suffering females become enmeshed – like sacrificial victims – in a repressively patriarchal or phallocentric world. Much Jamesian pathos is expended on the trials of the persecuted heroine; it was evidently easier to sympathize with a struggling butterfly in the net than with a free bird on the wing. *Hotel du Lac*, with its successfully independent but emotionally vulnerable novelist-heroine, might be seen as a crucial variant on a familiar Jamesian theme: as if Henrietta Stackpole (Jamesian *ficelle* and a largely functional figure in *Portrait of a Lady*) were suddenly retrieved from marginal status, endowed with the fine critical intelligence of James's invariably male artist-protagonists, and allowed to become the focal point of the narrative.

Other analogues with *Hotel du Lac* might include E. M. Forster's *A Room with a View* (where another predominantly English group are thrown together in a foreign hotel), and – more fundamentally, if less explicitly – certain novels of George Eliot: for the contrast of intelligence and physical attractiveness in Brookner's Edith Hope and Jennifer Pusey ('Virginia Woolf' to an 'Odalisque') recall such mutually exclusive pairs as Maggie Tulliver and Lucy Deane in *The Mill on the Floss* or Dorothea Brooke and Rosamond Vincy in *Middlemarch*). The thinly-veiled prurience of the Puseys, extravagant widow and regressive daughter, also raises in Edith's mind the whole question of 'What behaviour most becomes a woman' (40), a constant preoccupation of – say – *The Mill on the Floss*, with its investigation of social parameters for women: both intellectually (in the chequered history of Maggie's education), and later, emotionally (in the heroine's unhappy relations with Stephen Guest and Philip Wakem).[2]

The story of Edith Hope's escape from scandal in London to the anonymity of a Swiss hotel even has a superficial resemblance to the mechanics of a traditional marriage plot, although each stage is now refracted through a different narrative technique: Edith's virtual 'marriage' of *love* with art dealer David Simmonds (the discreet relationship to which she eventually returns) is contemplated by the heroine herself in a series of letters reminiscent of eighteenth century epistolary technique; her potential marriage of *sense* to the grey civil servant Geoffrey Long (a match promoted by her friend Penelope, and nullified by Edith's flight from the Registry Office) is recounted by the extradiegetic narrator in a lengthy analepsis deferred until the ninth chapter (of twelve); and her prospective marriage of *convenience* to the cynical voluptuary Philip Neville (whom she also ultimately refuses because of his indiscriminate philandering) is presented as 'first narrative' in present time.

Thus outlined, the novel's structure does not seem remote from the cyclical courtship plot of Emma, or the 'real' and 'parody' romances of *Wuthering Heights*.[3] But *Hotel du Lac* contrasts sharply with Austen (but not, of course, Brontë) in its heavy manipulation of story time, so that the three dramas are effectively played out concurrently, rather than consecutively; it differs from both authors, however, in its elaborately self-reflexive mode.

The latter dimension is established with the introduction of an intradiegetic narrator, popular novelist Edith Hope; her emergence during the course of the opening chapter is actually a far from simple development, as brief formal analysis will show.

The initial description of the hotel and its surrounding landscape apparently originates from what was once confidently described as an 'omniscient narrator'.[4] In an unexpected modulation, however, the second long paragraph introduces Edith Hope – writer of romantic fiction and protagonist of *Hotel du Lac* – now revealed as standing at the window, and possible focalizer of the initial, ostensibly extradiegetic description (8). The middle of the paragraph now introduces an internal monologue, an unmediated account of Edith's thoughts. Lasting for a full twenty-four lines without benefit of quotation marks or other typographical hints (and with only one verb of reflection, located in the second line of the passage), the shift in focalization seems carefully camouflaged, suggesting a distinctive narrative self-consciousness, rather than any naive inconsistency of representation.

This passage is followed by fourteen lines of extradiegetic narrative (' . . . she contemplated the room . . . '), six lines of internal monologue ('I shall be able to write . . . ', 9), five lines more of the external narrator ('it was to the other folder that her hands went', 10), before a radically new technical departure, the first of the narrator's five letters to David (10–12).

Three pages of letter are succeeded by new monologue ('Tea, she thought, I need tea') and further external narrative ('Unpacking took a few minutes'), before the long set description of the hotel itself – a full three pages as authoritative and solidly referential as any Balzacian topology (13–16). The extradiegetic narrator then brings Edith downstairs into the salon; a neatly inserted piece of transitional monologue ('How interesting, thought Edith . . . ', 17) permits an account of the salon itself and the activity of the guests inside to be mediated, at some length (ca. four pages [17–20]) and quite naturally, through the consciousness of Edith. The description of the salon and its occupants is followed by a two-page account of a walk (21–2), surprisingly devoid of any kind of direct monologue.

As Edith then retires to her room to dress for dinner, the extradiegetic narrator returns once again to fill the narrative pause (with benefit of 'omniscience'), offering a record (extending almost a page) of M. Huber, the hotel owner's, internal reflections (22–3). And here, with perhaps unconscious irony, the voice of male authority is allowed to bring the chapter to a close.

It is unnecessary to provide an account of similarly rapid shifts in focalization for the remaining eleven chapters of the novel; a more relevant point is whether such juggling actually serves any greater purpose than to demonstrate that the shortest distance between two (narrative) points is a straight line. There certainly *is* a greater significance, however, and one which emphasizes the need for a bridge between the methods of structuralist narratology exploited here and the procedures of more traditional thematics used broadly in other chapters. For such constantly shifting focalization as occurs in *Hotel du Lac* provides convenient access to one over-riding concern of the novel, the question of textual authority.

\*       \*       \*

In the second chapter of *Hotel du Lac*, there is an analepsis of almost five pages, reproducing a conversation at lunch between Edith and her literary agent. Here, Edith describes the 'potent myth' underlying her own variety of popular romantic fiction, according to which the tortoise defeats the hare, or, more specifically:

> it is the mouse-like unassuming girl who gets the hero, while the scornful temptress with whom he has had a stormy affair retreats baffled from the fray, never to return. (27)

She immediately dismisses this narrative model 'pleasantly, but with authority' as a lie. At the thematic level, one would immediately wish to point out the double irony that neither the 'myth' nor its rebuttal is entirely valid on this occasion: one 'scornful temptress' in the novel (Priscilla) does 'get the hero' (David) – with whom she enjoys the attenuated pleasures of domesticity; she remains unaware, however, that her husband is having an affair with the 'mouse-like unassuming girl' (Edith). Whatever the validity of the myth, moreover, it is perhaps the last occasion in the novel where Edith abrogates to herself such explicit and unquestioned authority.

The most light-hearted erosion of textual authority generally belongs to the novel's traditional script: thus, in her first letter to David, Edith twice jokes about 'the novelist's famed powers of imagination' (11) when she is unable to place people correctly, whether it concerns the profession of a fellow traveller on the plane to Geneva, or the social status of a fellow guest, the elderly Madame de Bonneuil. The joke resurfaces in chapter ten, when Edith's outspoken companion rubs the point home:

> I thought you were supposed to be a writer. Aren't you supposed to be good at observing human nature, or something? I only ask because you sometimes strike me as being a bit thick. (144)

Whether or not Brookner intends a comic allusion to 'the subject presumed to know', as the popular Lacanian tag for individual consciousness, she later finds the perfect emblem for Edith's erratic discursive practice in one of the pictures David auctions: Francesco Furini's canvass of *Time Revealing Truth* (88).

In any event, misunderstandings, confusions, premature judgments dog the text of *Hotel du Lac*. In the case of Monica, the elegant Englishwoman, Edith is also obliged to revise her original calculations:

the 'tall woman of extraordinary slenderness' (16) is at first marked down as a dancer, but by the second letter to David, the 'woman with the dog' must be 'adjusted upwards to lady, or rather Lady' – her husband is a member of the 'ruling class' (47). Even Edith's medical diagnosis ('A breakdown, she decided. A bereavement. Tread carefully') is also inaccurate, since Monica's problems are connected with infertility, and an inability to give her husband the heir he desperately wants.

But Edith's most significant errors concern the extravagant widow Mrs Pusey and her daughter, Jennifer. These also begin with miscalculations of age and social position: Mrs Pusey is first described as 'a lady of indeterminate age', whilst the daughter is judged to be 'about twenty-five' (19). Only a page later, however, Edith is adjusting the ages upwards (from 'upper fifties' and 'middle twenties' to 'upper sixties' and 'early thirties'), whilst in the following chapter – having heard Mrs Pusey refer to Noel Coward as 'that boy' – Edith realizes that 'ages would have to be revised once more' (34).

The process ends with the sensational revelation that Mrs Pusey is seventy-nine – and Edith's equally surprising, but more personally threatening, discovery that the fleshy and nubile Jennifer must actually be older than she is. One might trace the same process of textual revision as Edith attempts to place the Puseys socially. More serious psychological issues are introduced, however, by Edith's changing attitudes towards the Puseys. Even her initial reactions ('curiosity, envy, delight, attraction, and fear, the fear she always felt in the presence of strong personalities', 33) reveal a strong personal bias in favour of the couple. By the following chapter, however, this has changed to firm disapproval, derived from something more substantial than personal prejudice, and related to Mrs Pusey herself:

> For in this charming woman, so entirely estimable in her happy desire to capture hearts, so completely preoccupied with the femininity which had always provided her with life's chief delights, Edith perceived avidity, grossness, ardour. (38–9)

Edith's initially favourable impressions are certainly dictated by unhappy memories of her own mother. She thus 'writes up' Mrs Pusey in a letter to David, in terms more superficially glowing than genuine:

I adore Mrs Pusey. She is a totally serene, supremely confident woman who has, she laughingly suggests, simply made the best of what the good Lord gave her. (46–7)

But she interrupts her rhetorical exercise to recall the memory of the 'two women lovingly entwined as they saw her to the door', reflecting that there was 'love there':

> love between mother and daughter, and physical contact, and collusion about being pretty, none of which she herself had ever known. (48)

Chapter eight contains the long third letter to David, describing the birthday party, and Edith now admits to feeling 'something like pity, horror, compassion' for Mrs Pusey (107), although her 'final' judgement (final only inasmuch as it is the last one recorded in the text, and by no means definitive) is far less charitable. It is based on the stir caused by Mrs Pusey on discovering Alain – perhaps innocently – in her daughter's room. She is essentially a dishonourable person, ensconced in a 'monstrous cosiness' (144).

A similar process of representation (or literally continuous re-presentation) could be traced in Edith's account of Jennifer. The pattern is so common, in fact, that Edith's ongoing textual revision might be regarded as the major thematic concern of the novel's overt, traditional script. It is distinctly reminiscent of the aesthetics of a Conrad or Ford: for if, like Marlow in *Heart of Darkness*, Edith incorporates the process of (self)-discovery into her narrative act, like Powell in *The Good Soldier*,[5] she is often the most ignorant and least reliable textual focus.

The effect of Edith's narrative activity is to emphasize *Hotel du Lac*'s relation to the tradition of the self-conscious novel explored in Robert Alter's *Partial Magic*. Alter makes a clear distinction between the 'elaborately artful novel' – *Lord Jim* – where artifice serves the ends of psychological realism, and the self-conscious novel proper – *The French Lieutenant's Woman* – where 'artifice is deliberately exposed', thus testing the very 'ontological status of fiction' (Alter, xiii). When the intradiegetic narrator is also a professional author, Alter's categories may not always be mutually exclusive, and *Hotel du Lac* effectively questions the validity of this simple division.

The distinctive feature in the present case, however, is the retention of an extradiegetic narrator, whose reliability is often pitted against that of Edith. Not even the external presence of an 'implied author', however, is totally able to restore narrative credibility. There is a significant ambivalence in the conventionally explicit ending of the novel, with Edith's rejection of Philip Neville and her telegram to David ('Coming home', immediately modified to 'Returning'). Edith's message is well-meaningly glossed elsewhere by Brookner herself:

> 'Coming home' would be coming back to domestic propriety: 'home' implies husband, children, order, regular meals, but 'Returning' is her more honest view of the situation. To that extent she does break through to a clearer vision. (Haffenden, 29)

But the implications of the ending are hardly consonant with the author's initial design for the novel:

> I simply wanted to write a love story in which something unexpected happened, and in which *love really triumphed*. (my emphasis; Kenyon, 1989, 13)

As Edith 'returns' to David, loves's victory seems essentially pyrrhic – if not totally illusory – and the story reflects the terminal ambivalence of Brookner's beloved Dickens (say *Great Expectations*) rather than the pseudo-finality of Austen.

*Hotel du Lac* may often be read, therefore, as an ironic commentary on narrative credibility, intra- or extradiegetic; it provides an implicit critique of discursive practices explicitly institutionalized, in the English language at least, by the etymologically related concepts of *author* and *authority*. In late twentieth-century contexts, such authority is almost invariably written and male. In the first case, both writer and the written text are invested with special power and prestige: one consequence in our modern chirographic culture (as Walter Ong has described it)[6] is an atavistic belief in the finality, if not the infallibility, of the written word, a fetishism of the text. It is this 'authorial' (and, by unwarranted extension, 'authoritative') presence which the different narrative voices of *Hotel du Lac* playfully, but no less effectively deconstruct.

There is obviously a further ironic discrepancy between Edith's comic errors of judgement in placing people, and each finished authoritative statement – with its tendentious reaffirmations of traditional (and reactionary) sexual mythology – hailed as a 'modest but substantial seller' and disseminated (we are told) as far as Swiss provincial bookshops. Such unresolved tensions, however, seem to question the status of narratability in fiction rather than that of referentiality in the world outside.

If Edith's performance as narrator is regarded as in some way representative – not to say emblematic – of any narrative act, the reader is confronted with a paradox: according to this, the one reliable aspect of the present narrative is the implication that all narratives are *unreliable*, an *aporia* all the more striking for its presence in a 'conventional' or 'traditional' novel such as *Hotel du Lac*. In addition, therefore, to its character of charmingly wrought 'comedy of manners' – a commonplace among the novel's more patronizing critics (the covert gendering of the adjective being particularly appropriate) – *Hotel du Lac* thus suddenly acquires a metafictional dimension.

*         *         *

But if authority in *Hotel du Lac* revolves primarily around questions of narrative reliability and falls largely within the epistemological scope of the novel's traditional script or surface text, anxiety is ultimately situated at the deeper level of its enigmatic but ubiquitous subtext.

Modern literary theory provides many examples of contradiction or paradox as the normative condition of narrative. Such critical approaches are most obviously related to the kind of deconstructive poetics practised by Paul de Man (cf. *Allegories of Reading* 1979; *Blindness and Insight*, 1983), although, in a related context, Catherine Belsey has discussed Barthes's *S/Z* (1974) and Macherey's *A Theory of Textual Production* (1978). To Barthes's unravelling of Balzac, or Macherey's study of textual ideology unconsciously subverted by Verne, Belsey adds her own analysis of the presentation of women in Sherlock Holmes stories.[7] Brookner's fourth novel represents the author's most obvious example of the text which – in classic deconstructive terminology – simultaneously asserts and denies the authority of its own rhetorical mode.

The contradictions and paradoxes of *Hotel du Lac* may also be illuminated by the conceptual model of a textual unconscious, as found in literary applications of the theories of Lacan. In developing his model of the mirror stage, Lacan hypothesized the formation of the unconscious as occurring simultaneously with the acquisition of language and an individual's entry into the symbolic order; by the simplest of theoretical extensions, Lacanian critics have argued for the analogous formation of an unconscious within the literary text itself at the moment of production. The textual unconscious may thus be defined as 'the gap between the ideological project and the specifically literary form' (Belsey, 108).

In an essay on the application of Lacan's ideas to literary texts, Shoshana Felman has stressed the need to ask certain crucial questions: 'Where does it resist? Where does a text precisely make no sense, that is resist interpretation? Where does what I see – and what I read – resist my understanding?' (1981, 30). Success in answering these questions will clearly determine the reader's ability to recover this same unconscious dimension of the text.

In *Hotel du Lac*, one may confidently suggest several such sites, including the unexpected and even disturbing shifts of focalization in the opening chapter – together with various examples of seemingly obsessive repetition, each resistant to initial attempts at interpretation. The rest of the present reading therefore leaves the play of authority in the novel's traditional script to pursue the traces of anxiety present in its covert text.

Even if it were possible to read *Hotel du Lac* in a state of theoretical innocence, one would still surely be struck by certain repetitive patterns, among which, Edith's own state of almost constant anxiety is only the most prominent. As she writes her first letter to her lover, David, Edith momentarily panics (10); descending to the hotel dining-room, she is worried by an entrance 'always so difficult to negotiate' and the 'business of the meal to get through' (12); at dinner she recognizes her 'dread of the evening before her' (25); recalling her meetings with David she pictures herself 'Anxious in her nightgown . . . ' (29); opening her eyes again, she finds herself gazing fearfully around the still deserted salon' (30); after dinner she sits near the Puseys, 'as if to gain some bravery, some confidence from their utterly assured presence' (34); frightened in childhood by her mother and aunt, she would press her 'wet red face' against her father's hand (49); she contemplates the time 'anxiously' and considers telephoning David (56); on a bad morning she feels an 'instinctive shrinking' from food and company (65); she experiences an 'author's pang' when one of her novels is mentioned with slight reservation (74); after the champagne on Miss Pusey's birthday, she retires with 'fatigue, stretched nerves' (114); back in her rooms, she senses an underlying unease (116).

The external narrator's foregrounding of Edith's anxiety assumes almost obsessive proportions; and the significance of such over-representation may be related to two other prominent elements in the narrative as focalized through Edith: the emphasis on silence and a preoccupation with the physical appearance of Jennifer.

Events in the novel are characteristically enveloped in silence, but not merely the silence required by Edith for peaceful recuperation, or the successful conclusion of her latest novel. Edith is irresistibly drawn towards silence – a stillness or a becalmed 'immobility' of the kind that haunts Conradian protagonists. Her (female) fellow-guests are similarly enmeshed in silence.

At the hotel, Edith immediately notices the 'muted hush of the lobby' (13); in the garden outside 'the silence engulfed her' (20); the sound of her steps on the gravel are so loud as to seem 'intrusive' (22); she recalls her childhood as a 'pale silent daughter' (48); re-entering the hotel, she is struck by its 'dense, warm silence' (51); in the café in the town, she sits at a 'silent table' (52); one of the rare silences of the Puseys is described as 'ruminative' (56); Edith refers to her house in London and its 'quality of silence' (61); walking with Mr Neville after a crowded day, Edith is grateful for the 'silence of her companion' (74); the silence of Mme de Bonneuil's days is 'palpable' to Edith (77).

Contented in London, Edith had 'kept silent and yearned for David' (84); at the hotel, she appreciates 'the blessed silence and dimness of her room' (116); she sits 'alone in the silence' (117); she listens to Penelope's recriminations 'in silence' (132); in Mrs Pusey's evening salon 'there was a silence' (139); returning to the café, Edith and Monica 'ate in silence' (147); later, in her room, she is unwilling to exchange her silence for the pleasantries of the evening (155); Edith refers to the years of her youth spent in 'silence and wariness' (174); leaving Mr Neville and the Puseys together, she is 'aware of the pregnant silence behind her' (179). Even this list is by no means exhaustive, although – for the reader's sake – it is concluded here.

The third textual crux is the physical presence of Jennifer. Her external appearance – not least its sartorial detail – receives only marginally less attention than the narrator's anxiety or the prolifer-ation of silences. On her first entry, Jennifer is described as 'wearing rather tight white trousers (rather too tight, thought Edith) which outlined a bottom shaped like a large Victorian plum' (18); as

Jennifer rises to invite Edith over for coffee, she smoothes her black dress over her 'abundant hips' (34); she has an insistent 'physical presence' (37); or more specifically, a 'stolidity which verged on opulence' (39); in Edith's most elaborate description:

> Jennifer was a splendid specimen . . . Everything about her gleamed. Her light blue eyes, her regular slightly incurving teeth, her faultless skin, all gave off various types of sheen; her blonde hair looked almost dusty in comparison. Her rather plump artless body was, Edith saw, set forth by clothes which were far from artless and possibly too narrow; Jennifer managed to give the impression that she was growing out of them. Everything about her was as expensive as her mother's money could make it, but in a different style from Mrs Pusey's careful elegance. In her navy linen trousers and her, perhaps too tight, white jersey, Jennifer was determinedly *gamine*. (54)

When she is upset by the appearance of a spider in her room, she is revealed in a 'satin nightgown slipping from her plump shoulders' or – in Edith's sudden flash of insight – as an *odalisque* with 'quite a lot of very grown-up flesh'. For her mother's birthday she appears appropriately in pink *harem* pants and Edith comments 'I had not noticed how plump she was' (107). Her 'apparently uninformed voluptuousness' suggests a 'latency' (112). During the night crisis scene after Mrs Pusey's birthday celebrations she is shown with

> her face moody and flushed, her mouth set in a pout, her plump shoulders emerging from the slipping décolletage of a virginal but very slightly transparent lawn nightgown. (138)

And her final appearance, just before Edith's departure, is in 'another of her oddly immodest outfits' – 'a clinging low-necked blue silk sweater and a pair of white knickerbockers' (176).

Puzzling narrative shifts, anxiety, silence, the physical obsession: the objective of a second reading, made in accordance with the approach advocated by Felman, would be to reconcile such apparently disparate elements of the text. With the help of a Lacanian approach – supplemented by various gynocritical insights into language – this is not an impossible task.

One of the most lucid accounts of language under the sign

of what Mary Daly has called the phallocentrism of patriarchal order may be found in Dale Spender's *Man Made Language* (1980). Spender's comprehensive and convincing study of gender bias in both the semantic and syntactic fields is simply not reducible to what Brookner referred to dismissively in an interview as the 'all-men-are-swine-programme' (Haffenden, 28). Notwithstanding Brookner's disparaging remarks about feminism, *Hotel du Lac*, like virtually any text, indirectly illustrates the linguistic bias to which Spender refers. Thus, Edith defines the hotel by its absence of men – 'women, women, only women' (33), this 'gyneceum' (61) – and yet she can rather illogically only compare the present occupants to the 'respected *patrons* of an earlier era' (13) or else to other '*patrons* of long standing' (14). Etymologically, patron is unequivocally male in gender, and yet semantics would clearly preclude the alternative usage of the word 'matron'.

Elsewhere, Edith finds 'meals in public were not to her taste, even when she was accompanied' (25); the immediate association is her last meal before leaving England, eaten with her agent Harold Webb. Men accompany, as Dale Spender would certainly point out, whilst women are accompanied.

In a letter to David, Edith records that Mr Neville 'took me out on a very long walk'. A man takes a woman out for a walk; he also takes a dog out. A woman takes a dog out, whilst (in facetious usage at least) an unruly dog might take a man/master or woman/mistress out; man or dog might take a *mistress* out, and a man could of course take a *bitch* out. But what, then, is a mistress, and who, incidentally, is a bitch? There is ample material in *Hotel du Lac* for semantic juggling of this kind, which might even provide a source of amusement, were not the implications of male cultural bias so disturbing.

The linguistic insights of Spender and other feminist theorists, in conjunction with the notion of the unconscious text, throw much light on the 'secret corners' of *Hotel du Lac*. Edith Hope produces romantic novels vindicating the 'tortoise- and-hare' mythology (with good news for 'hares'); Anita Brookner set out to write a simple love story 'in which love really triumphed'; but the text itself re-enacts the dilemma of the female writer/reader/speaker trapped between communicating in a (patriarchal and authoritative) language that is not hers – with the inevitable anxiety this generates; or of totally rejecting this language – and retreating into a psychologically debilitating and ultimately inoperable total silence. This, then, may well be the latent significance of the insistent emphasis on 'anxiety' and 'silence' throughout Edith's narrative.

The emphasis on Jennifer's physical presence may also be linked to the ubiquitous textual properties of anxiety and silence. It could be explained at a conventional level of character analysis: Edith reveals a fascination tinged with envy both for Jennifer's more obvious physical attributes, but also for her freedom from the curse of self-consciousness under which she herself labours.

At another level of analysis, moreover, the figures of Edith and Jennifer may reflect the common tendency in Brookner's novels (a trait shared with George Eliot) to separate feminine intelligence from female sexuality – an insistence on mutual exclusivity which bears an ironic resemblance to reactionary male stereotypes.

At yet another level, however, Edith's reactions reflect a half articulated protest against the norms of the *scopological* culture in which she is inscribed, a culture in which woman may often be defined primarily as the object of male gaze. Mrs Pusey accepts such attentions quite happily (Before entering the dining-room, she 'assured herself that her presence had been noted'). 'I think you have an admirer' she informs Edith: admire – *admirare* – literally to look on; it is, however, a role which Edith is unwilling to assume, perhaps insisting on her Virginia Woolf cardigans to emphasize this refusal.

But if sexual stereotyping and linguistic bias are two ubiquitous elements of *Hotel du Lac*, the concept of the Lacanian textual unconscious emerges most explicitly in two otherwise puzzling passages. The first of these, already mentioned briefly, is the opening paragraph of the novel, with its peculiar modality used to describe the lake and its environs, temporarily concealed by mist:

> From the window all that could be seen was a receding area of grey. It was to be *supposed* that beyond the grey garden, which *seemed* to sprout nothing but the stiffish leaves of some unfamiliar plant, lay the vast grey lake, spreading like an anaesthetic towards the invisible further shore, and yet beyond that *in imagination only*, yet verified by the brochure, the peak of Dent d'Oche, on which snow *might* already be slightly and silently falling. (my emphasis; 7)

The description has a strangely hypothetical quality, not totally dependent on atmospheric conditions, 'It was to be supposed' – 'seemed to sprout' – 'might already be . . falling' – where the effect is less a questioning of referentiality than a resistance to any form of articulation at all. The landscape has a 'mysterious opacity' (8) and – most significantly of all – is later described as a 'toneless expanse' (9), a striking case of semantic ambivalence, suggesting not merely 'monochrome', but perhaps a 'soundless' or literally pre-verbal intimation. The key phrase of the opening paragraph, however, is surely 'in imagination only', where the text seems to refuse the Lacanian transition from inchoate imagination to the symbolic order of language, a language already convincingly demonstrated to constitute a fundamentally male preserve.

In the context of 'women's writing' there would be much to say. If the act of communication entails a re-enactment of the assumption into the symbolic order of language, Edith's narrative thus creates a double tension: spurred on to write by the simultaneous desire for economic independence and need for psychic relief (cf. Brookner's own references to abreaction and conversion hysteria: Haffenden, 26; Kenyon, 17), she nevertheless faces a world where woman is defined in socio-economic terms *by* and *through* men, and where her imaginings can only be articulated in a patriarchal or phallocentric discourse.

One final example will demonstrate the point quite explicitly: when she thinks of her house in London, Edith fondly recalls the little girl next door:

> At this time, she knew, her neigbour's child, a child of heart-breaking beauty whose happiness and simplicity were already threatened by a speech defect, would come out to see if she were there (but she was always there) and would slip through the hedge to say goodnight. (121)

As Edith watches her 'wrestling with the words, her thin body juddering with the effort to unlock them', the scene may be read in purely emblematic terms. The little girl is literally enacting the reluctant assumption by the (female) child into the symbolic order of (male) language.

        \*             \*             \*

I have suggested that *Hotel du Lac* is clearly related to a classic realist tradition. Its extensive use of *mise en abyme*, purely formal as well as thematically motivated – provides ironic comment on the concept of textual authority. The narrator's authority is nevertheless dogged by anxiety and – ultimately – by the threat of silence. These symptoms, in turn, may be related to both Lacanian and feminist insights into language; certain passages within the text would seem literally to enact female resistance to man-made language. At this point, however, the interpenetration of text and (male) critic becomes increasingly problematic; Brookner herself does not encourage feminist commentary on her novels ('You'd have to be crouching in your burrows to see my novels in a feminist way', Haffenden, 28); but the inducement to read *Hotel du Lac* from this perspective is very powerful when the results are so helpful in overcoming various points of resistance within the text.

## FAMILY AND FRIENDS

Brookner's fifth novel, *Family and Friends*, is a domestic chronicle, introducing a highly selective series of episodes, punctuated with narrative speculation and constructed round a series of wedding portraits. The first of these portraits, in the opening chapter of the book, introduces Sofka – widow and matriarch – together with her four children, 'handsome Frederick', 'little Alfred' and the sisters, Mireille and Babette – referred to thereafter as Mimi and Betty. If the sons are named after 'kings and emperors', and the daughters suggest 'characters in a musical comedy', it is because we have returned once again to well-trod Brookner territory, where 'the boys were to conquer, and the girls to flirt' (10).

Subsequent chapters alternate between the occasionally overlapping destinies of the four children, tracing a series of Brookneresque patterns, some now familiar, but others refreshingly new. The dashing and genial Frederick assumes responsibility for the family firm, whilst the brooding, adolescent Alfred is happiest shut in his room immersed in *The Conquest of Peru*. Mimi and Betty supplement piano studies under the irreproachable Mr Cariani with extra-curricular dancing lessons from his dreamy but affable son, Frank.

Alarmed by Betty's nascent sexuality, the matriarchal Sofka sends her daughter – under Frank's escort – to a boarding-school in Switzerland; but Betty progresses no further than Paris, where, having sent her unsuspecting brother home to England, she pursues an assignation with Frank Cariani. At Sofka's request, Alfred and Mimi leave for Paris in order to reclaim Betty, initiating another situation encountered in previous novels: Mimi, the ingenuous heroine – whom Frank actually admits to liking best – begins the long vigil at her hotel, waiting for the imagined lover who will never arrive. Edith Hope's waiting for her lover had virtually become a way of life; Kitty Maule's – like Mimi's – was actually consigned to a Paris hotel. In *Family and Friends*, however, Frank is 'stolen' by Betty. Mimi returns to England, and – like several of her predecessors in Brookner's fiction – is unable either to recover from her disillusion or even to share her grief.

Subsequent chapters concentrate on the courtship and marriage of Frederick and Eva (Evie) – the robust and determined daughter of a hotelier from the Italian riviera – and Betty's dancing career in Paris, with her eventual marriage to the nephew of a Hungarian film producer. Alfred buys a country home in Kent and provokes scandal by embarking on an affair with an old flame, Dolly, now married to a family friend. The destinies of the children continue to pass before us, captured momentarily as if in pictures from a family album, when not literally presented through the device of wedding photographs: Alfred as indecisive in love as in any other situation, Mimi peacefully married to Lautner, elderly manager of the family firm; Frederick becalmed in Bordighera, Betty humbled in Hollywood.

At the end of the novel, the family appears gathered once again (albeit without Frederick and Evie) just before Sofka's death, and the narrative ends with a final wedding photograph, from the marriage of Ursie, family maid and surrogate daughter.

\*        \*        \*

In providing the barest summary of a novel like *Family and Friends*, it is difficult to avoid an element of banality; and without endorsing Peter Kemp's unflattering comparisons with Barbara Cartland or his intemperate outbursts about 'palpitating sentimentality', one may indeed suspect elements of 'novelettish romance'. Such accusations may be easily countered, however, in either of two ways.

Firstly, numerous examples of established classics also suggest – in synopsis form – close affinities with popular literature: thus *Daisy Miller* or *Washington Square* might be made to sound considerably more novelettish than anything Brookner has written; even a plot summary of *Portrait of a Lady*, with due emphasis on socio-economic *specifica*, might seem to anticipate the anodyne patterns of modern television soap opera. Alternatively, one could point to a natural and inevitable process of cross-fertilization between 'major' and 'minor' literary genres, without for the moment considering the vexed question of what these ill-defined categories might encompass. Brookner should, in all fairness, be judged not on plot summaries which proclaim her relation to the sentimental novelette, but in her ability to transcend the limitations of the genre.

In the latter respect, admittedly, *Family and Friends* is not initially encouraging. The narrative sometimes seems content merely to repeat, rather than re-examine, patterns familiar from earlier novels, patterns which sometimes fail to rise beyond the level of *idée fixe*. Thus, in the meditations on the first wedding photograph in the opening chapter, narrative focus wavers precariously between Sofka and a familiar-sounding narrative *persona*. Mimi and Betty, like 'sheltered girls in that unliberated age . . . long to be married' (12). Through well-regulated flirtation with a number of young men, 'they need never know the grip of a hopeless or unrequited passion and be spared the shame of being left unclaimed' (13). But social insight merges imperceptibly with what seems almost authorial obsession in Brookner's fiction, as we learn of Sofka's determination 'that her daughters should be spared the humiliation of those who wait', prompting the narrator's pointed speculation '[p]erhaps she has had this experience herself?' (13).

Ironically, of course, the waiting role is precisely the one that Mimi will play, in spite of her mother's efforts; Betty herself will avoid the pattern, but only by being the immediate cause of her elder sister's suffering. Thus Brookner recreates, now in a context of sibling rivalry, the rudimentary polarization of female stereotypes reproduced in every previous novel – the naively innocent waiting woman and the selfish usurper. The verbal portrait of Betty in the third chapter shows an animus not entirely attributable to Sofka, but which may even reflect the bias of a now familiar authorial prudery. Betty is described as possessing 'a guttersnipe charm' (32) and as being more 'in touch with her own lower instincts' (37) than any of the other children. Betty's sexuality is 'unwelcome' to her mother, Sofka, and – one suspects – not to Sofka alone.

Thus in the third chapter, the supposedly detached, external narrator retails an extraordinary insight appparently originating in the younger sister:

> Betty knows that her mission in life is to be a woman who prevents men from staying with their virgin loves, and she is eager to embark on this career. (44)

It is an unlikely presentiment, more suggestive of extradiegetic narrative bias than of individual intuition by an autonomous agent.

Elsewhere, Brookner varies another familiar theme by showing a male figure (rather than the characteristically forlorn female) suffering under the inevitable burden of a good character. In this respect, both Mimi and Alfred

> stand for those solid and perhaps little regarded virtues of loyalty and fidelity and a scrupulous attention paid to the word or promise given or received. (52)

With greater ironic detachment, the narrator refers to the 'tiny but hardy flame of virtue which has sustained Alfred, much to his regret, for all of thirty years' (104); Mimi, however, seems more resigned to her own goodness, reconciled to the impression she gives of 'a maiden lady devoted to good works'.

But *Family and Friends* introduces another structural innovation, with the later recurrent contrast between dutiful and prodigal children. If the two 'good' children are neatly ranged against the two 'bad' ones, there is also a clear internal division or cross-reference: the frustrations of Betty, who left home, are paralleled by those of Alfred, who remained; and the contentments of Frederick, who also deserted the family, are matched in those ultimately enjoyed by Mimi, who remained to support it.

But as in *Hotel du Lac*, the story itself tends to undermine the narrator's authority, encouraging the reader to follow Lawrence's advice and trust the tale rather than the teller. In the opening chapter, the narrator speculates (with a sense of determinism characteristic of Brookner herself) on the future of anachronistically well-bred bourgeois girls:

> Is there something doomed about those girls, although they are in perfect health and devoted to their mother? What happens to young women, brought up to obedience, and bred to docility and virtue? What happens to such unprotected lives? How will they deal with the world or the world with them? (13–14)

The answer to these questions is clearly anticipated in the first reference to girls with 'something doomed' about them (13). And yet the events of the narrative seem to subvert such simple formulaic phrases. If Frederick achieves a life of calm and resignation away from the sphere of the family, Betty is not an advertisement for emotional fulfilment as she sits by the chemical blue of her Hollywood swimming-pool. And if Alfred frets over the responsibilities and sacrifices imposed on him, Mimi – once the most desperate of all the children – mellows with age to present an image of domestic contentment.

The real interests of *Family and Friends* are not, however, limited to such minor variations on established Brookner themes, but are linked with two striking innovations in narrative technique: a sophisticated self-reflexivity – signalling fresh recourse to a tendency begun in *Hotel du Lac* – and a new exploitation of the iconographic mode which will receive its most elaborate treatment in *A Misalliance*.

In the first of these contexts, the ironic examination of narrative authority initiated in *Hotel du Lac* finds a new application. Brookner alleviates occasional monolithic tendencies in the narrative of *Family and Friends* by a greater attention towards conflicting psychological impulses among her characters, together with an increased awareness of a sense of contingency: thus Sofka, paradoxically, comes to feel a greater sympathy for the two children who have defied her than for the two who remained loyal. And on the other hand, not even Mimi, 'the good daughter', is immune to the seditious urge: in Paris she feels that she had been 'the one most ready, most willing, to defect' (69).

But the experiences of Mimi in Paris have an added significance for both reader and subject. The former might now be moved to weigh more carefully the various components in what has virtually become a Brookner *topos* – the naively waiting and eventually abandoned woman.

The constituent features of the familiar erotic triangle may even be itemized in structural terms as: the timidity and insecurity of a young woman, more or less unconvinced of her own attractiveness; the selfishness and insensitivity of a man, more or less oblivious of the emotions he has inspired; and the power and determination of the other woman, corresponding in varying degrees to Brookner's stereotype of the 'sultry temptress'. All three agents are combined in a contingent situation, with its inevitable attendant misunderstandings, failures in communication, and other random elements. And if readers themselves ponder the relative importance of the situation's three constants and its numerous variables, *Family and Friends* is the novel where the protagonist is most explicitly shown to be doing the same thing, thus following *Hotel du Lac* in questioning the very foundation of textual authority.

Indirect reflection on the latter concept is introduced in a memorable analytical passage in chapter ten, where the narrator compares the contrasting capacities of Mimi and Alfred to escape their home environment:

> Unlike Alfred, Mimi has been too long disabled to fight her way clear. The enactment of Mimi's desires is all retrospective, in the mind. Mimi constantly *rewrites the script* that decreed that she should remain solitary that night in the Hotel Bedford et West End. It is not Frank for whom she yearns now but for that missing factor in herself that would have brought Frank to her side. (my emphasis; 126)

If Mimi's sense of loss and regret lies well within the sphere of traditional characterization, the reference to 'writing the script' introduces a broader theoretical perspective on the interpretation of experience – and, by implication, the subjective or arbitrary character of narrative itself.

There are presumably covert relations between Brookner heroines and their creator, and the possible nature of these links is discussed in the final chapter. But even at this point, it is clear that the portrayal of Mimi through conventional psycho-narrative stands in problematic relation to the *mise en abyme* of the narrative act, as represented by the challenging 'script' metaphor. The reference to a search for the 'missing factor' perhaps reflects an awareness – by both Mimi and her creator – of an inconclusive play of signifiers within the text, where meaning (according to one current orthodoxy) is no longer transparently recuperable, but only infinitely deferred. Or in the narrower context of Brookner novels, the issue of the 'autobiographical' quality of her fiction must be balanced by that of the 'fictionality' of her (or anybody else's) autobiography. In any event, the references to 'script' or 'missing factor' suggest a narrative sophistication, even an ontological awareness, otherwise easily belied by the apparent banality of the *topos* itself.

*             *             *

The second innovative aspect of *Family and Friends* is reflected in the novel's elaboration of iconography. *Hotel du Lac*, it is true, is liberally sprinkled with literary references, supplemented by an occasional effective use of the verbal icon. The comparison of Mimi waiting in her Paris hotel to the Lady of Shalott had been anticipated by an identical reference in relation to Edith Hope. In practical terms, it was perhaps the portrayal of Edith's lover, David Simmonds, as an art auctioneer that provided Brookner with an opportunity to introduce into *Hotel du Lac* the kind of iconography more conspicuously associated with the two succeeding novels. Certainly, painting provides *Hotel du Lac* with some of its most memorable 'images', such as the ironic reflection on Edith's own vacillating authority and constant textual revision, when David announces the sale of a painting attributed to Francesco Furini and entitled *Time Revealing Truth*.

Iconography proper acquires its most important thematic function in *A Misalliance*, but the process by which it is enabled to envelop – if not actually take over – a Brookner text may be followed as it emerges in *Family and Friends*. Even the more marginal figures of the story reflect the author's tendency to elevate individual agents to archetype or myth; Frank Cariani is thus:

> a throwback to some Sardinian shepherd who may just conceivably have engendered the entire Cariani line. He is dark, lithe, dangerously handsome; he is in addition both sulky and shy. In his white shirt, black trousers and black pumps, he looks like a wild creature whose nakedness is struggling to dominate his unaccustomed trappings. (35)

Frank is also the dancer, and his primordial qualities resonate suggestively with the metaphorical force which dancing acquires during the course of the novel. (As I shall argue later, if dancing is the metonymic adjunct to the first wedding photograph, it is the metaphoric undertow to the final portrait.)

Frederick's wife, suitably named Eva or Evie, is similarly translated (or perhaps merely restored) to the realm of fable: 'the spread thighs, the gleaming teeth, the shouting laughter, the springy yardage of hair' (75) overwhelm – in their different ways – both mother and son:

all these features speak a language which perhaps Sofka has never understood. But it is precisely this combination of animality that has hooked Frederick and knocked him out. (75)

More explicitly, Evie suggests 'a member of the species, in those days before the lava cooled . . . ' (73). In her role of Earth Mother, she entrances Frederick and removes him effortlessly from his biological mother's grasp. Frederick 'now seeks cataclysms and no longer cares for disguise'.

But Brookner's characteristic tendency towards mythologization (typically recorded in iconographic terms) emerges most clearly with Sofka's four children. The youthful Frederick is depicted lounging in a doorway 'with the nonchalant stance of the Apollo Belvedere' (17), although – in purely structural terms – he may later stagger under the weight of his own mythological ballast: now the archetypal English aristocrat ('out of the unpromising debris of a European family' 22); now 'the original *homo ludens*' (23); now the prodigal son who does not return and thus who 'makes the idea of goodness a mockery' (167).

The two sisters are effectively constructed by a miscellany of 'character-indicators',[8] most prominently – and again perhaps with a certain banality – by the songs they sing at the piano: Mimi interprets the provocative 'Les Filles de Cadiz' (with 'many a haughty glance and smouldering expression' 29), whilst Mimi ('the serious one') appropriates Massenet's *Elégie* ('O doux printemps d'autrefois'), which she will perform wistfully for many years to come.

Betty, in addition, is twice directly equated with Colette, although the terms of the comparison are revealing in unexpected ways. The adolescent rite of passage, as elsewhere in Brookner, is marked by the cutting of hair, making Betty resemble Colette (38); but Betty is described as bearing a 'marked resemblance' to Colette only six pages earlier, when she still has long hair. The true simililarity may lie less in physical appearances than in a partly repressed authorial distaste for the obvious sense of sexual emancipation that accompanies the younger daughter's gesture. There may even be latent sexual associations in what is described as Bettie's 'bushy triangular bob' (38).

In a passage of ironic contrast, Mimi later attempts to have her own hair cut short during her stay in Paris. The hairdresser refuses to touch it and 'amorously' brushes the 'red-gold waves':

smart women waiting for his attentions join in the chorus of admiration and suddenly Mimi is suffused with happiness. She sits glowing, her hair spread over her shoulders; (70)

Her reaction to the hairdresser and his female clientele, as she 'closes her eyes and takes a deep breath', may be read as a retreat from the processes of emotional or sexual maturation, and a simultaneous regression into the narcissistic world of childhood.

The most powerful pictorial analogy in the case of Betty is quite specific:

With the ivory cigarette-holder between her teeth and her finger-nails painted bright red, with her legs crossed high, her brooding eyes and her sharp teeth, Betty looks like a painting by Foujita, a native Parisian, a Bohemian a fallen angel. (40)

Mimi, on the other hand, is indexed alternatively by references to Rossetti's chaste *Beata Beatrix*, and to the repressed sexuality of Hunt's (or perhaps Millais's) *Lady of Shalott*.

In the course of their mythographic realization, Betty and Mimi may sometimes lie closer to stereotype than to archetype. Mimi is 'one of those women who marry early or not at all' (43); Betty is 'one of those women who believe in acting out a passion before they really feel it' (42); Mimi is 'not the type of girl who will, or indeed, can, do anything independently'; Betty is 'a woman who prevents men from staying with their virgin loves' (44). Here, as in other novels, the narrator flirts with cliché by an uncritical reliance on cultural codes (perhaps the 'Voice of Science' dismissed so scathingly by Barthes).[9] Barthes's references to the material accessible to the 'diligent student in the classical bourgeois educational system' – including maxims about 'life, death, suffering, love, women, ages of man etc.' (1974, 206) – raise more than fortuitous echoes in the ideology of the Brookner narrator.

Hardly surprisingly therefore, the most strikingly innovative character-indicators are not Betty's or Mimi's, but those of Alfred. It is in Alfred's case that iconography (based on classical myth or pictorial realism) is most explicit, replacing the literary cross-reference of the early novels as the chief means of indexing character. This process is evident both at the level of self-perception and in terms of external 'portrayal'. With his 'visions, largely nourished by reading' Alfred's behaviour anticipates the quixotic pathology explored more fully in *Lewis Percy*. Alfred explicitly compares himself with Henry V and Nicholas Nickleby (50), and is conscious of his own 'mythical quest for the grail'. More explicitly: The passage represents a point of convergence for self-perception and external narrative voice:

> Sometimes Alfred has a dream in which he is running through a dark wood; at his heels there are two beautiful golden dogs, his familiars, and with them he is running through the dark wood of his pilgrimage to the golden dawn of his reward. (103)

The latter source imagines Alfred 'intent on finding his mythical home' (106), or projecting his ideals into the creation of a 'mythical domain' (117); or else creates its own iconographic riddle ('In what glade, in what grove, can Alfred find his peace?' 110). To sustain the process of analogy, Alfred is explicitly seen as 'a character in classical tragedy or allegorical painting' (171). His own versions of pastoral – or the narrator's recourse to Arcadian myth – are Brookner's hitherto most elaborate exploitation of iconography. In *A Misalliance*, however, the technique will receive its most comprehensive and consistent application.

*       *       *

If the first three novels rely structurally on specific literary models – principally Balzac, Constant and Proust/Gide – the next three may be linked by their fruitful exploration of various iconographic modes. The very title of *Family and Friends* alludes to an ingenious technical solution for avoiding the potential voluminousness of the fictional family chronicle. A. N. Wilson, who considered *Family and Friends* Brookner's best novel to date, wrote appreciatively of how brilliantly the author (like Bennett in *The Old Wives' Tale*) had 'manipulated the inexorably dull march of time' (*TLS*, 6 September 1985). The same reviewer was even moved to speak of the novel's Chekhovian tone.

Brookner's method is to build her novel around a series of wedding photographs, and she provided an interesting response to Olga Kenyon's question of why she had chosen the form:

> Because it was easier. It was not a difficult book to write it was almost entirely free of anxiety. A chapter to each one is almost the easiest form. It was fascinating to write, as I could use

the reaction of an art historian to the photographs. (Kenyon, 1989, 19)

One would immediately wish to make two obvious comments: the formal pattern is by no means as rigid as Brookner would suggest – if one character provides the ground for a chapter, it is nonetheless impossible to isolate him/her from other family members; and the rather rudimentary kind of division to which Brookner refers is at least as evident in *Latecomers*.

Secondly, the novelist's descriptions (with an occasional familiar tone of *de haut en bas*) occasionally seem to suggest the fashion journalist or even the interior designer, as much as the professional art historian; the most imaginative and dramatically integrated use of icongraphy is in *A Misalliance*, where the contents of pictures are invariably focalized through the troubled consciousness of Blanche Vernon, rather than the medium of the external narrator.

In either novel, however, iconography is of paramount importance, as the narrative pauses regularly in deference to the 'verbal icon' – be it Blanche's paintings or Sofka's family portraits. With the shift from the incidental iconography of *Hotel du Lac* to a more intensified application in *Family and Friends* or *A Misalliance*, moreover, it is useful to consult the most comprehensive account to date of framing in the novel: *Reading Frames in Modern Fiction* by Mary Ann Caws (1985).

Caws pursues three major theses: firstly, that in many narratives certain passages stand out in relief from the general flow of the prose. In these contexts, we are aware of borders and an intensification of focus. These framed scenes may literally *reflect* or *contain* (the concealed metaphors are themselves striking) the thematic kernel of a work, and not infrequently stand in metonymic relation to a larger narrative 'picture'.

Secondly, these passages may mark an intrusion into the literary text of other genres: Caws specifies the structures of music, the perceptions of visual art, or the dialogue and gestures of dramatic form.

Thirdly, whereas in 'pre-modernist' texts, these passages generally emphasize the actual contents of the frame in terms of the field included, much modernist and post-modernist narrative stresses the very idea of framing rather than what the frame happens to include.

Caws provides extended analysis of Austen ('Pre-modern Borders') and James ('High Modernist Framing'), authors obviously of particularly interest in view of their relation to Brookner. And yet *Family and Friends*, it might be objected, does not use the frame analogue, but literally introduces photographs, as if Brookner sought to incorporate both vehicle and tenor within her text. But such an impression is illusory, since the narrative is conspicuous precisely for its alternation between genuine photographs and – to combine two of Caws's categories – 'dramatic *tableaux*'. A brief re-examination of the novel should illustrate this process.

The anonymous narrator proceeds from a series of wedding photographs (and several analogous tableaux), preserving the context – and even occasionally the discursive syntax – of an excursion through a family album. Thus, the opening words ('Here is Sofka, in a wedding photograph . . . ') introduce the matriarchal figure who will dominate much of the novel, together with her four children and numerous other vague or unspecified individuals. The whole of the opening chapter actually consists of description and speculation stimulated by the figures in the picture. It may also be significant that the accounts of wedding photographs are the only occasions in the novel which introduce the comments of a first-person narrator ('I assume' . . . 'This I know to be the case'), thus recalling Brookner's reference to being shown an 'old family photograph' (Kenyon, 20) and suggesting a relatively unmediated response to the picture.

The second wedding portrait proper is introduced in chapter six on the marriage of Frederick and Sophie ('a very jolly occasion', 82), but in between these two points the narrative will make a number of direct appeals to the visual imagination, be it the framing of Mimi as Rossetti's 'Beata Beatrix' (70) or – even more striking for its opening injunction to the reader – the scene of the family at Sunday lunch:

> *Picture them* at the table. Alfred, flourishing carving knives, prepares to exert his patriarchal will on a large roast of beef, for Sunday is devoted to the consumption of traditional English food. (my emphasis; 77)

And in fact, the description of seating arrangements is not unlike the emblematic reading of some ancient guild banquet preserved on an old master's canvas:

> Alfred sits at the head of the table because Sofka has decided that he deserved this distinction. She herself sits at the foot, and

Frederick is on her right, where he prefers to be. These positions seem so appropriate to the natures of the two brothers that neither of them would think to dispute them, although Alfred has a lingering nostalgia for the days when Frederick sat at the head, and he, the cherished younger son, sat at Sofka's side, where, as a boy, he could turn to her and whisper requests. On Alfred's right sits Mimi, who seems to have lost a little weight or to have let her hair grow rather untidily; . . . (77)

Sofka explains the removal of a chair on the other side of the table with a reference to her younger daughter 'completing her education' in Paris! (78) – an interpretation of absences no less than presences – and the allegorical reading is complete.

The next wedding photograph proper is from the marriage of Mimi and Lautner:

Here they all are in the photograph. Lautner looks radiant. Sofka wears a dress of parma violet, with a little hat of violet petals. (I have this on record.) Here are Nettie and Dolly, looking as unlike each other as it is possible for half-sisters to look. Strangely enough, these two have never got on very well. Dolly looks stunning, in a burnt orange two-piece. Nettie wears a pale blue, which sets off her still beautiful hair. (136)

In its general banality, the actual description, which – had it been focalized by one of the novelist's less self-conscious female figures – could well have passed as subtle characterization by psycho-narrative, does little apparent credit to the intelligence of an *external narrator*. We remember once again dismissive comparisons of Brookner's fiction to romantic novelettes; but we now also sense that – if the use of wedding photographs is an ingenious structuring device – then the weighty thematic climaxes implied by such high bourgeois weddings ensure that such scenes do not remain an ideologically neutral motif.

The narrator's imaginative projections onto the first wedding photograph thus appear in a new perspective. Here, the husbands are assumed to have found a 'precarious harmony':

the sudden look of worldliness their faces assumed as their lips closed voluptuously round the fine Romeo y Julietas [sic] and they lifted their heads a little to expel the bluish smoke reminded their wives – censorious women, with higher standards – why they had married them. (9)

If the visual detail reflects the skilful evocation of a period piece, the particular brand of cigar referred to may also suggest a sceptical reference to Romantic myth. The implicit belief that female discipline tames male desire reinforces the image of moral rectitude by which Brookner indiscriminately identifies her heroines *in fabula* and herself in interview (cf. Kenyon, 20, Guppy, 159). It also once more suggests her easy acceptance of the 'Voice of Science' (as the phrase is disparagingly used by Barthes) and its conventional cultural codes.

Another form of sexual hierarchy is illustrated by Mimi and Lautner in a second striking pseudo-photographic scene:

See how patriarchally he places encompassing arms on the back of the sofa on which Mimi is seated! See how he stands when she enters the room and opens the door when she leaves it! (182)

The passage is also remarkable, however, for the use of a discursive syntax exactly appropriate to the study of a photograph album. The analogy between certain dramatically framed scenes and the old wedding photographs is of course recognized by the narrator, too, as in Sofka's deathbed scene:

Truth to tell, the atmosphere in that drawing-room is not unlike one of those weddings at which the whole clan foregathered. (169)

But two other occasions provide the most interesting technical and thematic applications, respectively, of Brookner's photographic technique. On the first of these, the pictures from Mimi and Lautner's wedding are sent to Betty and Max in Hollywood. Max 'pores keenly over the photographs' and speculates on the identity of the wedding guests, thus effectively providing a *mise en abyme* of the narrator him/herself, an impression reinforced by an earlier narratorial comment when Betty first meets her future husband in Paris: 'Max Markus and his uncle see eye to eye in the making and framing of images' (96). At a purely technical level, the introduction of *mise en abyme* relates *Family and Friends* to *Hotel du Lac*; the thematic implication of the device may nonetheless be to subvert the novelist's essentially ordered vision ('I do like a rational world', Haffenden, 26) by the suggestive implication of vanishing perspectives, or of endless deferral without a final term.

The second example is even more interesting, however, and concerns the final picture – a genuine photograph from the wedding of George and Ursie ('Here they all are, family and friends in the wedding photograph. It is the last one in the album', 187). The first and last scenes of the novel are thus conspicuously wedding photo-graphs, and the final lines of the narrative even suggest an explicit verbal echo of the novel's opening pages: 'See the resemblance. Wait for the dancing to begin,'

In the first chapter, it seems reasonable to suggest that the image of dancing possesses a purely metonymic function:

I have no doubt that great quantities of delicious food – things in aspic, things in baskets of spun sugar – were consumed, and that the music struck up and the bride and bridegroom danced . . . (9)

But as we contemplate the last photograph in the album ('here they all are, family and friends') the activity is surely transformed into metaphor:

See that look on Vicky's face, that imperious stare, so unlike a child, so like Sofka. See Alfred's hand proudly clasping her little shoulder. See the resemblance. Wait for the dancing to begin. (187)

Dancing has become a metaphor for life itself.[10] The final image is impressive evidence of a certain thematic density amassed during the course of *Family and Friends*, and which confirms its position as one of Brookner's most challenging and rewarding novels.

## A MISALLIANCE

It seems unlikely that an internationally established art scholar could have begun to write fiction without any trace whatsoever of her previous scholarly interests. Brookner herself is admittedly unhelpful in this respect, and denies any link between the two activities ('The awful thing is that I see no connection at all. It's a sort of schizophrenic activity as far as I'm concerned', Haffenden, 27). These comments, however, may merely reflect may reflect a disarmingly ingenuous side of the author's personality.

In the context of art history, moreover, it is worth pointing out that even the simplest bibliographical details of Brookner's academic career are sometimes obscured: thus, a note to the paperback imprint of her novels (Grafton Books) gives the misleading impression that she has actually published *three* studies in art history, the first of which was entitled *Watteau, the Genius of the Future* (!), followed by monographs on Greuze and Jacques Louis David. This would appear to suggest that Brookner's 'genius of the future' was Watteau, although we are of course dealing here with two quite separate books.

The *Genius of the Future* – with its studies of the art criticism of six French 'men of letters' – may actually possess some interest and relevance for Brookner's own writing. None of the writers studied by Brookner here – Diderot, Stendhal, Baudelaire, Zola, the brothers Goncourt and Huysmans – were primarily professional art critics; only Baudelaire, moreover, had any practical artistic talent. And yet all of them were successful in synthesizing their ideas on art with their own creative writing. Zola in *L'Oeuvre* (1886) and the brothers Goncourt in *Manette Salomon* (1867) even wrote novels centred round the life of an artist. Brookner is similarly eclectic: she realizes herself that her own critical approach as an art historan may be distinctly literary, with its emphasis on psycho-biographical speculation, a tendency particularly pronounced in *The Genius of the Future*.

Elsewhere, moreover, her placing of Greuze within the context of eighteenth century sensibility owes much to her familiarity with contemporary literary history. The interrelation of literature and art remains important as the art historian begins writing fiction, since the novels – above all, *Family and Friends* and *A Misalliance* – are intimately linked with pictorial elements. If one regards Brookner's fiction in evolutionary terms, in fact, the fourth and fifth novels represent the writer's emancipation from close French literary models, and an increasing reliance on analogies between the image and the written word.

Brookner's denial of connections between her fiction and her art history should therefore be carefully scrutinized. She can reveal a clear nostalgia for art, and there is, for example, a mixture of admiration and envy in her remark to Haffenden on the respective roles of painter and novelist:

> I think you love the world more as a painter. Painters have a healthy appetite for life. I think my personages could be reactivated, if the times were right: I hope so. (30)

In another context, she saw her studies in art history as 'steps in the painful process of self-realisation' (Kenyon, 10), an idea sufficiently close to her declared motives for beginning to write fiction: 'I wanted to control rather than be controlled, to ordain rather than be ordained, and to relegate rather than be relegated' (Haffenden, 25). Her self-evaluation as an academic, moreover suggests a creative imagination unconsciously seeking an outlet in fiction:

> I see myself as a speculative art historian rather than a scholar, and am sometimes worried that I might not be rigorous enough. (Kenyon, 10)

More specifically, the structuring of *Family and Friends* through a series of family photographs is explicitly related to her previous career as an art historian ('It was fascinating to write, as I could use the reaction of an art historian to the photographs', Kenyon, 19). All of the novels regularly use cross-references to painting as an important means of indexing character and situation. Reduced occasionally to the level of mannerism, the device may recall the clumsiness of certain references in the novels of Hardy; used more subtly, it is only comparable to effects obtained by James. And yet Brookner obviously knows more than either of these writers about the history of art.[11]

Critics of James have long been aware of this author's close links to painting and the plastic arts, not merely in thematic terms – reflected in a fondness for the artist-protagonist figure – but also structurally, in a characteristic technique of 'freezing' a scene and effectively reducing it to tableau. Viola Hopkins, in her classic essay 'Visual Art Devices and Parallels in the Fiction of Henry James', even attempted to relate her author more precisely to the Italian mannerists – specifically Caravaggio.

Among more recent critics, the authoritative study of literary 'framing', by Mary Ann Caws, draws widely on a close study of James. With benefit of hindsight, however, Caws could also have devoted space to Brookner: for it may be reasonably claimed that, in the three novels immediately succeeding *Look at Me*, iconography and framing supplant French fictional models as the central structuring device.

The technique of framing was most obviously anticipated in *Look at Me*, however, when Frances pauses on her nightmare walk through the London streets, to stand motionless before a lighted shop window:

> I lingered outside Harvey Nichols, watching a small electric train racing silently round and round. When I raised my eyes from this, it was to meet my own reflection, small, slight, undeniably chic. Not a hair out of place. Still poised, still terrified, still murderous. A person, you would say, of no overt desires or needs. (164)

In a patent piece of symbolism, the racing electric train suggests Frances '[r]unning like an acolyte to those who did not need me', as she describes herself in the following paragraph; but in iconographic terms, it is Frances, rather than the train, who is effectively framed by the lighted shop window.

The use of the verbal icon then receives increased emphasis in *Hotel du Lac*, with Edith's imagination readily conjuring up an image of David's mysterious 'rooms': 'large divans in whitewashed houses shuttered against the heat of the afternoon, a dreaming, glowing idleness, inspired by Delacroix' (56). It is nevertheless in *Family and Friends* and *A Misalliance*, that pictorial analogies reach their highest point of development. Each of these novels uses increased numbers of artistic references; but whilst *Family and Friends* – through the alternation of literal photographs with dramatic tableaux – carries framing to its logical limits, *A Misalliance* – by its central thematic emphasis – finally raises iconography to the level of ideological system. In other words, if the pictorial analogies of *Family and Friends* represent an ingenious attempt to overcome technical problems inherent in the family chronicle novel, the links with the pictorial arts in *A Misalliance* are far more fundamental: for, as the following analysis will show, Brookner effectively develops a coherent and consistent iconography to reflect the dominant thematic concerns of the novel.

*          *          *

Blanche Vernon is 'humbled and baffled' by divorce after twenty years of marriage to a man who has left her for Amanda (or 'Mousie'), a young graduate in computer sciences without the 'slightest spark of imagination' (30).

As she leaves her house each morning (immaculate 'down to the last varnished finger nail', 5), it is tempting to see her as an older, more intellectual – but equally doomed – version of Kitty's friend Caroline in *Providence*. Blanche divides her time between the 'flowerless streets of West Brompton' (13) and the National Gallery or the Wallace Collection, much as Caroline alternates between Harrods and Harvey Nichols. In her outdoor environment, Blanche studies the '[e]lderly, tired and overdressed' widows of the neighbourhood ('the over-painted lips smiled, revealing the ghosts of girls long gone', 11); in the galleries, she becomes obsessed with the 'smile of certain nymphs'(8) in the Italian rooms. The faces of these creatures taunt Blanche with what she has either lost or never possessed, just as the sight of 'scaly widows' in South Kensington mocks her with premonitions of what she will become.

Loss of companionship, for the Brookner single woman, is inevitably linked with loss of social status, a point emphasized by Blanche's encounter with her neighbour, the dentist's wife Phyllis Duff. '[M]odest and superior', Mrs Duff could never be mistaken for the 'new breed of woman who takes on the world'. Neither, apparently, could Blanche, and friends like her sister- in-law Barbara hope vaguely that 'she might effect her re-entry into society by marrying again' (26).

For two days a week Blanche dispenses tea for the outpatients of a local hospital, and it is on one of these occasions that she meets and mentally 'appropriates' silent and self-contained three-year-old Elinor. Sally Beamish, the child's adoptive mother ('spectacular, vivid, obtrusive', 39) creates an immediately unfavourable impression. As Blanche later becomes involved with child and mother, the insights gained from hours passed in the National Gallery are thoroughly developed, and used to reinforce a polarity long familiar to Brookner readers; this is now articulated with particular precision by Blanche in the fourth chapter:

She saw suddenly and precisely something that had previously only appeared to her in a vague and nebulous light: a great chasm dividing the whole of womanhood. On the one side, Barbara with her bridge evenings and her gouty husband, Mrs Duff with her girlish respectability, and her own awkward self, and on the other Mousie and her kind and Sally Beamish, movers and shakers, careless and lawless, dressed in temporary and impractical garments, and in their train men who would subvert their families, abandon their wives and children, for their unsettling companionship. (64–5)

Blanche's friend and one-time admirer, Patrick Fox, expounds the same thesis in less emphatic terms:

'It is simply that some women make one restless. Others one knows will always be there to come home to. It is as simple as that.' (167)

A familiar Brookner division, now firmly established as the Christian versus the Pagan, is also bolstered by the iconographic resources of the National Gallery, which thus underpin the entire thematic structure of the novel.

If the first artistic reference in *A Misalliance* is to Turner and his remark that the sun is God (7), then love itself is soon identified with 'the passing favour dispensed by the old, cynical, and unfair gods of antiquity' (20). It is the 'passport to the landscape where the sun shone eternally and where cornucopias of fruit scented the warm air' (20). But as Blanche prepares for bed and studies her own reflection, she sees conversely a face in the 'clouded mirror' with 'the anxious look, the lugubrious bleached look, of an inhabitant of medieval Flanders' (21).

In a passage of striking emblematic power, Blanche retires to bed, 'ribbed Gothic feet' shining palely below her long white nightdress (21), among images of darkness and damp:

Over the dark and silent garden a silent cat stalked. The trees were motionless under their weight of moisture. From the sodden earth came an exhalation of damp. Hearing the owl, Athena's attendant, hooting in the far distance, Blanche let down the curtain, took off her robe and went to bed. (21)

It is Sally Beamish, reluctant stepmother to the mute child, Elinor, who comes to embody the features of the 'invulnerable and patrician nymphs of the National Gallery's Italian Rooms' (46). By an unexpected choice of word, Blanche's first description anticipates the mythological implications of Sally's appearance:

> The ichor of extreme and abundant youth and fertility made its pulse felt in the sheen of her skin, the coarseness of the red hair, the limbs swimming in their layered cotton garments, the small black feet bare in their black leather sandals. (39)

The *ichor* – or fluid which flows like blood in the veins of gods – is united with a face wearing the 'smile of a true pagan' (41), an 'unfettered body' beneath 'strange black cotton clothes' (43) and an appearance that mirrors a 'free-running emotion' (44).

After one afternoon spent child-minding, Blanche returns Elinor to her mother's untidy apartment, now depicted as the grotto of a classical nymph, and reflects ironically on Sally's shortcomings as a mother:

> . . . Mrs Beamish's mythological status would give her a careless attitude towards children; nymphs are not known for their maternal feelings, although they lend themselves, for brief periods, to the business of nurture. (61)

But the insistent presence of Elinor also has broader thematic implications. For if the biography of Brookner's earlier protagonists usually encompasses childhood, and *Hotel du Lac* presents the emblematic figure of a young girl, *A Misalliance* is the first novel to incorporate a child as an important external agent. Elinor may most obviously reincarnate the heart-breakingly beautiful child with a 'crippling speech defect' who makes a fleeting appearance in *Hotel du Lac*, but she also acquires a substantial secondary dual role. At a purely metonymic level, she arouses protective, perhaps maternal, feelings in a lonely and childless divorcée; metaphorically, however, she is clearly a counterweight to her own mother, and even symbol and analogue of Blanche herself:

> For the child in Blanche had recognized the loneliness of the little girl in the Outpatients' Department, had recognized too that her inability to speak was not organic but deliberate, that she refused, out of some terrible strength, to come to terms with the world which she perceived as abnormal, unsatisfactory, deficient. The steadiness of the child, as opposed to the effortlessness, the

weightlessness, of the mother, indicated a desire for an ordered
structured universe, with a full complement of the fixed points
of an ordinary, even a conventional childhood. (48)

Blanche's sense of identification with Elinor resonates throughout
the novel, as in her hints to Patrick ('I know all about lonely children. Some people are lonely all their lives', 169), or her admission
to Bertie ('I suppose I was thinking about children and how they
present you with a version of yourself', 175). Structurally, the effect
is one of increased symmetry, as Blanche's thematic association with
the child comes to parallel that of the supposedly unscrupulous
Sally and Mousie; in the novelist's characteristic search for significant form, the child has become the fourth term.

Sally's cavalier treatment of her adoptive daughter is in stark contrast to the 'daughterly trap' of responsibility (this too, a recurrent
Brookner motif) into which Blanche herself had fallen. As she
reflects on her strange dream of rowing her mother – dressed in
beige chiffon and a large straw hat – to the Isle of Wight, Blanche
recognizes 'the life of forbearance, prudence, fortitude, humility: all
the Christian virtues' (70) forced on her by a 'calculating parent'.
The novelist's 'grudge' against Christianity emerges once again.

But now Blanche's increasingly subversive attitude encourages
her to abandon what she begins to regard as her Molly Theale-like
existence (73), although it is characteristically the pictorial image
rather than the fictional analogue which she finds best expresses
her feelings:

> thinking that she had not learned the right lessons, she mourn-
> fully set herself to learning more. But she did not quite trust
> the books, which had left her unprepared, and tried a different
> discipline. *The pictures told her another story.* (my emphasis; 95)

Bertie's girlfriend, the incongruously named Mousie is – like Sally
– also identified with an irresponsible pagan world, in explicit
contrast to Blanche's own life of duty and self-denial. Once again,
the National Gallery brings these principles 'into focus and into
opposition':

> On the one hand she had seen the fallen creation and its mournful
> effegies – the bleached virgins, the suffering saints, the uncalled

for martyrdoms – and on the other the carefree mythological excesses of those who did not, or did not need to, know of the alternative convention. (120)

Blanche associates Sally with various mythological images of the more obviously carefree type, such as the smile of the Goddess with the Pomegranate (47) – a figure that haunts her dreams; or Danae with the shower of gold (130) – an ironical reference to Sally's unspecified economic resources; when she is not reduced to harsher analogues with an 'emotional gangster, given to hijackings and other acts of terrorism' (51).

The polarity of Christians and Pagans runs insistently through the novel: Adam and Eve themselves are remembered not only for their associations with a gloomy Christian typology, but also – with witty irreverence – for their embodiment of another Brookner motif, children's relations with a problematic parent! In contrast to our first parents are the *kouroi* of her dreams 'with their blandfixed smile' (153), or (after yet another visit to the National Gallery) '[a]ll those deities carrying on their uninhabited lives. In full view' (176). Confronted by 'the blind fixity of the archaic smile' (151), Blanche waits for 'a sign of grace, a sign to displace her worst imaginings' (150), but naturally no sign comes.

Sally's husband, Paul, works temporarily for a wealthy American couple touring Europe, hoping to obtain a lot of money in a short time, in order to return to the kind of lifestyle that his wife clearly expects. As Blanche becomes involved with Sally's precarious existence, she indirectly reveals her lack of illlusions about the kind of person she is trying to help:

> she had begun her visits to the National Gallery, to be met there only with the austere visions of saints, the dolorous lives of virgins and martyrs, and, most singularly, the knowing and impervious smiles of those nymphs, who, she now began to see, had more of an equivalence in ordinary life, as it is lived by certain women, than she had ever suspected. (89)

In an effort to unravel Sally's personal and bureaucratic tangles, Blanche enlists the aid of a former admirer, Patrick Fox.

The characterization of Patrick introduces thematic variation as the narrative momentarily ignores the devastating influence of the nymph/temptress/parasite on the female protagonist, to consider instead the latter's effect on a male character, a subject that will not be fully worked out until *Lewis Percy*. Greater emotional distance succeeds in producing an ironic, if not satirical, portrait of the recessive and self-contained bachelor, Patrick. Forced to spend an 'occasional evening' at home, he paces his apartment, sometimes striking a 'poignant note' from his harpsichord, and wondering if his housekeeper will leave him if he brings home a wife:

> One thing led to another on these evenings of abstinence, and he would tell himself that all he required after a hard day at the office was half an hour with the Meditations of Marcus Aurelius and a couple of Brandenburg Concertos: anything else would be redundant. (92)

Memories of Blanche's 'raciness and delicacy', however, would eventually lead him to the telephone.

Patrick later becomes infatuated with Sally. He makes improbable plans to take her away on holiday, and sees this initiative in terms of cutting loose after years of attendance on a widowed mother. Like earlier Brookner heroines, he is prone – as Blanche rightly surmises – to feed on

> vague and elliptical remarks, marvelling at the sheer unfamilarity of it all, and believing that unaccountability contains erotic messages, messages of intrigue, of favours withheld, of penalties meted out. (168)

But there is also bitterness in the portrait; when Patrick is asked to intercede with Paul's American employer, he is able to cite his (female) analyst's prohibition against such potentially traumatic involvement. Blanche remarks sarcastically 'I wish I could have an analyst who would stop me doing things like this . . . Is she very expensive?' (130), but the restriction is clearly not only a financial one. There may even be a concealed autobiographical link. Brookner's interviews suggest familiarity with psychiatry, and it was Haffenden who asked whether she had been through psychoanalysis, to be told: 'No, and I wouldn't do it now: it would take too long.' As with Blanche, the real reason for avoiding the analyst's couch may be a more fundamental form of resistance.

Eventually it is Blanche who must go and confront the Demuths over Paul's alleged financial irregularities, an experience which provokes a powerful mental crisis. As Blanche struggles home after her interview with the American couple, Brookner produces possibly the most powerfully evocative passage of human suffering in all her fiction, surpassing even the nightmarish walk of Frances at the end of *Providence*. Inching forward 'under the glare of the unconsummated storm':

> she forced herself to think ahead to the white bed that awaited her, and saw herself, shriven, in a long white robe, waiting by her window, one hand holding back the curtain, for the first drops of rain to fall. I must get home before the storm, she thought, but she saw no means of doing so. (147–8)

In her distraught state, the experiences of the previous months return in grotesque fantasy form. Looking for saints, she can only find 'nymphs and deities'. Feeling herself to be one of the pilgrims on earth 'seeking their glimpse of salvation', she can only see the gods, 'striding with all their ideal muscularity into new liaisons' (148). Christian and Pagan worlds clash in some ghastly *Götterdämmerung* enacted entirely inside Blanche's head:

> Not, then, the confusion of Adam and Eve, mawkishly, stupidly, ashamed, half-heartedly instinctive, and instantly, massively rebuked, but the plunderers, the conscienceless, the plausible, scattering their children, seeking their pleasure, vanquishing their rivals, and, always, moving on. (148)

When she reaches home, Phyllis Duff, the good angel (like Nancy in *Providence*) appears to offer support (her gossipy comfort has the 'charm of a fairy tale', 154). Like the traumatic experiences of earlier heroines (Kitty Maule, Frances Hinton), Blanche's crisis also has many of the archetypal associations of rebirth; and after her eventual recovery, the last cycle of Blanche's narrative begins, a repetitive pattern reminiscent of *Providence* and *A Start in Life*.

She symbolically allows herself to sit in the sun ('the Sun is life'), cuts her hair, pays a last visit to Sally Beamish – pointedly empty-handed – and remonstrates mildly with her ex-husband: 'if only you knew how tired I am of doing the right thing', 175). She plans a Continental holiday in autumn sunshine, but as she retires to bed and sinks into a relaxed sleep, she is awoken by the sound of a key in the lock:

> For an insane moment she imagined herself pursued by the entire
> Beamish family – Sally, Paul, Elinor, the grandmother – each
> member of which had somehow managed to furnish itself with
> a key. (192)

It is Bertie who has returned.

The ending of the novel might seem promisingly ambiguous, but
it is more probably the compulsive repetition of a dramatic pattern –
of raised expectations and ironic reversal – present in every previous
novel except *Hotel du Lac*: it is difficult not to read the final scene as
a deterministically conceived defeat for Blanche in her struggle for
freedom and self-fulfilment.

But even when allowances have been made for strong 'family
resemblances', Blanche provides notable variations on the familiar
Brookner protagonist. Most obviously, she is the oldest and maturest
heroine to date, and it is in fact easy to trace a cumulative sequence
in the early Brookner novels.

*A Start in Life*, like the classic *Bildungsroman*, emphasizes the
protagonist's childhood and adolescence; the rapidly sketched aftermath of the final chapter – with Ruth's perfunctory marriage,
immediate widowhood and attainment of the age of forty – may
owe less to generic conventions than to the actual structure of
Balzac's model text. *Providence* considerably reduces the amount of
space devoted to the heroine's adolescence, but gives a correspondingly fuller account of her pursuit of an academic career. Frances
in *Look at Me*, a less academically successful but more creatively
talented figure than Ruth or Kitty, is also – for the central span of
the narrative – conspicuously older than either. And Edith Hope
in *Hotel du Lac* is an experienced and independent writer in her
mid-thirties, whose childhood history only emerges from a series
of brief flashbacks.

The pattern is clearly broken by *Family and Friends*, resembling
*Latecomers* with its 'quartet' of chief characters; and the protagonists
of *A Friend from England* and *Lewis Percy* have become progressively
younger.

With twenty years of marriage behind her, Blanche therefore represents the furthest point along an evolutionary path, although even
she is obviously an attractive and well-preserved woman. Brookner
has not yet written her *Mrs Dalloway* or *The Middle Age of Mrs Eliot*.
Observations of this kind would obviously have a certain bearing

on the autobiographical approach, even without the novelist's own well-documented reactions to her early heroines.

In this context, she is unequivocal ('Poor little things, I feel sorry for them. They're idiots: there's no other word for them', Haffenden, 30 / 'Sometimes I'm fed up with them . . . They're stupid', Guppy, 20). There is a fairly rudimentary form of identification ('I may have had more experience, but I've learned just as little as those characters'), together with a marked tendency towards thematic generalization ('They're aware of what life should be, but not of what it is' Haffenden, 28). The insights of a later more sophisticated protagonist, however, may not be all gain: of Rachel Kennedy (*A Friend from England*), it might thus be suggested that she is conversely aware of what life is, and not what it could be.

Predictably, *Look at Me* and Frances Hinton provoke the author's strongest reaction:

> I despised her for her suceptibility, her lack of divination, her stupidity. I felt myself getting madder and madder with her as I wrote it. (Kenyon, 13)

Blanche is also largely regarded as the simple embodiment of a theme ('that even good behaviour can go wrong'), although Brookner's extended comment on her character is both shrewd and sympathetic, as it expands to reflect deeply held personal beliefs:

> There is a personal dislike directed against Blanche Vernon, because you can't blame her for anything, except perhaps for being a prig. Now that is a very minor vice in my book. The point is that there are a lot of women like her: nice, innocent, but boring. Nobody likes them and as a result they lead very miserable lives. They are not fun to be with and in England you've got to be *fun*; you must be a *fun* person, having fun all the time! It's very superficial, but there it is. (Kenyon, 166)

The autobiographical link would again appear self-evident, but I refrain from developing it further at this point.

\*       \*       \*

Brookner's easy conversancy with Pagan and Christian iconography provides a solid structure with which to foreground the thematic concerns obliquely announced in the earlier novels, and increasingly insistent with each subsequent book. In her most substantial and revealing interview (Haffenden, 1984), Brookner allows herself to be questioned on precisely these motifs, and makes no attempt to conceal a deeply felt grudge against Christian ideology. Her own ideological sympathies show consistent affinities with the kind of eighteenth-century rationalism illumined in her art criticism, and reflected in certain of the earlier novels.

One may conclude the discussion of the novel providing the virtual apotheosis of Brookner's iconographic technique with a brief reference to jacket illustrations – more specifically, those of the paperback editions of her novels; these are the form, after all, in which most readers have become familiar with her fiction. Few contemporary writers have been so fortunately served in this respect. Most of the paperback editions of Brookner's novels reproduce portraits – or details from larger paintings – of women or young girls. *A Start in Life*, for example, shows a detail of Renoir's *The Daughters of Catulle Mendès at the Piano*. The pale and delicate features of a young girl, framed by beautiful thick red hair, offer a brilliant evocation of the literary portrait of the adolescent Ruth ('with extraordinary hair that made her head ache', 11) found within the pages of the novel.

The cover of *Providence* features Moise Kisling's portrait, *Kiki de Montparnasse*, an adolescent girl with short dark hair cut in a fringe, large brown eyes and delicately oval – even bird-like – features. The sad, distant expression of the face, emphasized by Kisling's severe neo-Egyptian stylization of its features also cleverly evokes the remoteness and vulnerability, together with the essential foreignness, of Kitty Maule.

The illustration for *Look at Me* reproduces a detail of André Derain's portrait of *Madame Rita Van Leer*. The fatigued expression of the subject – head cocked to one side and resting on the hands – the small almond-shaped eyes in an otherwise featureless and slightly puffy face, the insistent almost neurasthenic gaze fixed intently on the spectator, all suggest that sense of being a remote and passive observer which is such an essential part of Frances Hinton's self-perception.

The sequence of female heads is broken with *Hotel du Lac*, but *Family and Friends* continues the series with a detail from Gustav Klimt's portrait of *Gertha Felsöványi*. The subject is now a mature woman (perhaps thirty years old) with pale, narrow, but attractive features; the cheeks are slightly rouged, and the whole face is dominated by large blue eyes. The short and tousled auburn hair is perhaps a genial reference to the novel's central ritual of cutting hair, defiantly undergone by Betty, and unsuccessfully attempted by Mimi.

*A Misalliance* reproduces a detail from Kees van Dongen's *Woman with a Siamese Cat*. Here, the subject is a handsome but serious-looking woman of about forty, with an oval face, large dark eyes, slim nose, small delicate lips and short light brown hair just covering her ears. The woman has a long graceful neck and gently sloping shoulders, and wears a mildly décolleté pink dress with a necklace of single pearls. The portrait suggestively combines the formal elegance and even the physical attractiveness – together with the composure and aloofness – which all help to define the character of Blanche Vernon.

With *A Friend from England* and Norman Hepple's *Portrait of a Young Woman*, however, the remarkable sequence of motivated illustrations may break down: for the novel contains no direct physical description of its first person narrator, Rachel Kennedy. Hepple's subject has a broad forehead and solid features, dominated by large dreamy eyes. But if the almost placid face of Hepple's portrait reproduces Heather Livingstone's 'milk-fed appearance' (19), its thick shoulder-length auburn hair does not correspond to Heather's brutal *garçonne* crop. The cover designer may here of course be one step ahead of the literary critic: the broad forehead and powerful but attractive features might thus be regarded as contrasting with large, soft and beautiful brown eyes gazing into a remote distance; and the portrait's simultaneous impression of solidity and sensitivity may echo the actual bifurcation of the female protagonist suggested in my analysis of the novel itself.

With *Latecomers* and *Lewis Percy*, the evocative sequence of female portraits – previously broken only by *Hotel du Lac* – virtually comes to an end. *Latecomers* reproduces part of Jan van Huysum's *Basket of Flowers*. Perhaps in an imaginative response to certain thematic associations of the novel's title – 'You are not a survivor. You are a latecomer', as Hartmann tells Fibich (141) – the painting shows a brown butterfly alighting on the unopened bud of an autumn flower.

Finally, *Lewis Percy* – with its cover illustration of a detail from Victor Pasmore's *Lamplight* – shows a softly lit interior, bathed in warm reds and golds, revealing on closer examination an indeterminate female figure in the background: perhaps a subtle evocation of the barely discernible presence of Lewis's mother, Grace, in Parson's Green.

It is, of course, all too easy – if one is familiar with a Brookner novel – to project certain characteristics of a protagonist onto a cover illustration. On the other hand, some contemporary theoretical trends would encourage an approach to the text which embraced any extrinsic factors of textual production and presentation – not excluding matters of 'external packaging'. Furthermore, the high level of iconographic emphasis in all of the novels suggests that the choice of cover illustration would not have been a haphazard affair.

*A Misalliance* closes the cycle of Brookner's most overtly experimental novels and marks the transition to a new creative phase. The third group of texts is the most heterogeneous of all, and the three novels are probably best characterized precisely by their individuality. The combination of innovative structural methods with more traditional thematic material is nevertheless retained as the common denominator of *A Friend from England, Latecomers* and *Lewis Percy*.

# 4
## Creative Returns

In placing the last three novels under the heading of Creative Returns, I have drawn on two possible meanings of the word return: the sense of simple retroaction or reversion to earlier models, and that of profit or gain from past experience. In one respect, *A Friend from England*, *Latecomers* and *Percy Lewis* are all technically conservative novels, without the overt experimentation and insistent self-consciousness of their immediate predecessors. They reflect a nineteenth-century realist tradition to which the author herself frequently refers.[1]

In thematic terms, too, the three novels are retrospective: *A Friend from England*, in particular, represents a virtual compendium of familiar Brookner motifs. On the other hand, if the first three books, with their high dependence on French literary models, may in some ways be regarded as a distinguished fictional apprenticeship; and the next three are regarded as the most innovative and formally challenging of the novels; then the third group displays the technical assurance, and often the virtuosity, of an experienced and accomplished writer.

The opening pages of *A Friend from England* describe how Rachel Kennedy, thirty-two years old, unmarried, and part-owner of a bookshop, has 'inherited' her accountant Oscar Livingstone, from her father. In the course of her journeys to the Livingstones' home in Wimbledon, she is 'admitted to the family circle', which she regards initially as an entirely happy development. She finds in Dorrie Livingstone's face something that 'reminded me of the wistful, complicated attitudes of my own mother' (16).

The growing attachment is further motivated by Rachel's feelings of domestic isolation, and she recognizes her own tendency to 'gravitate towards those families whose domesticity was so engulfing that all I had to do was listen and marvel' (26). Her relationship with the Livingstones becomes so important, precisely because the family represents 'fixed points of reference in a slipping universe, abiding by rules which everyone else had broken' (31). Rachel says virtually nothing about her biological parents, but is correspondingly candid about the special appeal of Oscar and Dorrie:

> the return of the Livingstones signified that I was in some way free once more, as if their rootedness gave me the security to be rootless, to test my vagrancy against their stability, my preparedness for adventure against their bourgeois world. The contrast was perhaps necessary to me for reasons which were present in me, not as reasons, but perhaps as instincts, as if I and they existed to offset each other in a way to benefit both conditions, . . . (67–8)

Rachel's attachment to the Livingstones' home is thrown into relief by the feelings of desperation and the reluctant sense of identification she experiences in her own small apartment:

> It was, I saw, a flat to get out of rather than one to stay in. It was a machine for eating and sleeping in, a suitable dwelling for a working woman, whose main interest is in her work. I disliked this version of myself, which seemed to negate my other activities, reduced them to after-hours amusements, whereas I had always thought them pretty central. These mute white walls had been silent witnesses to many encounters; nevertheless, they withheld comment, and their very withholding struck me as unfriendly. '*Unheimlich*' was the word which came to mind when I stood on the threshold of my bedroom: . . . (123)

And Rachel does not consider the translation 'unhomely' strong enough to express the sense of alienation she feels.

Her relationship with the Livingstones' daughter generates the major source of tension in the novel, and her criticisms echo those of various Brookner protagonists – Edith Hope, Blanche Vernon, Kitty Maule – towards women they regard as spoilt, parasitic or childishly irresponsible – the Puseys, Sally Beamish or Jane Fairchild, respectively. Personal resentment and envy mingle suggestively with an emergent sense of feminist awareness in two comments on the Livingstones' daughter:

> But of course she had always been the protected one, allowed to remain a child for as long as she wished, and then presented with a set of grown-up toys when the passage of time demanded them. I felt sorry for her, but I felt impatient too. . . . I felt a spasm of distaste for her and for all those women like her, women who work for fun and marry for status, and still demand compensation. The only excuse for such women is incurable frivolity. And Heather was not even frivolous. (109)

The gradual adoption of Rachel is paralleled by the simultaneous emancipation of Heather. As in *A Start in Life* and *Providence*, there are two cycles of liberation. Heather first marries Michael Sandberg, whose chief virtue would appear to be that she has discovered him by herself, without family interference. But the relationship ends as conclusively as any romantic attachment in Brookner, when Michael is revealed as homosexual.

Heather decides to remarry almost immediately, having fallen in love with Marco, the brother of her Italian friend, Clara. Opposition now comes less from Heather's parents than from Rachel herself, who feels that Heather's plan to move to Italy is selfish and irresponsible. The narrative ends as Rachel travels to Venice – ostensibly for the sake of the Livingstones – to make a final appeal to their daughter's sense of filial duty. The outcome of the second romantic cycle is uncertain, although readers may draw their own conclusions as Rachel, overcome by 'shame, penury and the shock of truth', last sees Heather vanishing down the *Calle de la Vida* – the 'street of life' (204).

In accordance with a familiar Brookner procedure, the Romantic motif is introduced iconographically, through external cultural reference: Rachel takes Oscar and Dorrie to a performance of *La Bohème* in chapter two, referring amusedly to the spectacle of 'Oscar and Dorrie holding hands tightly throughout the last act', and 'dabb[ing] their eyes when the curtain went down'. Ironically, the Livingstones regard their surrogate daughter as a daring figure, a 'feminist' and a 'romantic' who 'ruled over a sort of Bohemia', although Rachel herself hastens to add that the truth was 'somewhat different' (31).

Rachel is apparently unequivocal on romanticism – and particularly so on the subject of romantic love: 'Some women avoid love – I do myself – because they fear its treachery' (105); or in a passing comment on the Livingstones more significant for what it reveals of Rachel:

> I had been softened and amused by the solemnity with which they had accepted all the farrago of romantic passion. For to me it was a farrago, both on the stage and in real life, something archaic and unmanageable, unsettling and devastating, and to succumb to such a passion would be a quite voluntary step towards self-destruction. (117)

It is a finely ironic characterization of an increasingly unreliable narrator, and – with the novel's conclusion in mind – one need do no more here than note the psychological implications of such vehement denials, or the dramatic potential of such overweening *hubris*. On the first score, the Rachel of the final episodes in Venice has reached a state bordering on psychosis; whilst, in a fine piece of structural irony, it is precisely Rachel's evocation of another life ('Deceit. Control. Arrangements. Mismanagement', 198) which had strengthened Heather's resolve to turn her back on English middle-class convention and remain in Italy.

As Rachel travels reluctantly to Wimbledon to discuss Heather's intended remarriage, it is she herself who is most affected by the meeting. Dorrie explains with equanimity, 'It's all very romantic. Apparently it was love at first sight' (182), adding a final comment particularly devastating for Rachel:

> 'And we'd rather know that she had had this chance. I didn't like to think of her growing older and not knowing what true love was.' (183)

Rachel has presumably never known it, and it is therefore easy to undertand her feelings of irritation if the Livingstones have not lost a belief in romantic love. And yet, for all its cliché-ridden, threadbare quality, this particular narrative allows Oscar and Dorrie to accept Heather's departure more serenely than does Rachel's vaunted scepticism.

Dorrie proudly introduces Rachel to her sisters as a 'feminist' (68), and Rachel does in fact revive the debate on the protected versus the independent woman (familiar from Edith's remarks on Monica and the Puseys in *Hotel du Lac*). In her shrewdest and most extensive comment on the topic, Rachel begins characeristically from personal experience:

> The lives of idle women fascinate me, and yet such women always bridle when you speak to them of your commitments, your plans, your calculations, as if you were casting aspersions on their own industriousness, which they will then go on to demonstrate. (171)

Her deadpan comment ('It will be a pity if women in the more conventional mould are to be phased out, for there will never be anyone to go home to', 171) is worthy of Austen herself, and so too is the waspishness of her conclusion:

> It pleases me, in some obscure way, to conceive of women as timorous, delicate, in need of special treatment, of deference, waves of sympathy and praise lapping at their feet as they perform some quite ordinary task, or simply preside at their tables, family acquiescent around them. Born to serve, as it might be thought, such women seem to triumph, and many of them preserve a good conscience at the same time. It is quite an achievement. (171)

In an earlier passage with double-edged overtones for the feminist debate, Rachel had also elaborated on her sense of socio-cultural divide among women: from her own more liberated position, she looks back with a scorn not devoid of envy on women as a 'protected species':

> Women have come a long way, of course: we can all be left alone at night now. But sometimes it seems a high price to pay. We can also open the door cheerfully to strangers at any hour, deal with obscene telephone calls and mend fuses. It has never occurred to me that someone else would do the locking up . . . It has never occurred to me because I do all these things as a matter of course. But Dorrie and her sisters still belonged to the protected variety, safe to express fear, anxiety, distress. (139)

Rachel's own emancipation is certainly linked more closely with 'self-repression' than with 'self-expression'. She identifies her own reluctance to express emotions as an attempt to 'avoid certain conditions that I refused to think about', adding perceptively: 'After all, I was in line for them myself' (139). There are inescapable references in these comments to such recurrent Brookner themes as loneliness, isolation and the marginal status of the unmarried woman.

                    *          *          *

Rachel Kennedy's story also marks a return to first person narrative – together with Frances Hinton's account in *Look at Me* – the exception in Brookner's fiction. *Hotel du Lac* of course alternates between first and third person narrative, although grammatical distinctions of person often fail to correspond to divisions in focalization. As I suggest later (in the context of *Lewis Percy*), psycho-narrative and (third person) narrated monologue are as important, as problematic, and occasionally as subtly ambivalent as they are in Austen herself. Rachel is an even less sympathetic focalizer than Blanche Vernon in *A Misalliance*, as illustrated for example in her painstaking decription of the Livingstones' home:

> The house – a substantial but essentially modest suburban villa – was furnished with voluptuous grandeur in approximations of various styles, predominantly those of several Louis, with late nineteenth- and early twentieth-century additions. Heavy coloured glass ashtrays of monstruous size and weight rested on inlaid marquetry tables of vaguely Pompadour associations. At dinner we drank champagne from ruby Bohemian glasses: the meat was carved at a Boulle-type sideboard. 'Regency' wallpaper of dark green and lighter green stripes was partially covered by gilt-framed landscapes of no style whatsoever. (12)

Brookner the art historian is clearly in evidence, and as an exercise in *l'effet du réel*, her performance would not have disgraced Balzac. Barthes distinguished between informants – minor descriptive details merely reinforcing the 'reality effect', and indices – elements requiring a decoding process (Barthes, 1982, 75–84; cf. Martin, 113).[2]

In the present case, the decoding process inevitably focuses on narrator rather than object: for if Oscar and Dorrie's Wimbledon home suggests – at worst – fussiness or eclecticism run riot, the tone of *de haut en bas* in Rachel's description reflects an almost stupefying condescension. The description must either be read, therefore, as a masterpiece of indirect characterization, or as Brookner's own initiation into the grand English tradition – exemplified by Waugh, Maugham, Powell and many others – of cultural snobbery. It is hard to imagine such true exotics of the English novel as Conrad or Koestler bothering to record a Boulle-*type* sideboard.

The reader's irritation may be reinforced by a kind of world-weary superiority in Rachel's references to 'paying one's dues' (41) or the tedious *rite de passage* of Heather's fiancé being introduced to the family. But the narrator's knowledge is not limited to the kind of 'knowing in apartness' which Lawrence found so distasteful in Jane Austen. It may actually reflect a structural fault in the novel, whereby Rachel literally knows too much for a first person intradiegetic narrator. Her eerily accurate prognosis for Michael Sandberg and his father may be a case in point.

But Brookner's methods are vindicated by the fine ironic build-up over the last two chapters, when Rachel undertakes to bring Heather home from Venice. As a plot structure it is reminiscent of Mimi's abortive trip to Paris in *Family and Friends* to retrieve her sister Betty; a further structural analogy between the two novels appears in terms of motivation, as Rachel's *hubris* and Mimi's emotional naivity produce the inevitable ironic reversal at the end of their respective narratives.

After two inconclusive meetings with Heather at home, the trip to Venice had seemed doomed from the start, and this is also the understanding of Rachel as retrospective narrator. On this score, however, the exact amount of self-awareness invested in her narrative is not immediately clear. Rachel may have been initially insensitive to her own prudery and prejudice; she thus makes no attempt to censor such harsh and personally unflattering references as those to Heather 'awakening in the arms of a knowing Italian' (148) or 'sit[ting] in some dingy apartment, waiting for her prospective mother-in-law to serve her with a plate of soup' (186). But when she describes herself, immediately prior to departure, smoothing the 'leather of conqueror's boots' against the calves of her legs, the element of retrospective self-irony can hardly remain in doubt.

Towards the end of *A Friend from England*, Rachel attempts to visualize the outcome of Heather's second attempt at emancipation from her parents:

> her mother would really die without her, and perhaps her father
> too, but die of a broken heart, that heart they had in common
> where Heather was concerned. I did not at the time think that
> any of this was melodramatic. Looking back much later I came
> to see it as something from the pages of a nineteenth-century
> novel, . . . (166)

Such a forecast seems to bear little relation to the parents' true
feeings when Rachel next meets them. Oscar admits that they will
miss their daughter, but insists that Heather must have her chance
to be as happy as he and Dorrie have been. Dorrie exemplifies, and
even to some extent justifies, belief in what Rachel dismisses as the
farrago of Romantic love ('I didn't like to think of her growing older
and not knowing what true love was', 183).

It is true that Dorrie subsequently gives way to tears and
gratefully accepts Rachel's offer to go to Venice and intercede
with Heather once more, but there is a clear suggestion that such an
initiative is prompted more by Rachel's barely concealed obsessions
than by Dorrie's own emotional needs; Rachel's judgement is thus
unreliable, and the further the narrative progresses, the less the
reader is inclined to accept her predictions on any subject at all.

Thematically, the entire episode reflects the confrontation of spontaneous romanticism with intelligent scepticism which is so frequently at the heart of Brookner's fiction. The contrast is heightened
here, moreover, by a clever structural irony, according to which
romantic love is defended by the utterly conventional Livingstones
and vindicated by the shadowy, recessive Heather, whereas the
'voice of reason' belongs to Rachel, fast succumbing to alarming
psychotic impulses. As the author herself ruefully suggests elsewhere, 'in certain situations reason doesn't work, and that's the
most desolate discovery of all' (Haffenden, 28).

The full force of this particular dichotomy is invested in the
word 'melodramatic' in the passage quoted above: for it is unclear
whether the adjective refers to 'story' or 'discourse', the objective
(but presumably irrecoverable) circumstances of the Livingstones'
future lives, or the projections made for these lives by an increasingly unreliable Rachel.[3]

Less ambivalent, however, are Brookner's references in interviews
to the great Victorian novelists, and even the suggestion that her
own story – like Heather's – belongs to a novel of the period. She

thus traces the 'moral rectitude' of her characters to a personal 'grounding in nineteenth-century novels and nineteenth-century behaviour' (Haffenden, 27); these characters, like their creator, 'obey all nineteenth-century rules of morality and duty and serious- ness'; they are 'nineteenth-century families, without the nineteenth century to give support' (Kenyon, 20). She admires the 'decent feelings' of Trollope 'whose moral standards are clear within the framework of the novel' (Haffenden, 25), in addition to the 'indig- nation' of Dickens and the 'moral scruple' of James (28). Brookner and her protagonists in fact rarely transcend Victorian perspectives, although the latter – on the evidence of her novels at least – appear to delude far more than they are able to sustain.

The brief digression on the autobiographical dimension of the nov- els is made advisedly at this point. For if Brookner tends to see her fiction in terms of impure ('autobiographical') or pure ('invented') novels, the critic is tempted to find ubiquitous autobiography of some kind, now appearing as surface matter, and now as deeper structures.

The points of contact between Rachel Kennedy and the collec- tive persona of the Brookner interviews are particularly striking. Their subject, like Rachel, had also felt herself to be a 'grown-up orphan', whilst her 'dreary Victorian story' anticipates the 'very old-fashioned moral tale' (Guppy, 166) which is *A Friend from England*. One might also point to the creative dynamics of the novel, and recall Brookner's remark that her characters exasperate her – as she finds herself deeply exasperating (Haffenden, 71). It is a highly significant pattern – duplicated in Rachel's attitude towards Heather, the reader's towards Rachel, or even in Rachel's attitude towards herself. In retrospect, we recall the author's brief anticipatory remarks on *A Friend from England*. Such remarks seem more accurate for their comment on the thematic structure of the novel than for the presumed distinction between author and protagonist:

> It is about an extremely emancipated young woman – whom they will not be able to think is me! – who is drawn into a family of blameless innocence whom she feels called upon to protect, but by whose innocence she finds herself finally vanquished. She can't measure up to it. (Guppy, 167)

  *                    *                    *

But if Brookner feels hamstrung by the legacy of Victorian ethics, *A Friend from England* itself successfully exploits themes and techniques associated with various nineteenth-century novelists: Dickens, Austen (in spite of the author's reservations towards this writer) and James are the most prominent of these.

On the evidence of the interviews, at least, Dickens's formative influence on Brookner was particularly strong. At the suggestion of her Polish father, she began reading the novels (at the age of seven) 'to unveil the mysteries of English life' (Haffenden, 28). This anecdote about her father is suggestive enough to be repeated and elaborated in successive interviews ('he thought Dickens gave a true picture of Engish life, where right always triumphed', Guppy, 149; 'he fed me with Dickens from the time I was seven', Kenyon, 9).

In the novels of Dickens, critics have long drawn attention to the prominence of the 'orphan' motif, together with the high incidence of failed or absent biological parents and the corresponding importance of substitute figures.[4] Brookner's novels, too, are conspicuous for their high incidence of orphans, as well their numerous portraits of misguided, inadequate, or merely irresponsible parents.

If *Providence* (Kitty Maule) introduces the orphan motif, and *Look at Me* (Frances Hinton) portrays the taking-up of the solitary heroine by a group of contemporaries, *A Friend from England* is the first novel to introduce a genuine adoptive family. But Rachel's surrogate father, Oscar Livingstone, does not correspond entirely to the fairy-tale figures of the Cheerybles or Mr Brownlow: most significantly, he has a twenty-seven year old daughter of his own; whilst the age and status of the 'orphan' figure, independent and self-employed Rachel Kennedy, also suggest a context far removed from archetypal Dickensian patterns. In view of the biological daughter's passivity and apparent social inadequacy, moreover, the Livingstones' motives for cultivating the more worldly Rachel as a companion for Heather are not entirely altruistic.

And yet the orphan myth once again provides the most powerful correlative for the oppressive sense of cultural and emotional alienation from which the Brookner heroine suffers. Rachel appreciates her 'place in this family circle' (50) and delights in 'the seduction and the novelty of a fixed point' (63). Her adoption by the Livingstones is moreover expressed in terms of another familiar Dickensian motif – most conspicuous in *Providence* – the communion provided by the shared meal.[5] The fusion of these two thematic elements appears most clearly in a reference by Rachel to Dorrie's hospitality:

I supposed that all parents worried about their children's diet. Mine had not, which was why I found it so delightful to sit and be fed by Dorrie, whose food was a *magnificent celebration*. (my emphasis; 22)

But the orphan motif also merges within the familiar sphere of reciprocity or conflict between the female protagonist and her existential (characteristically sexual) rival.

Rachel's personal narrative begins as Dorrie Livingstone invites her to dinner (11), a meal which their daughter Heather would significantly never attend (14). Rachel's virtual substitution for Heather in various filial contexts – she visits Dorrie in hospital, when Heather is not even aware of her mother's illness – recapitulates another Brookner theme, the selfishness of the prodigal offspring. In *A Friend from England*, however, the contrast (prominent in *Family and Friends*) between 'good' and 'bad' children is further refined by the way in which Rachel's adoption has its exact structural and thematic counterpart in Heather's gradual emancipation from her parents. Rachel comes to regret the process, as she admits in a more candid moment:

I felt that Heather had usurped my independence and was in effect using my time to enjoy the equivalent of my habitual adventures. (148)

The two women effectively become sisters, although Heather's suggestion to Rachel – 'You're part of the family now' (41) – cannot, in the broader thematic context of Brookner's fiction, be regarded as an unmitigated blessing; the point is reinforced by a later reference to the 'additional curse of happy families' (131). But as Heather's and Rachel's incompatibility declines into antagonism, and so much of the novel becomes concerned with Heather's marriage(s) – with all the attendant pressure from well-meaning parents and intrusive relations – it is tempting to seek parallels in a second nineteenth-century novelist, Jane Austen.

After the dismantlement of the Austen myth by critics such as D. W. Harding and Marvin Mudrick, it become possible to understand better the human and even the artistic shortcomings of the novelist, together with the frustrations and resentments of her world.[6] One of the finest of such post-lapsarian studies – John Halperin's critical biography – has laid particular stress on the prominence of sibling rivalry both in the life and in the fiction.

Such a general thematic parallel between Brookner and Austen is probably of greater interest than, for instance, more specific links with *Mansfield Park* through the orphan/adoption motif. *A Friend from England* obviously differs from Austen novels in its use of a first person narrator: critical comments on Heather ('pale milk-fed appearance', 16; 'bovine expression', 65; 'mulish' silences, 91) thus stem directly from Rachel.

But this distinction is less fundamental than it might appear: for if Austen actually alternates between an external narrator and focalization through the psycho-narrative of a central character, Brookner uses a similar narrative split: Rachel's unflattering comments on Heather's appearance are part of an unreflecting synchronous narrative, whereas her more considered judgements ('What surprised me was the hatred that seemed to have sprung between us', 199) clearly belong to a process of retrospective focalization. A more obvious analogy might be the dual focalization of Pip as child and adult in *Great Expectations*, although the parallel with Austen remains valid.

Such a binary pattern acquires great prominence in the carefully articulated contrast and nascent rivalry between two sisters – biological, as with Elinor and Marianne Dashwood, or adoptive, as in the case of Rachel and Heather (the latter perhaps also comparable to Fanny Price and Mary Crawford). Brookner's 'sisters', like Austen's, are effectively complementary or reciprocal: Rachel's supposed experience is an obvious counterpart to Heather's inexperience, whilst her process of increased family involvement has already been identified as a neat inversion of Heather's movement towards emancipation.

There is, moreover, an inevitable sense of quasi-mechanical symmetry in both writers, suggesting the actual splitting of a single character. This impression is reinforced in *A Friend from England* by the partition between Rachel and Heather of so many elements common to previous Brookner protagonists: Rachel, an orphan figure, her livelihood derived from books, has – like Frances Hinton – been traumatized by painful and barely suppressed erotic experiences; Heather, introvert and unformed, achieves emancipation through the process of romantic love (a cycle which – like Ruth Weiss and Kitty Maule – she attempts twice).

It is precisely this type of division which distinguishes certain female pairs in Austen's later novels. The novelist apparently censored *Pride and Prejudice* for being 'rather too light, and bright and sparkling' and much of the novel's tone may be traced to Austen's heroine. In the weightier *Mansfield Park* – the argument runs – she is naturally unable to suppress her characteristic verve; and so maintains an extensive role for an anonymous and authoritative external narrator, whilst producing a kind of mental bifurcation (or splitting of types) between the two main female characters.

If Elizabeth Bennet is the prototypical Jane Austen heroine, her attributes are now divided between Mary Crawford and Fanny Price, Mary retaining Elizabeth's wit and dynamism, and Fanny inheriting her virtues of constancy and moral sense. In *A Friend from England*, Brookner also apparently sought greater artistic detachment, as appears from her claim to have created a protagonist 'whom they will not be able to think is me!' (Guppy, 167).

The third major presence in *A Friend from England* is that of James; the latter's influence is not, however, limited to the kind of 'moral scruple' to which Brookner vaguely refers, but also extends to stylistic elements. Critics have long drawn attention to the Jamesian tehnique of sustaining an 'extended' or 'expanded' metaphor throughout the length of a novel:[7] thus *Portrait of a Lady* – mentioned explicitly by Brookner in an interview (Guppy, 159) – pursues greater cohesion by constant recourse to images of art and collecting. *A Friend from England* introduces a comparable extended metaphor with its prominent water imagery.

Such imagery in the novel is admittedly insistent rather than consistent in character. On some occasions, too, wet weather may belong to the sphere of natural description. Rain may be pure metonymic detail, although – in a hydrophobic narrator – its hidden significance must surely never be discounted. In the long history of reading illness as metaphor, traced in Susan Sontag's classic study,[8] Rachel's hydrophobia (like Tissy's agoraphobia in *Lewis Percy*) is yet another manifestation: either state is the effective correlative for the unspecified mental sickness to which a female character is subject.

But from the point at which Rachel agrees to go swimming with her colleague, Robin, in an attempt to overcome her fear, the more universal associations of water imagery – a metaphor we live (and die) by – become increasingly apparent. Such associations are not new to Brookner; in the first letter to her lover, David, in *Hotel du Lac*, Edith Hope had referred to her flight from marriage to Geoffrey

Long, neatly inverting the title of Stevie Smith's poem, arguably the most celebrated reworking of water and drowning metaphors from our collective cultural repertoire.

> For a moment I panicked, for I am myself now, and was then, although this fact was not recognized. Not drowning but waving. (10)

If dancing, in *Family and Friends*, emerges as the privileged trope for living itself, water is now the central metaphor for the site of this activity.

It is associations of this kind – even with all their inconsistencies – which now become the common currency of *A Friend from England*. Thus Heather is seen as 'a swimmer in calm and protected waters', powered only by the 'healthy movements of a beautifully functioning organism' (28); for Rachel herself, the Livingstones are 'the dry land to which a hapless swimmer such as myself might cling for safety' (66).

The alternative for Rachel is her recurrent dream of drowning: even thinking is accompanied by a '*wave* of sadness', and she opts for a 'life on the *surface*' (62). With her adoptive family, however, she can '*drift* contentedly on the *stream* of their desultory talk', although she regards the Livingstones themselves as 'living at some subterranean level, *immersed in a sea-dream* that never rose to the surface' (63). Ultimately, of course, even Oscar and Dorrie are not immune to the ' *troubled waters* of a family drama' (185).

Rachel expresses growing concern for her own situation with the comment that her life was 'perhaps a little *adrift*' (81), and – in a characteristic mixing of metaphors – begins to sense the limitations of her ' landlocked freedom' (82); Heather, on the other hand, had sought the 'safer *haven* of marriage'. Rachel refers to the '*drowning waters*' of her dreams (117), and remembers the '*storms* of childhood' (160). Or when the overwhelmingly literal London rain finally impinges on her figurative world, she records the womb-like experience of sitting ' submerged in the taxi's dark little cave' whilst the '*waves of water*' seem to part under its wheels (161).

Tropology and pathology merge in a dramatic climax worthy of James, as Rachel pursues Heather to Venice ('the ultimate nightmare: a city filled with water', 186). (Meteorology certainly compounds her sufferings, since it rains hard for much of her stay). The apotheosis of the novel's water imagery occurs in a richly

emblematic final scene: Rachel, 'conqueror's boots' notwithstanding, remains 'blocked by water' (203) as her quarry seems to
disappear into the 'impenetrable shadows' of the city of water.
Later that night, she awakens from a 'dream of drowning' and
remembers Heather 'vanishing down the Calle de la Vida' (204) –
metaphorically and literally, the street of life.

Among the horrors of 'darkened lapping water' below her, Rachel
forces herself to visit the *Accademia* (191). The dramatic quality of
the scene is doubtless enhanced by the fact it provides the only
sustained use of iconographic reference in the entire novel. Rachel
passes 'gold polyptichs', the 'flailing limbs of several martyrdoms'
and Bellini's *Madonnas*, to reach the only picture she wanted to see:

> The woman suckling her child had a heavy face, immanent with
> meaning, but from which all explanation had been withdrawn.
> To her right, on the left of the picture, stood the mysterious
> and elegant knight, intense and remote, his face in shadow.
> The storm that broke on the scene bound the two together in
> puzzling simplicity. (191)

Rachel may in fact be following a pattern of childhood regression common among Brookner protagonists; and in the portrait of
Giorgone's *The Tempest* she is presumably able to discover both her
parents and herself.

At an earlier point in her narrative, as her mental condition deteriorates, Rachel describes the totally debilitating effect of wet weather:

> The weather put a stop to all my activities. Every evening I got
> into bed earlier and earlier. It was as if I were travelling back-
> wards, back into childhood. I slept voraciously and was aware
> of dreaming copiously, although I always forgot my dreams as
> soon as I woke. (121)

But such oblivion does not prevent Rachel – in a fine piece of
dramatic irony – from insisting that 'these dreams were of no
consequence to me or of interest to anyone else' (121)!

In her interview with John Haffenden, Brookner emphasizes the
role of abreaction in the composition of her novels, and the whole
complex of hydrophobia in *A Friend from England* may even represent the imaginative tranference of some unspecified a personal

fear. Alternately, the persistent water motif may be read in terms of some of its commonest associations within our culture: *currents* of feeling, *stream* of consciousness, *depth* of emotion, fertility, birth and even life itself.[9] Ultimately, perhaps, the narrative may rest on an imaginative synthesis of both of these dimensions.

*        *        *

In a memorable review that has already made fleeting appearances in this study, Peter Kemp belabours Brookner with the weight of Henry James. It is true that she lacks the massiveness and density of James, but she equally avoids a number of Jamesian shortcomings. There is thus much to be said for writing fiction, as she does, in which plausible figures invariably perform recognizable functions in comprehensible language within a limited compass. In view of the strengths and subtleties of *A Friend from England*, moreover, to dismiss Brookner as the 'fictional specialist in migraines, flushes and female malaises' (Kemp, 1989) can only be evidence of a particularly cloddish male sensibility.

## LATECOMERS

*Latecomers*, like its successor *Lewis Percy*, also justifies the kind of judgement implied by the phrase 'creative returns'. For all its impressive evidence of thematic innovation, however, it may be useful to begin by concentrating on familiar elements in the novel, and relate certain narrative strategies to those of earlier works, particularly *Family and Friends*.

Brookner described the latter as fairly schematic ('four children, two of each sex'), and characterized its writing as 'almost entirely free from anxiety'. Her remark on structure ('A chapter to each one is almost the easiest form', Kenyon, 19) refers explicitly to the subjects of the first photograph in *Family and Friends*, but is equally valid as a general approach to narrative methods. Thus *Latecomers* also begins with a chapter for each major character in the story; and in this respect, certainly, the conventional pattern of minor cross references between essentially monolithic narrative blocks, together with the recurrence of habitual Brookner motifs, may obscure what is original in the novel.

The first and third chapters are devoted to Hartmann and Fibich, lifelong friends and successful business associates in a firm manufacturing facetious greeting cards; chapters two and four present their respective wives, Yvette and Christine. The two men are the more remarkable pair; described as 'metaphorically and almost physically twin souls', sharing background and status – even a common first name – it is impossible not to regard them as another example of the bifurcation used in *A Friend from England*.

If the two men are indeed opposite poles of a single identity, the essence of this polarity would lie in their contrasting capacities for dealing with the legacy of the past. As a twelve-year-old refugee at an English boarding-school, Hartmann's sense of alienation is no less than that of his companion and compatriot, the seven-year-old Fibich:

> Doubly, even trebly an outsider, he knew, even on his first day, that he was doomed. Had it not been for the accident of being paired with Fibich – but both were forbidden to speak German – he would have died or killed himself. Only the knowledge that someone else's experience reflected his own reality saved him, . . . (10)

Reading *Oliver Twist*, Hartmann marvels that 'Dickens had had such an acute understanding of the misery of boys' (12). The reference to the archetypal orphan figure of the Victorian novel anticipates the laconic notice a page later that the parents of both Hartmann and Fibich are dead.

Unlike Fibich, the adult Hartmann makes determined and largely successful efforts to come to terms with his past: his methods are a conscious and disciplined process of repression. In the attempt to 'screen out the undesirable, the inadvertent', much is 'consigned to the dust, or to that repository that can only be approached in dreams' (7). There is discomfort from certain elements which can never be forgotten, but the even tenor of Hartmann's life appears to justify this 'extreme form of censorship' (23). It is an equilibrium which Fibich will never possess:

> Fibich *remembered*. Fibich *remembered* Aunt Marie, whom he called 'Aunt', and the flat filled with implacable Gothic furniture where he had spent so many years wondering if his bewilderment would ever end. He *remembered* blundering through his life, never knowing or indeed discovering whether his actions were acceptable or whether they were as futile as he believed them to be. (my emphasis; 33)

If Hartmann's past is thus exorcised, Fibich's is either grossly distorted or simply and involuntarily lost, even as its painful legacy remains. In this respect, the hours spent with his analyst are of little help: plagued by dreams of his own inadequacy, he can only recover isolated fragments from a 'mass of fear':

> He had, for example, an image of himself as a very small, very plump boy, engulfed in a large wing chair which he knew to be called the Voltaire, feeling lazy, replete, and secure in the dying light of a winter afternoon. (33)

The 'crucial' element of fatness – 'since for all of his adult life he had been laughingly, cadaverously thin' (33) – may echo the insistent division in Brookner between solid and ethereal female characters, but also suggests the infant's inevitable association of repletion with care and affection. The contorted quality of Fibich's memory also contrasts markedly with the selected reminiscences of Hartmann:

> He remembered his father, in a magnificently odorous and gleaming emporium, pointing with his cane to a pineapple, a box of peaches, and asking for them to be taken out to the car. Or himself, when tiny, walking with his nurse in the Englische Garten. Or first love, at the age of ten, and a game of hide-and-seek with the beloved at Nymphenburg, beside the long paths rustling with fallen leaves and the commotion of birds. (7)

Described ironically as 'scenes that might have been devised by Proust', Hartmann's recollections of a vanished Central European idyll also possess a Nabokov-like nostalgia, an element of playful invention quite at variance with the disturbing fragments dredged up by Fibich. Even in his reminiscences, Hartmann is a voluptuary.

The relation to the past, so fundamental for Hartmann and Fibich, is also the crucial formative influence on their wives, although this dimension is sometimes overshadowed here by Brookner's characteristic determinism, which prompts her to equate female physical appearance with certain behavioural traits. Yvette Hartmann is thus often portrayed with a regulated hatred which Austen herself might have envied: frivolous and narcissistic, she has Iris Pusey's ability to enter a room 'with a sort of preemptive bustle, as if drawing on herself the attention of a crowd', 19). Safe 'in the land of husbands and wives, on whom society smiles' – always a sensitive issue for the author and her unmarried protagonists – she is happy to have brought the 'business of flirting' to an 'honourable conclusion' (31). Such a coldly calculating Brookner woman, so physically unresponsive and socially unliberated, almost inevitably possesses

> a body that might have been designed by a Salon painter of the Second Empire, by Baudry or Bouguereau, one of those legendary hourglass shapes that bloom extravagantly but harmoniously above and below a narrow waist. (27–8)

In this respect too, Yvette is an obvious antithesis to the homely but angular Christine Fibich, although an equally interesting if more original contrast is reflected in the respective attitudes of the two women towards the past. Yvette has almost obliterated memories from before the time when she had assumed control over her own life. What she cannot repress, she attempts to embellish, as in her image of a train journey from Paris to Bordeaux with her young widowed mother; she had sat tiny and docile with a *tartine* in her hand, whilst her mother urged '*Mange, mange, ma fille*' (23). The words 'had been accompanied by the cast shadow of her protective body' (24), clearly echoing Fibich's own pre-oedipal association of the mother's food with comfort and security.

But if the externally mediated account of Yvette's childhood reminiscence is thematically analogous to Fibich's own memories, it is structurally quite distinct, since it is followed by a direct critique from the implied author of Yvette's credulity:

> To Yvette the story had no resonance except as a novelette, the kind in which she believed implicitly, despite her relative sophistication, and this too was a common position among women in the days that preceded enlightenment. (24)

The reader is then given the 'real' version of events, although it remains unclear whether the diegetic revision of the idyll is focalized through Hartmann, or simply the assertion of a bluntly authoritative external narrator. In either case, we learn how Yvonne's mother was in reality 'fuelled by a desperate and unyielding purpose' – she had been wondering how to obtain a divorce even as her husband was killed (24). If the new version is indeed Hartmann's, Brookner habitués will be forewarned: a man's word may generally be accepted before a woman's, particularly if the latter possesses an hourglass figure!

Drab, colourless Christine Fibich has clearer memories of child-hood – clearer at the moment of recall, and apparently clearer, too, in the actual act of narration. And since the nourishment of children – in every sense – is so prominent a motif in Brookner, the story of the *tartine* finds a significant and predictable counterpart in one particular memory of Christine's parents:

> When Christine came home from school she would find them both asleep, discordantly, and she soon learned to make herself a sandwich and to take it to her room. (49)

We might have returned unawares to the childhood neglect of Ruth Weiss.

Another example of the pervasive structural parallelism of *Late-comers* may be seen in the respective attempts of Yvette and Fibich to unravel their past by visits to Berlin and Nice, respectively (and indeed in Hartmann's contrasting reactions to the two initiatives). Taken obligingly by her husband to Nice, Yvette discovers how her father, a handsome and unscrupulous art-dealer, had collaborated with the Germans in wartime Paris, and later been shot in a private act of revenge. Her natural evasiveness is beautifully brought out in her spontaneous re-editing of the story: '"Handsome, you say?" said Yvette. "An art dealer? That must be where I get my taste from"' (164).

On the other hand, Hartmann had been extremely sceptical about Fibich's journey to Berlin ('Back to Berlin? Are you mad?' 141). His misgivings obviously reflect a deep love and subtle understanding of his lifelong friend, but may equally spring from the fact that the submerged details of Fibich's history are also linked with unhappy fragments of his own. In the event, Fibich's painful reconstruction of his lost childhood becomes a moving rite of passage explicitly heralding a rebirth, and prefiguring the theme of 'latecoming' announced in the title of the novel.

The ironic description of Christine's early life is markedly different in tone to the accounts of the other three. '[D]eprived of childhood' (125), her virtual 'orphan' status owes less to absence than to inadequacy of parental figures. Christine's mother dies soon after the birth of her daughter, and Mr Hardy, a morose widower 'out of sympathy with women in general' marries Rita Gifford, a divorcée from his Bridge Club, 'who liked being married, or rather who liked the status of marriage, for she did not care much for men' (48).

Mr Hardy's deathbed scene and the final exchange with his anxious daughter – 'Father. Tell me what to do' . . . 'Don't sell Glaxo' (52) – represent Brookner's most conspicuous foray into black humour. The parting words of Christine's stepmother, as she leaves without warning to become a hotelier in Bournemouth, are no more encouraging – although they are a familiar form of counsel to Brookner female protagonists:

'Buy yourself some new clothes or something,' said Mrs Hardy. 'You look awful. And take that expression off your face. Men hate a misery. As far as that goes' she added, 'the best of luck. You'll need it.' (53)

By this point, the savagery of Brookner's narrative transcends the mere 'regulated hatred' of late Austen, to recall another emotional casualty of twentieth century insensitivity, Evelyn Waugh.

Parental irresponsibility and neglect – with the related orphan motif – is a recurrent Brookner theme: the distinctive sharpening of tone in *Latecomers* may reflect some more personal investment in the story, and not exclude the possibility of displaced autobiography.

Christine is quick to recognize Fibich as 'one of her own' – effectively a fellow-sufferer – although marriage temporarily transforms her, bringing a happiness 'tinged with wonder'. She takes to love-making 'with unexpected ease and delight' (58), in pointed contrast to the 'usual reluctant performance' of Yvette with Hartmann (22). After her previous reticence, Brookner's sexual references are encouragingly explicit in the later novels. As the years pass, however, the 'distant, self-absorbed' Fibich succeeds in passing his fears on to Christine, who now 'began to feel, as she had once felt in her father's gloomy house, an outsider' (59).

The constant analogies, cross-references and correlations between Hartmann, Fibich and their wives give the opening chapters a fluidity which their quasi-mechanical symmetry might have been expected to inhibit. The same kind of rigid parallelism neverthe-less recurs throughout the novel. The fifth chapter, for example, describes the birth of the two children: plain, passive and self-effacing Marianne to the sociable Hartmanns; handsome, robust and unruly Toto (Thomas) to the retiring Fibiches. Even the pregnancies are explicitly contrasted: Marianne suffers hers reluctantly, irritated by the loss of her hourglass figure; Christine is possessed by an 'inner strength, sign of the divine afflatus' ('for the first time in her life she considered herself to be of some consequence', 67).

Later, each child forms a compensatory relationship with the couple that are not its biological parents, effectively transforming them into foster parents, and once again resurrecting the orphan/adoption motif.

Thus Marianne is the only person able to dispel Fibich's melancholy ('He adored her, looked on her as their ruined inheritance made good.' 65); but she is also close to Christine, who sees in her 'the temperate child whom she would have so much preferred to her turbulent son'. Toto, in turn, likes and admires Hartmann 'who had given him his first glass of champagne and wafted a cigar under his nose, urging him to appreciate the aroma' (83); with Yvette, his relationship is even more intimate – as a boy, he watches entranced as she performs her toilette; in his youth, he comes to appreciate this self-love ('the love that never fails'), and in Yvette's narcissism he sees 'the ratification of his own' (91).

\*                    \*                    \*

Superficially, in its character of family chronicle, and more substantially, through consistent parallelism of this kind, *Latecomers* is closest in character to *Family and Friends*. It nevertheless uses a number of motifs familiar from other novels.

Toto admittedly breaks fresh ground by going to Oxford, where he makes his greatest impression in the theatre, whilst acquiring the reputation of a lady-killer; he graduates with a poor degree and a large following. Marianne's higher education, on the other hand, follows a path taken – with minor variations – by other Brookner heroines: study at London University, although here not French but English literature (allowing the introduction of textual references to Dickens, Collins and Trollope). Upset by the 'impingement of the real world', however, she abandons her studies and begins to work – like Blanche Vernon in *A Misalliance* – for a charitable organization. Her anxious parents find a suitable husband for her in the company accountant, Roger Myers – a convenient figure whose age and appearance recall Roddy (*A Start in Life*), and whose loyalty and professional status suggest Lautner (*Family and Friends*).

The account of a West End shopping trip by Yvette and Christine allows some discussion of the contemporary situation of women, but otherwise – at the exact mid-point of the narrative – functions essentially as interlude, before the return to the strict parallelism of the early chapters. Each of the four major characters now undergoes a kind of spiritual crisis: Christine is upset primarily by her unsatisfactory relationship with her son; Fibich is obsessed by the need to retrace his past in Berlin; Hartmann takes the morning off from the office to face his own feelings of 'dereliction'; Yvette confronts her sense of *Torschlusspanik* – 'the panic of the shutting of the door' (160). It is the latter sensation, in fact, which prompts Hartmann to arrange the ill-fated trip to Nice.

The narrative then returns briefly to what – in their occasional banality – seem almost random events from a family chronicle. Toto leaves Oxford, and, together with two university friends, spends six months living with his parents, before achieving his first successes in the cinema. Fibich, in what might have been a suitably dramatic climax, eventually returns to Berlin; the visit is explicitly treated as a rite of passage or spiritual rebirth, and yet immediately after his return to England, Fibich breaks down over lunch with Hartmann.

Implicit, too, in the latter half of the book is the idea of 'latecoming' which gives the novel its title. Hartmann, who finds increasing equilibrium with Yvette as the years pass, sees this process as an 'entering into possession', a 'latecoming' (115), and attempts to reassure Fibich:

> You are not a survivor. You are a latecomer, like me. Like Yvette, for that matter. You had a bad start. Why go back to the beginning? One thing is certain: you can't start again. (141)

The narrative ends arbitrarily, as it might seem, with the birth of a second child to Hartmann's daughter, Marianne, and the short family memoir that Fibich sends to his son in America.

One might trace other familiar Brookner motifs in the novel, such as the North-South opposition: Yvette, on her shopping trip with Christine, thinks of the 'cruel burden of the north' (111); Fibich, returning from Berlin, suffers from the *fatigue du nord*, whilst Hartmann in the cab beside him dreams of selling up and going to the sun, 'the source of all life' (220).

Art and literature play their customary role as an ironic commentary on character and theme at various points in the novel: Yvette thus reads *La Princesse de Clèves* (31) – the story of a woman of the highest character, who can offer her husband loyalty but not love; in Berlin, Fibich visits the Dahlem museum and rejects the German exhibits for the quintessential Englishness of Gainsborough's *Joshua Rigby* – confident and unthreatened (197).

It is nonetheless the insistent reliance on binary pattern – developed almost to a kind of structural symmetry – which contributes most conspicuously to the *overt* significance of a novel in which some readers might complain that very little happens. It is precisely this latter characteristic, however, which may provide the key to a highly suggestive *covert* dimension of the text. For there are indeed several points in *Latecomers* where the reader is particularly aware that nothing happens: a dramatic hint is thrown out, only to remain undeveloped; narrative directions are suggested which are never actually followed. The phenomenon may be illustrated by three quite different examples.

On the eve of her marriage, Toto takes Marianne for dinner at the Savoy Grill; Marianne's sense of alarm is expressed revealingly ('On more than one occasion she had shrunk from his exuberance, as a cat shrinks from hissing rain', 104) – perhaps an echo of the hydrophobic imagery of *A Friend from England*; and an extremely subdued evening ends with the exasperated Toto kissing Marianne by force as he delivers her home.

Marianne's subsequent escape ('the skin round her mouth rubbed raw', 106) is followed by Fibich's extraordinary outburst, when he calls his son a burglar and asset-stripper – the comically incongruous term may in turn be an ironic echo of the equally inappropriate commercial obsessions of Christine's father on his deathbed. A few pages later, however, while discussing Yvette's easy acceptance of prosperity, the narrator comments:

> she had never experienced the secret treachery of her own flesh, as Marianne had done in Toto's embrace, had never had time for the meekness that had settled on Marianne when left behind by more adventurous friends, and, more important, had never known, never would know, longing, as Marianne was to know it in the years to come, when a young man's hasty but expert appropriation had awakened in her the knowledge of what she

was throwing away in marrying her so unexciting husband. (115–16)

The passage seems strangely at odds with the external narrator's account of the scene, where there is not the least indication that Marianne is 'betrayed by her own flesh' in Toto's arms. There is not even any comment afterwards, either directly from the narrator or focalized through Marianne. Without the narrator's subsequent remarks, the kiss might have passed as an unpleasant and embarrassing incident, but one more memorable for the extraordinary outburst it provokes from Fibich, than for any lasting effect on Marianne.

No further reference is made to treachery of the flesh, adventurous friends or even longing, as Marianne later sinks into a life of placid domesticity with Roger Myers. Acts of open sexual aggression are virtually unknown in Brookner's fiction (although Lewis Percy occasionally entertains sado-oral fantasies involving Tissy); one is therefore tempted to find a hidden significance in Toto's symbolic violation, perhaps buried in the consciousness of a narrator too traumatized even to project personal experience onto autonomous character.

Whatever its thematic significance, however, the episode remains formally the novel's most memorable example of a narrative line not followed, what might be described as a *refusal of emplotment*.

There are two other hardly less striking examples of the same process, the first of these concerning Fibich's return to Berlin. The initial motive given for the visit is Fibich's sense of existential void, the need to know that he 'had a beginning' (141). The joyful fantasies of recognition which he allows himself are touchingly similar to Hartmann's presumably more authentic memories of Nymphenberg or the *Englische Garten* (7):

> He longed to know what his life had been before he could remember it. He longed to walk a foreign street and be recognized. He imagined it, the start of wonder on an elderly person's face. Is it you, Fibich's boy? You used to play with my children. That was what he longed for. That, and the suddenly restored familiarity of the foreign street, that café, that theatre, that park. (142–3)

The subsequent journey is rich in symbolic resonance, with its powerful synthesis of pilgrimage, holy quest, epic descent into the underworld and explicit spiritual rebirth. As the time of departure approaches, Fibich feels the 'slow, sad opening of the abyss' into which he momentarily thinks he might vanish:

> He felt layers of the life he had sought heroically to maintain as reasonable peeling away and leaving him as sorrowful as a medieval sinner deserted by his God, the God in whom he, Fibich, had never believed. (191)

An earlier reference to exploring 'the heart of darkness' (141) with his analyst also suggests the kind of figurative level at which Fibich's journey should be read. On the flight to Berlin, however, where his thoughts inevitably run on death ('the only solution he would ever be permitted to his insoluble lifelong problems'), he also redefines the purpose of his journey, now describing it as:

> This pilgrimage, undertaken for Toto, to answer Toto's questions, to furnish Toto with a lineage that would survive the death of his parents. (191)

At the very end of the novel, Fibich writes to Toto in America (a structural parallel, perhaps, to the letter his mother had written to Oxford) enclosing the short memoir, 'which contains your history and as much of mine as I can remember', 237). Fibich's moving letter reveals the names of Toto's grandparents, but refers to the enclosed notebook for further information. But nothing in the narrative indicates that Fibich had ever discovered anything about his parents' identity whilst in Berlin; there is no suggestion that he even attempted to do so (he admittedly knew their names, but these would presumably have been recorded in the original letter he received as a child from Switzerland).

Certain descriptive details of the trip itself evoke an archetypal journey, or at least some form of sacred knightly quest: arrival at dusk under a 'huge dark blue sky, moonless and starless, stretched over the curiously silent city' 193); the city lights 'like heraldic devices or the badges of ancient guilds'; Fibich's deep sleep ('so uninterrupted, that when he awoke he felt peaceful and even faintly optimistic', 194); the literal 'underground' journey (195); the explicit associations as he squeezes through the narrow door to the Eastern sector of the city ('so like a symbolic birth that he laughed', 200).

The episode ends with a remarkable incident on the return journey at one of London's airports, when a woman faints in the heat
and Fibich feels the 'stirrings of the old panic':

> As he knew he must, he turned, in time to see the figure of a
> woman, collapse into the arms of her husband, who bent over
> her to lay her on the ground. Together they formed a mourning
> group, ageless, timeless without nationality. His mouth dry, his
> heart beating, Fibich pushed on, stumbling now, his peace and
> calm destroyed, . . . (205)

The scene is a cruel replica of Fibich's last sight of his own parents
at the Friedrichstrasse station over half a century before.

Such an untimely conclusion to the journey perhaps suggests that
the absence of most details from the past may ultimately be less
traumatic than the presence of those few which remain – for this
presence is ubiquitous and oppressive; it may also confirm Fibich's
earlier insight that 'his purpose in life had been not to find his own
father but to be a father himself' (203). What it does not do, however,
is mediate between Fibich's experience of an essentially *metaphorical*
journey to Berlin, and his quite *literal* search for detail concerning
his lost past. Seen in this perspective, the omission of any account
of an actual process of enquiry whilst in Berlin cannot be simply
regarded as a case of justified narrative ellipsis. It is the second
striking example of Brookner's mysterious refusal of emplotment.

The final instance is far more trivial when viewed in purely thematic terms, although it might have proved sensational in relation
to the simple mechanics of plot. After Hartmann discovers that the
splendour of his wife's body is 'limited to what could be displayed
rather than enjoyed', he takes a mistress – Elizabeth – and several
pages are devoted to describing this relationship (29–31). When,
much later, Yvette and Christine make their West End shopping
spree, they finish at a shop (described suggestively as 'near the
office') and owned by a lady called, precisely, Elizabeth.

Most novel readers will assume that the two women are one and
the same person, and feel the suspense created by such a contingent
encounter; the identity is, in fact, neither confirmed or denied,
and no Elizabeth whatsoever reappears in the narrative. The same
over-susceptible readers may merely be the objects of a narrative
joke ('Elizabeth' may, after all, be Brookner's 'man in a raincoat'),
and yet the two incidents can also be seen as a further example of

emplotment denied or deferred. It remains to consider, therefore, whether the three highly distinct but equally striking examples have any common narratological significance that might throw light on the rest of the novel.

At a simple pragmatic level, the so-called 'refusal of emplotment' could be reduced to basic writing habits. In the three major interviews widely quoted in the present study, Brookner is helpfully explicit about her methods of composition. For Shusha Guppy, who is particularly interested in such details, the novelist explains that she never rewrites:

> It is always the first draft. I may alter the last chapter; I may lengthen it. Only because I get very tired at the end of a book and tend to rush and go too quickly, so when I have finished it I go over the last chapter. (Guppy, 164)

She admits to letting 'organic growth' take over, adding candidly: 'I have an idea, but I don't know exactly what will happen.' The approach seems to be confirmed in the Olga Kenyon interview two years later. When Brookner began her first novel, there were 'no secret notebooks, not a scrap, not a sentence', and she has continued in the same style:

> No, there are no drafts, no fetishes, no false starts; there simply isn't *time*. I write straight onto a typewriter, as though the novels had been encoded in the unconscious. (Kenyon, 11)

Such a process of essentially linear composition inevitably recalls the great serialized novels of the Victorian age – an age, moreover, with which Brookner identifies in so many other contexts. And of all the major novelists that she mentions, the clear precursor – in spite of ostensible differences of scale – is Dickens, particularly the Dickens of the earlier less planned and therefore less structurally coherent novels. *Latecomers* might therefore have unforeseen analogies with Dickens, analogies not limited to a sense of 'indignation' (stressed in all three Brookner interviews), or the prominence of orphans and surrogate parents.

A second less obvious point emerges from a brief reconsideration of the author's comments on her own writing methods. The three sets of interview answers, in spite of their sometimes uncanny verbal similarities, are not simply artless and transparent. Any subject offering so much purportedly candid and revealing information as Brookner supplies about herself and her work will necessarily introduce – consciously or not – elements of ambiguity, inconsistency or reticence. In interview, no less than *in fabula*, it is possible to 'give too much away' (Guppy, 168).

In the present context, the second of the above quotations is probably the more revealing: for whether or not entire novels really are 'encoded in the unconscious' as it claims, a concept such as the refusal of emplotment is not affected. The argument is as follows: either Brookner is a meticulous writer, and in a narrative with such an elaborate web of cross-reference as *Latecomers*, it seems unlikely that she would knowingly allow three different hares to course unpursued, in which case the procedure would be unconscious. Or even if such a refusal of emplotment *were* conscious (and the encoding process not as complete as Brookner suggests), the actual motive for this refusal would still presumably remain unconscious.

The examples of textual suppression which the refusal of emplotment works to produce provide potential material for the kind of psycho-biographical approach pursued in the final chapter of the present study.

One anticipatory observation, however, may be made in the present context, by way of completing the analogy with Dickens proposed above. Brookner is not in any derogatory sense a limited novelist; and yet the psycho-biographical tendencies of my conclusion – together with the structural analysis that precedes it – reinforces the reader's impression of a restricted range of characters in the nine novels, combined with apparently compulsive repetition of certain situations.[10]

The female protagonists (and even their later male counterparts) have an unmistakable family resemblance; the strong polarity between naive, virtuous heroines and their 'bold' and 'wicked' rivals is equally striking. The male antagonists (at least those of the early novels) constitute another quasi-collective figure. Seen in the most reductive terms, in fact, virtually the entire Brookner cast might well appear to be derived from facets of the novelist's own personality, augmented by a very small group of family and other unidentified familiars; the narrow range of incidents, moreover, may have close links with the particular circumstances of the novelist's own life.

But if the protagonists seem fragments of a single identity, and the events of the novels are simple reworkings of a single text, the writer's achievement is all the more remarkable. For although the characters may be literary constructs embodying a limited number of recurrent traits (illustrating what current narrative theory would call a semiotic model of character), a number of these figures – Edith Hope or Lewis Percy, for example – give a convincing impression of complete inner autonomy (thus going far to vindicate complementary mimetic theories of character).[11] It may be precisely the ability to individualize figments of a single obsessive, even tortured, imagination that provides the final and most far-reaching analogy between Brookner and Dickens.[12]

*       *       *

It remains to comment briefly on the actual novelty of *Latecomers*, the extent to which it may be said to extend the author's range as a novelist. Brookner has often been criticized for writing to a formula, an accusation which the present study should easily refute. If the first three novels relied heavily on literary parallels (less obvious but still pertinent in *Look at Me*), the next three were more open to formal innovation, exemplified by *mise en abyme* in *Hotel du Lac*, literary framing in *Family and Friends* and the elaboration of iconography in *A Misalliance*. Brookner herself incidentally made claims for the originality of the latter:

> [A] *Misalliance* is much longer and has a broader canvas. It is quite different from the others, not at all deterministic, and rather sentimental. (Guppy, 165)

But for genuine extension of thematic or even dramatic range rather than more specifically technical innovation, it is necessary to go to the last three novels; although here, too, the rubric 'fictional returns' is intended to suggest the ambivalent qualities of this group. Of the three books, *A Friend from England* – inscribed within nineteenth-century fictional parameters and demonstrably related to the fiction of Austen, Dickens and James – has the most distinctively traditional aspect.

*Latecomers* and *Lewis Percy* are more genuinely innovative: the former, amongst other reasons, for the creative leap that produces strong empathy with two male characters, and an ability to transform or transcend a sometimes rigidly symmetrical structure; *Lewis*

*Percy* for its new thematic advances and – by its broad use of parody – a novel generic dimension.

## LEWIS PERCY

Brookner's claim that her ninth novel, *Lewis Percy*, represents a complete departure from her earlier fiction (Haffenden, 32) should not be exaggerated. It is marginally longer than all her previous books; and it repeats the strategy only previously found in *Latecomers* (with its sympathetic portaiture of Hartmann and Fibich) of assigning the principle point of focalization to a male consciousness – research student, librarian and future visiting professor, Lewis Percy.

Seen from another perspective, however, the novel also reproduces a central thematic contrast familiar from earlier works: the discrepancy between the passive sedentary life of the writer or academic, and some barely apprehended but infinitely more attractive life of excitement and achievement in the world beyond. It is a dualism which was particularly evident to early female protagonists, from Ruth Weiss (*A Start in Life*) through Kitty Maule (*Providence*) to Frances Hinton (*Look at Me*).

Brookner made her prophetically bleak entry into the world of fiction with the opening words of *A Start in Life*, 'Dr Weiss, at forty, knew that her life had been ruined by literature'. And Ruth is sensitive enough to find parallels between her own destiny and that of Eugénie Grandet, although it remains for the shrewd extradiegetic narrator to provide an ironic commentary on the heroine's existence through regular references to a web of earier texts, from Balzac and other writers.

At the high point in her search for self-fulfilment, Ruth is installed in the Dixons' Paris flat, happily involved in her burgeoning relationship with Professor Duplessis, ready to abandon her identification with Eugénie Grandet and 'training herself to be a winner'; during this period 'Balzac stayed in her briefcase for whole evenings at a stretch' (139).

Kitty Maule is an able teacher and scholar, but her extensive experience of literature does not prepare her (and may even handicap her) for her dealings with the external world: the relationship of her lover, Maurice Bishop, with her own pupil, Jane Fairchild, thus comes as a total surprise.

In *Look at Me*, finally, literary inclinations are an obvious complement to what Fanny candidly refers to as 'her lack of experience in the wilder and more interesting areas of human conduct' (75). The traumatic conclusion of Kitty's relationship with James Anstey hastens her choice of 'literature' over 'life': 'In future I would become subsumed into my head, and into my hand, my writing hand' (179). And in the final chapter of the novel, Brookner echoes the structural irony of Proustian 'autobiography' as she turns back to study James Anstey and the other characters ('I must know them once again at first hand', 190). Her final sentences – 'I pick up my pen. I start writing' – are not, of course, the prelude to fresh authorial activity, since – as with *À la Recherche du Temps perdu* – the novel is already written.

*Lewis Percy* also returns to the thematically fertile encounter of literature and life. In his role of research student writing a thesis on the concept of heroism in the nineteenth century French novel, the hero's position is almost identical to that of the original Brookner protagonist: Ruth Weiss (likewise a research student, and spending time in Paris) was working on the women in Balzac's novels. The central situation of *Lewis Percy* is also closely paralleled in *Providence*, where Kitty Maule's study of the Romantic tradition is an integral element of the novel. ( There is even a passing reference to the academic world in *A Misalliance*, although Blanche Vernon's momentary urge to finish her thesis on Mme de Staël may represent an example of authorial self-irony, and therefore even an in-joke for her keener readers).

The contrast between other people's vigour and his own sedentary existence comes home clearly to Lewis sitting – as Ruth Weiss once sat – in the *Bibliothèque Nationale*:

> The high vaulted room seemed to be scholarship itself, putting a finger to its lips, urging silence, but his youthful body demanded movement. After such austerity he desired gratification, simple sustenance, the prospect of adventure. Yet in the street, it was hard for him to shake off the peculiar thrall of his day, the palpable silence that kept him wrapped in his thoughts, unprepared for, perhaps unequal to, the challenge of real life. (11)

His return to Paris a few months later is a frustrating experience ('He was no longer content with things as they were, with small pleasures, small perspectives', 43), and his single visit to the *Bibliothèque Nationale* is, by any standards, brief.

Back in London, a trip to the local library with his mother is
equally oppressive ('He felt doomed, irritated, yet at the same
time submissive. Here was destiny staring him in the face', 46).
Or, to add narrated monologue to psycho-narrative: 'The British
Museum was his refuge, but it was also his prison' (54). His
sense of foreboding seems largely justified, since – for most of the
narrative – he remains employed at his old college library under the
flamboyant Goldsborough. His final rescue by the *deus ex machina*,
Millinship, with the offer of a visiting professorship on his own
terms seems highly improbable. At this point, the external narrator,
too, might qualify for the judgement passed on Lewis by the exotic
and perhaps promiscuous Emmy: 'You fantasize too much. You've
probably read too much' (203).

*       *       *

But in addition to reproducing the life *versus* literature dichotomy
of the early novels, *Lewis Percy* also maintains a constant stream
of literary references and parallels – analogous to the iconography
discussed with reference to the middle novels (of the eighties) – thus
providing a kind of index, or even a metacommentary on the events
of the text.

The process begins after the death of Mrs Percy, when Lewis
enters his mother's room to collect her old library books ('sober tales
of love and loyalty that reflected the moods of women as he wished
to consider them' 42). As he removes a nail-file from *The Song of the
Ark,* he half smilingly acknowledges that his mother's tastes are his
own. Still feeling the full effect of bereavement, he borrows Edith
Wharton's *The Age of Innocence* and *Ethan Frome* (which he races
through in two days), following them up with an Elizabeth Bowen
and a Margaret Kennedy.

In terms of lowest common denominator, all three writers are
'women's novelists' in the senses discussed in the introductory
chapter with reference to Kenyon and Waugh; they may only
represent what Lewis regards, with a hint of patronage, as 'tender
fictional worlds' (54), but they are also 'salutary' in their attention
to 'normal concerns'. In any event, they differ from his 'official
reading', firmly characterized – the irony is now surely the narrator's – as dealing with 'grown-up theories about heroism, and
nineteenth-century heroism at that' (53).

Literary references are also, of course, a device used by Lewis
Percy himself as a form of characterization. His wife is like one of the

automata from the *The Tales of Hoffman*, coming to life when Lewis is absent (98); Millinship, his dapper American visitor, is compared to a character in Edith Wharton or Henry James (223); and as a single parent for his daughter, Jessica, Lewis sees himself as a kind of Silas Marner.

The whole tissue of literary reference is held together by regular appearances in the text of Lewis's own monograph, *The Hero as Archetype*: regarded by his supervisor (in a finely judged piece of academic twitting) as too revolutionary a title for the original dissertation) (82); assailed by Tissy and her mother as 'the equivalent of an infidelity' (110); and providing an ironic comment on Lewis's own existence when he receives six complimentary but unwanted copies from his publisher (175).

Modifications in Lewis's reading tastes are an amusing but reliable index of his emotional development. At one crucial point in the narrative he retires to bed with his mother's copy of *The Constant Nymph* ('It was all easier in books, he thought, especially in books written by women', 75), but for once he finds that his mother's old books have nothing to say to him. His eventual rejection of 'all those women's novels' heralds a new devotion to the 'gentlemen' of Trollope – *The Eustace Diamonds* (86) and, later, *The Prime Minister* (103). In the latter, Lewis notes, the admirable Mr Wharton made his 'round of the parks every Sunday' (103), whilst he himself 'merely trudged from his house to the bus-stop every morning, and from the bus-stop to his house every evening' (103).

Plot resolution in *Lewis Percy* is nevertheless marked by the protagonist's ultimate rejection of such tendencies towards identification: 'The old Lewis Percy, the Lewis Percy who had wanted to be a character in a book, and had not managed to be one, had bowed out long ago', 230); or in the final paragraph:

> Now, if ever, was the moment to behave like a hero, to summon up ineffable resources. But he was tired of such fantasies, and when his flight was called he straightened up immediately, picked up his bag, anxious to get it over and done with. (261)

Brookner's characteristic technique of fictional cross-reference is the equivalent of a kind of literary shorthand. For all its wit and intelligence, however, it occasionally risks degenerating into a kind of literary short cut – diegetic *ersatz* rather than authentic narrative performance.

In this context, it is comparable with the equally prominent use of iconography of her novels. But just as *A Misalliance* is the first novel to provide a comprehensive and structurally integrated use of such iconography (based on a Christian/Pagan polarity), so *Lewis Percy* is the first narrative to enact a similar kind of integration for its web of literary cross-reference. This effect is achieved by the habitual presentation of the protagonist in terms of a Romance idealism, undercut with equal consistency by epistemologically and generically dissonant counter-narratives: a naive empiricism well spiced with satire, *bathos* and even a suggestion of Mock Epic.

Thus Lewis's return to his room in the Avenue Klber after his day's work at the *Bibliothèque Nationale* is ironically compared to 'the wage-earner's homecoming, the warrior's repose' (14). His customary offering to the yearning spinsters in the house – in a detail poised teasingly between alimentary metonym and phallic metaphor – is a soft piece of Camembert and a bag of cherries. Lewis is moreover in thrall to his mother by the sodden Common in 'unfashionable Parsons Green'.

To an intelligent young man studying the concept of heroism in the nineteenth-century novel, a certain discrepancy between art and life (particularly his own life) can hardly fail to become apparent. Lewis twice quotes the words of Julien Sorel: '*Laissez-moi ma vie idéale . . .* ' (41), although his own reactions to the external world owe less to the vigour of the Romantic hero than to the cerebral fantasies of chivalrous romance. Even more than Hartmann, Lewis Percy is Brookner's great idealizer of woman, an attitude which is regularly deflated by the irony of the extradiegetic narrator: Lewis thus sees his mother, nymph-like, as a 'genius of the place' (49), when she is actually engaged on nothing more than shopping expeditions; and the banality of certain of her pronouncements ('Good women are better than bad women' . . . 'Never buy cakes unwrapped' ) further reduces her mythical aura. He also sees the pale and recessive Tissy return from the library each night, to be 'subsumed' into a 'dark blushing cave' with its glowing red walls (59): a captive damsel in the custody of her ogre-like mother.

In retrospect, even the unworldly Lewis feels slightly uncomfortable at the ease with which he is accepted as suitor to Tissy ('Surely a feeling of conquest should be more liberating than this!' 64). But his new situation now approximates more closely that of the knight-errant and his lady; with an 'accredited girlfriend', he feels he has passed one of the many 'tests' awaiting him ('for he did not doubt that there were many tasks ahead,' 68), and that he is now on the way to adulthood and even possibly 'heroic stature'.

In a characteristic Brookner division, the narrator is external, but the focalizer – by a process combining narrated monologue with psycho-narrative – is the hapless protagonist. Thus Tissy Harper is explicitly described as 'an ineluctable part of his quest', or – with a banality scarcely worthy of a 'brilliant' research student – as 'the Sleeping Beauty, whom he would awaken with a kiss' (68). Lewis's ingenuousness is short-lived, however, and he is soon wondering 'what impulse of chivalry had ever made him want to rescue her', realizing that he himself would need to be rescued, 'before he could contemplate so quixotic a course' (79).

As in the case of his Spanish avatar, the fictional realization of Lewis fluctuates between plausible individual – a comic but sympathetic figure – and purely literary construct – the textual site for delusions of near manic proportions. He thus interprets his sore throat as a symptom of love (87), regards Tissy as a patiently waiting damsel (89) and invokes heaven ('Please let me do well', 91) at the outset of his knightly quest. But his idealization of womanhood even extends absurdly to the cleaning woman, Mrs Joliffe, whom he is surprised not to find 'the cheerful independent paragon on whom he had set his sights' (83); and the obsessive quality of Lewis's behaviour pattern emerges clearly through the long succession of other female figures on whom he projects his image of the ideal woman: beginning with his mother, these include various female guests at the Avenue Kléber, Tissy, Emmy and even his own daughter Jessica.

And as with Cervantes's hero, Lewis Percy's own process of disillusion is likewise a long and painful one. The concluding image of the novel suggests, moreover, that the process is by no means final and irreversible. The hero soon renounces his earlier expectations of 'marriage as a kind of saturnalia' (92); there is no 'folly and licentiousness' and very little of the 'almost mythological state, a metamorphosis' which he had envisaged (93). Tissy is adept at countering the 'amorous thought' ('I can't linger Lewis. I'm washing the paint', 95); he still feels a heroic devotion towards his wife and – in the admittedly unlikely event – would 'defend her to the death' (120); and yet, his characteristic feelings as a married man are a 'dryness, interspersed with spasms of desire', together with a longing for 'one real upward flight' (116).

It is immediately after this confession that Lewis's friend Pen
Douglas comes to dinner with his provocative sister, Emmy (her
'usual half-bottle of Mimosa cologne' poured into the 'well of
her bosom', 119). The narrator handles the scene with particular
relish, undermining Lewis's idealism with a further series of comic
touches. The memorable comment of Pen's voluptuous sister as she
attacks her dessert ('You'll see more of me in the autumn,' . . . 'Oh,
this tart! Divine!', 122) – with a possible dietary pun and an even
more tenuous sexual one – at least lends itself to simple *double
entendre*; but the over-reaction to Tissy's conventional after-dinner
formulae ('Coffee everyone?' etc.) has a characteristic and inescapable irony:

> It was at this point, hearing his wife utter these appropriately
> wifely sentences, that Lewis realized that the evening had been
> a complete success. (123)

In another brief episode, Lewis combines romantic amorous intrigue
with the chivalry of an older and harsher code. The picnic in Hyde
Park with Emmy leads Lewis to the Serpentine, the 'secret depths
of the park' and eventually to an embrace by the 'Italian Garden'
(134–5): a quasi-allegorical setting reminiscent of the emblematic
technique of the Sotherton scenes in *Mansfield Park*. But after this
episode, Lewis reawakens to what he sees as Tissy's 'fragility',
'docility' and 'virginal lack of independence':

> This gave her a legendary quality, rather as if she had stepped out
> of the Unicorn tapestry, or wore a metaphorical wimple. Above
> all, she carried about her an aura of chastity, which was, he saw,
> never to be entirely confounded. These qualities still moved him,
> mixed though they were in his mind with his own impatience,
> exasperation, and a degree of bewilderment that began to reach
> epic proportions. (140)

Brookner habitués will here anticipate a frame of literary reference incorporating a familiar ideological and iconographic polarity:
Pagan joy and Christian gloom, attended by implicit sympathy and
wistful envy for the former. And surely enough, Lewis comes to
feel a disgust at his own virtue, or the whole idea of 'virtue in its
diminished Christian interpretation: continence' (141). As he notes

ironically: 'Great deeds were not always undertaken virtuously, nor were great loves blamelessly consummated' (141).

Shortly after this, Tissy leaves Lewis – in reaction to his presumed infidelity with Emmy – and returns to her mother. The remainder of the novel might be regarded as a virtual ragbag of figural devices, drawing equally on myths of Christian redemption and Pagan contingency: the hero's long period of 'dereliction' representing the purgatory through which he must pass before spiritual rebirth (through the agency of the *deus ex machina*, Millinship); the offer of a visiting professorship in the United States marking the assumption into paradise, or at least the 'new life'.

It is clear, however, that no real psychological transformation takes place; Lewis frequently acquires new ideas, but these do not allow him to abandon earlier ingrained attitudes. Meeting his old Paris acquaintance, Roberta, in Selfridges, he reflects that he is still 'seduced and beguiled by the company of women' (144); in the light of Emmy's contempt after his resistance to her, Lewis questions his own 'chivalrous behaviour', but retains his 'love for women in general and his wife and putative mistress in particular' (145).

In a surely emblematic gesture, he refuses to revise his doctoral thesis, in spite of painful new insights into the heroic ideal; the most he can envisage is an updating of the work with the addition of a second volume – the hero enters the twentieth century.

When his morale is at its lowest point, Lewis actually wonders whether either Tissy or Emmy had ever been worth all the trouble; and only pages later, he is upset by the way in which both women had crudely reduced the nocturnal visit to Pen's house to its simple sexual component: whilst Tissy had merely asked 'Did you or didn't you?' (without incidentally waiting for an answer), Emmy had likewise demanded 'Will you or won't you' (166). In a particularly genial pun conflating chivalry and eroticism – whilst effectively deflating them both – the narrator suggests ironically that: 'a passage of arms was what had been in mind' (166).

The novel's ending is open to conflicting interpretations, depending essentially on whether or not its structure is read as analogous to that of other Brookner narratives. The arrival of Emmy at the airport 'plunging through the crowd, necklaces flying' (261) – to join Lewis as he departs to take up the previous offer of a visiting professorship – might signal the crowning expression of Lewis's happiness; against this, however, such an ending would ironically represent a pitch of romantic fantasy far in excess of anything portrayed (and effectively subverted) in the course of the novel.

According to an alternative, and more consistent reading, therefore, the finale would correspond precisely to a familiar Brookner pattern of ironic build-up succeeded by final disillusion. Thus, Ruth Weiss ultimately abandons her demoralizing identification with Eugénie Grandet, only to be denied existential freedom by the imposition of family commitments; Kitty Maule finds a new optimism and self-confidence, only to discover that her lover has left her for another woman; or – in perhaps the closest parallel of all – Blanche Vernon finally completes the painful process of post-divorce readjustment, only to find her penitent ex-husband on the doorstep; by analogy then, the same kind of structural reversal in *Lewis Percy* would seem to suggest – in accordance with Brookner's characteristic blend of shrewdness and honesty – that, just as the hero's new life was beginning, the arrival of Emmy marked the start of a new destructive cycle.

\*               \*               \*

Up to this point, *Lewis Percy* may be usefully related to a literary model of long ancestry, where the protagonist is unable to distinguish between the world of 'literature' and that of 'real life': a more restricted variant of the infinitely vaster but correspondingly less manageable category of the 'appearance versus reality' dichotomy. The *locus classicus* of the latter in European literature is clearly *Don Quixote*, although it is safe to assume that this particular conflict is as old as imaginative literature itself. If the English novel has produced nothing as substantial in the genre as Flaubert's *bovaryisme*, there is nevertheless a significant minor tradition built on the theme: it would include the various more explicit eighteenth century imitations of Cervantes (*The Female Quixote, The Spiritual Quixote* etc.) and such broader structural analogues as *Northanger Abbey*.

But a reading which regards *Lewis Percy* merely, or even essentially, as an ironic treatment of romantic sensibility overlooks another important focus of the novel: it is not simply a satirical fable of 'a man who loved women too much', but the Brookner narrative where woman figures most emphatically as subject, and not merely as object.

The novel is also noteworthy for its extended critique, paradoxically by a female writer, of various aspects of women's behaviour, a critique both implied by a skilfully internalized male protagonist and more explicitly articulated by a degendered external narrator. The naive condescension of Lewis's early assumptions about women remain as familiar echo: they are a 'congenial and compassionate sex' (3), a 'beneficent institution' (7). He later admits, however, that they may be a source of trouble ('He thought of a hundred Madame Bovarys waiting for a lover', 147): the female mind worked with an 'irrational faultlessness', it could display an insistence that was 'irregular, almost gangsterish' (165). And by the end of the novel, in the restaurant scene, a painfully disabused hero watches with detachment the 'childish' efforts of Jeannine Millinship to regain her husband's attention, or the undisguised boredom of another beautiful female diner behind her (235).

At two other points, however, there is a far more devastating critique of the novel's principle female characters. The relevant passages must be quoted at some length, to demonstrate a particular technical problem – and its only partial solution – within the frame of the narrative. In the first example, Lewis comments on Tissy's new 'niceness' towards him during the period following their separation:

> Yet there was a distance in the niceness which proclaimed: I have made my decision, I shall never go back on it. The other life that I lived with you was so benighted that you cannot expect me to admit it to my newly raised consciousness except to laugh at my folly. Of course, I serve as an example to the group. Remember how I couldn't go out alone? Shackled, you see, by false expectations. And look at me now. I earn my living, I've got friends, I'm *involved*. And I don't have to bother with men any more. That's what's so wonderful. We have a very good social life, the three of us: we go to exhibitions, see the new films, have plenty to talk about. Mother looks after Jess. It's given her a new lease of life; she was getting so low before. Now that she's got something to occupy her mind she's a different person. The baby's fine. She doesn't miss me. And later on, when she's older, she'll have me as a role model. That's extremely important for a girl. (194)

As an oblique parody of Tissy's newly found feminist views, this is quite impressive. There are admittedly phrases ('laugh at my folly'

/ 'Shackled . . . by false expectations') which seem disconcertingly close to what may be the Brookner 'house style', but the weakness of the passage appears at a higher narratological level.

For as the narrator awkwardly points out, 'She did not, of course, say any of this' (194): and the passage is mediated not by means of an external narrator, but through a male protagonist who has previously shown no interest in – or familiarity with – feminist discourse. One is tempted to conclude that the narrator (or even the author) is settling scores with 'the modern woman', and again imposing her own views on an ostensibly autonomous character.

This question of ambivalent focalization is perhaps even more evident in another passage; here, Lewis himself is apparently reflecting on paradoxical similarities between Tissy and Emmy, although his textual ironies may be shared with the consciousness of the extradiegetic narrator, and – by implication – that of the author herself:

> With her charm, her power, her inventiveness, [Emmy] was born to be a mistress. And knowing this, had come to hate men, the men who would not marry her but preferred her as she was. Tissy probably hated men too, he now thought, but for a different reason. There was nothing of the mistress about Tissy. But she considered that she had been sold into slavery, and all her efforts now were in the direction of emancipation. In the group she had probably learned to compare herself with ethnic minorities or the working class, on whom it was beholden to rise in revolt, to claim freedoms that had been denied to them. Apparently that was what they were both doing. Emmy would marry her rich man and revenge herself yet again by despising or deceiving him, probably both. And Tissy, presumably, would never look at a man again. In many ways they had a lot in common. (205)

Although I would hope to avoid the more arid kinds of formal analysis, the passage is worthy of closer examination for the light it sheds on narrative strategies highly characteristic of Brookner. The opening lines seem ambivalently located between narrated monologue and a purely external voice, although the introduction of a verb of reflection in the fifth line ('he now thought') suggests that the previous lines may in fact be quoted monologue:[13] (the unexpected shift of perspective incidentally recalls the opening paragraphs of *Hotel du Lac*).

In the next few lines, the narrative seems to drift back imperceptibly to a psycho-narrative presented in a progressively 'dissonant'
mode (my terminology is borrowed from Dorrit Cohn's *Transparent
Minds*, discussed nore fully in the opening chapter).[14] Emmy thus
felt 'beholden' to rise in revolt (the archaic verb form reflects ironic
distance); and 'would marry her rich man and revenge herself yet
again . . . ' (an obviously cynical conclusion). If the whole passage is
indeed focalized through Lewis, it recalls the excessive worldliness
of Ruth Kennedy (*A Friend from England*), making it increasingly
hard to believe that Lewis would be rash enough to fly off into the
sunset with Emmy.

If the passage is essentially external narrative, however, its profound scepticism may reflect the vulnerable sensitivity of a controlling intelligence behind the novel. As so often in Brookner's novels,
the implications are less fictional than autobiographical.

There are also pertinent comments to be added here on Kemp's
dismissal of Brookner, made precisely in a review of *Lewis Percy*.
At a purely critical level, Kemp's comments show a naive (or
wilful) disregard for any distinctions of voice: the story is often,
after all, focalized through Lewis himself, even as it is narrated
by an extradiegetic voice often quite as scathing as Kemp. Thus,
the novel's 'archaic sounding vocabulary' ('an apanage of allowable
distractions', 'indicted as a poltroon') cannot really be a function of
Brookner's 'style'. Such expressions belong to a kind of narrated
monologue originating in Lewis himself, absorbed in his world of
chivalry and myth of knightly quest. Can Kemp really have missed
the narrator's irony in referring to Lewis's fretfulness at the 'added
weight' of his pink-rimmed National Health spectacles, even if he
misses the witty cross-reference to the new heavier glasses Lewis
acquires in chapter ten?

*        *        *

Seen in the perspective of Brookner's earlier novels, then, *Lewis
Percy* contains a congenial blend of the old and the new. One thinks,
for example, of the now familiar polarity of North and South: the
hero returns from his contented existence in Paris to a London of
'post-war blight' in a land of 'ruminative half-shadow' (15). Fibich,
on his return to Berlin in Latecomers, had been overcome by the
*fatigue du nord*' (197); Frederick, in *Family and Friends*, contrasts
the 'greyness of England' with his life on the French *riviera*; such
cultural patterns are not uncommon.

Woman's status inside and outside marriage is another recurrent theme, which receives its classic expression in Mr Neville's cynical speculations in *Hotel du Lac*. *Lewis Percy*, incidentally, provides male and female points of view: if Tissy's status, 'which had been augmented by marriage, was precious to her', 96), Lewis loves Tiffy for her 'wifeliness', which 'established him as a man with a social position' (95).

The fertile subtext of literary and iconographic reference reflects another familiar Brookner device. With regard to the former, the various attractions of Stendhal, of Trollope, of James and Wharton, or of Mrs Percy's 'women's novels' have already been discussed in the context of Lewis's psychological development. Pictorial analogues – either casual or more significantly developed – are also prominent: Howard Millinship might have stepped from an El Greco canvas ('one of the mourners at the burial of *Count Orgaz*', 220) and Goldsborough appears in an Aristide Bruand hat. Lewis's first impression of Tissy at the local library returns to a more fully evolved iconography:

> That pose of the head, held slightly on one side, as if listening to an inner voice, those narrow slightly hunched shoulders, those prayerful hands, set him thinking of pale virgins in stone, the kind he had seen in the Victoria and Albert Museum. (51–2)

The reductive physical typology of Brookner women has occasionally been satirized by critics, and it is true that the timid, recessive Tissy has her predictable physical and mental counterpart in the bold, uninhibited Emmy. There is even a similar contrast between the mothers of Lewis and Tissy: ethereal *Grace* Percy and bold *Thea* Harper, with perhaps another echo of Brookner's most elaborate refinement of this polarity – pale Christian virtue and smiling Pagan license – in the iconography of *A Misalliance*.

The lonely hero himself, finally, is merely the latest in a succession of alienated protagonists, inevitably traceable to the hauntingly remote figure emerging from the author's own interviews. In the light of such recurrent patterns, moreover, it is surely less sensible to speak of the easy solution of novelistic formulae than the oppressive force of personal compulsions.

But there are several other features to suggest that *Lewis Percy* represents new developments, and that the author has by no means exhausted the potential displayed in her earlier novels. Brookner's advances may be linked with her changing attitudes towards the actual process of writing, attitudes eloquently described in the three highly articulate major interviews. *A Start in Life* was ostensibly written 'in a moment of sadness and desperation' (Guppy, 150), whereas by the time of *Look at Me*, the heroine, Frances, could describe writing as 'a penance for not being lucky' (151). Consciously or not, Brookner identifies directly with Frances at this point in the interview, but now claims a change of attitude:

> . . . since I wrote that sentence I have changed. Now I write because I enjoy it. Writing has freed me from the despair of living. I feel well when I am writing; I even put on a little weight! (Guppy, 151)

There is a more ambivalent, but nevertheless essentially positive, version of the same process in the most recent of the interviews:

> I can't really explain. I don't usually enjoy it. There's a terrible exhilaration, like having a high fever, which comes on me. Writing is my form of taking a sedative. It's almost a physiological process. When I'm actually writing, I feel so fantastically well. I even put on weight – and when it's over, I feel ill. (Kenyon, 12)

To Guppy, Brookner also claims that writing has made her 'softer, more understanding, more observant', and whether or not this increased sensitivity applies to the novelist's personal relations, it is certainly apparent in her fiction. There is a mellowing process in which she loses something of her customary tautness and frigidity. *Lewis Percy* even lets its author invest in self-irony: retiring to bed with his mother's copy of *The Constant Nymph*, the hero is allowed to reflect that 'It was all easier in books . . . especially in books written by women' (75), and later immersed in *The Eustace Diamonds*, he begins to feel 'a certain distaste for all those women's novels' (86). It is the kind of gently ironic but self-debunking humour which provided such an important element of *Hotel du Lac*.

Another significant development in *Lewis Percy* is Brookner's re-entry (after *Providence*) into the world of academic satire, with portraits of Lewis's supervisor, Professor Armitage, or the college librarian, Goldsborough. The former figure, 'too modest to have made his mark' worries at the examiner's possible reaction to a thesis entitled 'The Hero as Archetype':

> Save your archetypes for the book, if there is one. Gravity should be your watchword for the time being. What about 'Studies in behaviour in the nineteenth-century novel in France'? Or the nineteenth-century French novel. Whichever you prefer. (82)

Goldsborough is described rather misleadingly as a 'practitioner of the new criticism' (100), thus inviting confusion with the obsolescent New Criticism proper, but his most famous witticism is 'Only deconstruct' and the *vignette* is convincing enough:

> . . . he was a marauder, a manhandler, busy taking the text away from the author and turning it into something else. In Goldsborough's hands no writing was safe. He trembled on the verge of intoxicating double meanings, inadvertences, involuntary confessions. Most of his time in the library was spent corresponding with colleagues in France, sacking the temple of language and redistributing the spoils. (100)

The passage seems almost comparable to the classic satire of Swift and Pope in its simultaneous capacity to reveal in its author an essentially conservative disposition, even as its conceals a thin-skinned sensitivity.

Finally, *Lewis Percy* dispels common preconceptions about its author's reluctance to confront sexuality in her novels. Tact and restraint, in this context, should not be confused with reticence or prudery. The sex-food association common to Brookner, and the specific hunger of the reluctantly chaste Lewis, achieve their apotheosis in the extraordinary oral sadism of tea with the Harpers:

> Tissy now appeared to him to be composed of the same fondant yet friable material as the cake she was so dedicatedly eating. Tissy, in this setting, seemed to him to be composed entirely of cake. If he nibbled her ear it would break off and melt in his mouth like marzipan. Her pale delicacy almost invited assault; making love to her would be like violating a nun. (67)

The abiding impression of reading (and re-reading) Brookner is of a thematic and indeed an intellectual ambivalence. The main generative power of her fiction lies (as I have previously suggested) in an almost constant tension – in narrator, protagonist and author – between intellectual detachment and emotional susceptibility in relation to the Romantic myths. The most striking novels in this respect are those which, whilst reaching satisfying conclusions in purely formal terms, nevertheless reject naive and spurious resolutions of this thematic conflict: in practice, *Hotel du Lac* and *Lewis Percy*.

It is a critical judgement with clear autobiographical implications, and therefore provides a suitable point of transition to the concluding chapter of this study.

# 5

# Fictions of the Self

## NARRATIVE STRICTURES

There are so many analogies and parallels between different
Brookner novels – in structure, theme and even the smallest
incidental detail – that it is natural to ask whether all nine may
not in fact be variations on a single subject; or even, in some sense,
related versions of what is essentially one monolithic fiction. Such
hypotheses may be tested by a judicious combination of structuralist
narratology and the autobiographical approach.

The search for structures common to all of Brookner's novels can
be pursued, at its simplest, either in terms of characters or events.
Among 'functional' models of character emerging or resurfacing in
the sixties, the best-known are the new actantial theory of Greimas
(1970, 1983)[1] and the older *Morphology of the Folktale* by Propp (1968,
first published 1928).

Propp's analysis, limited to a specific type of Russian folk-tale,
identified characters with 'spheres of action' and categorized them
according to seven general roles: the villain, the donor, the helper,
the sought-for-person and her father, the dispatcher, the hero and
the false hero. Propp's hypothesis, it must be admitted, now seems
to have a largely historical interest, and is rarely encountered outside 'primers' of narratology (cf. Chatman, 1978; Rimmon-Kenan,
1983; Bal, 1985).

Greimas's model, replacing the personalized role of *actor* by the
abstract function of *actant*, reduced Propp's seven roles to six general
categories, as follows:

$$\text{sender} \rightarrow \text{object} \rightarrow \text{receiver}$$
$$\uparrow$$
$$\text{helper} \rightarrow \text{subject} \leftarrow \text{opponent}$$

Greimas makes modest claims for his theory:

this model seems to possess, because of its simplicity and for the analysis of mythical manifestations only, a certain operational value. (Greimas, 1983, 207)

Such moderation might have been expected to dispel liberal, humanist prejudices against a purely functional model, although – among literary critics in general – this has not normally been the case. Brookner's novels, with their conspicuous elements of fairy-tale and myth, respond encouragingly to Greimas's actantial model.

Alternatively, we may consider the actual repertoire of events in Brookner's novels. A close reading of all nine suggests, once again, that there are striking family resemblances, with major sequences of events (and even circumstantial details) repeated from novel to novel. The expression of these as some form of fictional paradigm would also be revealing. Here, too, structuralist narratology can offer two distinct models: the first of these – based on the concept of a number of propositional functions – was also elaborated by Propp, who suggested thirty-one of them. Not all needed to occur (or did in fact occur) in every story; those that did, however, always seemed to appear in the same order.

Propp's 'determinism' was criticized by Claude Bremond, who constructed a model which was more logically than temporally oriented, and able to take into account potential bifurcations of plot at different points in the story (Bremond, 1973). It basically assumed the three stages of possibility (or potentiality), process and outcome: a defined objective could thus be actualized ('steps taken') or not actualized ('steps not taken'). The process of actualization could, in turn, be a success or a failure – resulting in a new *status quo* etc.

\*                    \*                    \*

The Brookner plot has, at the very least, sufficient overtones of fairy-tale and myth for this kind of approach to be taken seriously. *A Start in Life* is quite explicit in this respect, with the young Ruth falling asleep 'enraptured' as her nurse promised her 'Cinderella shall go to the ball' (7); *Providence* and *Look at Me*, too, have their obvious analogies with the Cinderella myth. *Lewis Percy* has its own fairy-tale pattern, with its central parallelism between Tissy and the story of *Sleeping Beauty*. *Latecomers* (in Fibich's trip to Berlin) draws on such archetypal patterns as the night journey and rebirth; *A Misalliance*, with its elaborate contrast of Christian and Pagan iconography, develops an entire mythological matrix.

For the first three novels, in fact, one might tentatively apply Propp's scheme for characters and 'spheres of action' as follows:

|  | *A Start in Life* | *Providence* | *Look at Me* |
|---|---|---|---|
| hero(ine) | Ruth | Kitty | Frances |
| donor | parents | Louise/Vadim | mother/Nancy |
| helper | Anthea | Caroline (the Bentleys?) | Olivia |
| dispatcher | headmistress | clairvoyant | Nick/Alix |
| sought-for-person (and father?) | Richard | Maurice | James |
| false hero | (Richard) | (Maurice) | (James) |
| villain | (Mrs Cutler?) | Jane | Maria |

Even at this level and in the early novels, however, there are anomalies and loose ends. It is perhaps acceptable that, for Brookner, 'sought-for-person' and 'false hero' are typically synonymous: for unlike their fairy tale counterparts, her heroines do not normally live 'happily ever after'. But the *sought-for-person* does not have a visible *father*, unless – in the case of Richard and Maurice – it is a heavenly one! In the absence of a Jane or a Maria, furthermore, Richard's Christian good works may be the effective *villain* that thwarts the *hero(ine)*.

But Ruth Weiss identifies literature as the 'villain' of her life – a situation which might also be argued as applying to Kitty (for the false expectations it creates of a Romantic hero), or even to Frances (who virtually 'lives' in inverse proportion to what she writes). Perhaps, therefore, the higher level of abstraction permitted by Greimas's concept of *actants* is more suitable in the present context.

According to this model, one might adduce the following pattern for three exemplary Brookner novels. In *Providence*, Louise and Vadim are the *sender*, whose *object* is 'success' for their granddaughter in work as in love; the *receivers* are therefore her 'richly endowed provincial university' and Maurice, respectively. Alternatively, Kitty is the *subject*, Caroline – and indirectly the clairvoyant – is the *helper*, and Jane Fairfax the *opponent*.

*Look at Me*, on the other hand, is hardly less problematic for Greimas's model than it is for Propp's: if Frances is the *subject*,

James the *receiver* and Maria the *opponent* – thus producing the 'eternal triangle' of a novelette, as much as the archetypes of a fairy-tale – the other actants are more difficult to identify: the *helper* would be any or all of Olivia, Nick and Alex, and even the maid Nancy; Frances's lack of attention (forcing her into the role of some latter-day Scheherazade), and her need for affection (resulting in her discreet pursuit of James) might each presumably be classified as either *sender* or *object*.

*Lewis Percy*, finally – once gender transformations have been observed – corresponds quite clearly to a pattern that emerged in the first two novels. Mrs Percy is the *sender* who prepares the *object*, her son Lewis, to be husband and father; the *receiver* is primarily Tissy, and (when the cycle is repeated) Emmy Douglas. Alternatively, the *subject* is Lewis, himself, the *helper* is Emmy's brother, Penn, and the *opponent* – if not actually personalized – can be convincingly defined as Tissy's new state of awareness induced by her feminist friends.

In practice, therefore, even the Brookner novels ostensibly closest to fairy-tales offer considerable resistance to the theoretical models of Propp or Greimas. Are *A Start in Life* and *Lewis Percy* – with their distinctive repetitive pattern – to be considered, for instance, as 'compound' fairy tales, or double versions of a single tale? How is one to analyse *Hotel du Lac*, with its 'triple marriage plot', and how should one regard the polyfocalism of *Family and Friends* or *Latecomers*?

The classic formalist and structuralist models of Propp or Greimas obviously reflect a perennial methodological problem. Experience shows that either model – but particularly that of Greimas – may be applied to many characters in much fiction, but that there are invariably remainders and misfits which can only be found actantial status by means of fairly arbitrary textual interpretation. Alternatively, one may start 'at the other end' and elaborate some kind of *ad hoc* model, which will fit individual texts or authors rather well, but become increasingly inappropriate the further afield one moves.

As the present study is confined to a single author and generally empirical in character, the latter approach may be preferable; it is also, as it happens, quite rewarding.

The early Brookner novels may thus be seen as prototypes of a model characterized by five easily distinguishable features.

Firstly, the protagonist has 'orphan' status – literally so, in the case of Kitty (*Providence*) or Frances (*Look at Me*); virtually so, in the case of the neglected Ruth Weiss (*A Start in Life*).

Secondly, an obvious corollary of 'orphan' status – the parental role – is inadequate or non-existent, and childhood and/or adolescence correspondingly unhappy. Even Kitty's kind and well-meaning surrogate parents, Louise and Vadim, are unable to equip their granddaughter for an alien English world.

Thirdly, the protagonist achieves 'emancipation' from the childhood home through academic or 'artistic' talent: doctoral dissertations and university teaching for Ruth and Kitty, creative writing for Frances.

Fourthly, the protagonist becomes involved in an unsatisfactory emotional relationship with an unsuitable 'love object' – Richard Hirst, Maurice Bishop, James Anstey, respectively.

And in this process, fifthly, the protagonist is aided and abetted (or sometimes hindered) by a contrasting helper/antagonist figure: Anthea (*A Start in Life*), Caroline (*Providence*) or Nick-and-Alix (*Look at Me*).

Here too, some of the novels apparently resist such codification, although these narratives may in turn be explained as fairly simple displacements or metamorphoses of the original pattern. *Providence* and *Look at Me* are the clearest examples of this procedure; *A Start in Life* repeats the initial pattern in identical terms, when – in the middle of the narrative – Ruth finds herself alone in Paris, an 'orphan' once more and lodging with her surrogate parents, the Wilcoxes. Emancipation comes again through the academy, now in the form of the *Bibliothèque Nationale*; the new 'love object' is Professor Duplessis; the helper-antagonist role is filled, in turn, by Hugh and Jill Dixon.

*Lewis Percy* – albeit with a simple gender switch – also reproduces the structure of the earlier novels. The hero's childhood is passed over, but the absent father and the painfully recessive mother produce what is effectively an 'emotional' and 'intellectual' orphan. In a blatantly repetitive detail, Lewis's emancipation also comes through a dissertation on the French novel; he even does research in Paris. The role of helper-antagonist is played by Penry Douglas, who counterbalances Lewis's idealism of the female sex by suggesting that he needs either a wife or a cleaner. The 'love object' is initially Tissy, although, in terms of chivalresque obsession, Lewis's feelings are later transferred to Emmy Douglas, and even perhaps

– intermittently – to his daughter, Jessica.

The structures of the other five novels could all be regarded as recognizable transformations or displacements of the four I have already discussed. *Family and Friends* and *Latecomers* are most obviously similar to each other, with their four-way splitting of the protagonist function – two brothers and two sisters in the former, two married couples in the latter.

In *Family and Friends*, the orphan motif is clearly attenuated (only the father figure is missing), and remains subordinate to the theme of cultural alienation in the family transplanted from Central Europe. The children's inadequate upbringing – the novel may be read as an indictment of certain bourgeois values – may be blamed on the intimidating matriarchal presence of Sofka.

Plot structure is obviously modified by emphasis on the subsidiary Brookner theme – discussed by the author in her interviews and specifically elaborated in *A Start in Life* – of the child obliged to sacrifice its own life for the parent(s). Frederick and Betty are identified as the 'two who got away', Betty achieving her emancipation through artistic talent (more specifically, her ability to dance), and her love object is Franco Cariani – for whom she absconds in Paris.

In actual fact, Franco is as much the helper-protagonist, stolen by Betty from her sister, to be exploited and later discarded; the 'true' love object will be the statuesque Max, although – in conformity with Brookner's fictional morality – the escape into marriage will be an illusory one. Betty will ultimately be no happier than the deceived sister, Mimi, who remains at home. The contrasting destinies of Sofka's daughters might, in fact, be seen as illustrating Bremond's concept of *potentiality*, with Betty and Mimi exemplifying, respectively, the processes of *actualization* and *non-actualization*.

If the two brothers, Frederick and Alfred, seem more individually differentiated, they are nevertheless – both thematically and structurally – counterparts of Mimi and Betty: Frederick escapes from the home environment, whilst Alfred dutifully remains. In accordance with his greater autonomy as character, moreover, Frederick's process of emancipation is also the least explicitly formulaic, according to the terms I have outlined.

The elder son's fate is determined by marriage to an elemental figure even more powerful than Sofka, one who 'seems to promise, on her own, the propagation of the race': not inappropriately, she is called Eva! As Frederick retires to Bordighera, he is admittedly able to 'revert to being a violin player' (73), but it is not really artistic talent that has played any part in detaching him from his home environment. Evie, besides being the love object, virtually fills the role of helper-antagonist, as well as providing the means of emancipation.

Alfred, with a function analogous to that of Mimi, also represents potentiality unfulfilled: by the end of the book, he is a lonely figure, faithful to the family firm; his brief infatuation with Hal's beautiful but petulant wife, Dolly (!), proves as inconclusive as his search for another home. He thus remains unemancipated, and without helper or love object. He literally finds himself with nowhere to live and no-one to love.

The multiple focus of *Family and Friends* recurs in *Latecomers*, with a new quartet of characters. All four figures are authentic, or at least metaphorical, orphans: Hartmann and Fibich, whose shared Christian name also suggests the literal splitting of a single type, are a virtual compendium of Brookner motifs: refugees from Central Europe, orphans at an early age, immersed in an alien culture, oppressed by unhappy formative experiences (in this case, English boarding-school). Emancipation lies in business acumen as much as artistic talent, but Yvonne and Christine emerge quite predictably as the conventional love objects.

Hartmann constructs for himself a harmonious and essentially self-contained existence without any obvious helper figure: the process may be an implied critique of the helper-protagonist function, whether embodied as *shaman* (Fibich's analyst, Tissy Harper's family doctor or Kitty Maule's clairvoyant) or *matchmaker* (Penelope and Monica in *Hotel du Lac*, or Caroline in *Providence*).

Yvonne and Christine are also virtual orphans: the former had escaped with her mother from wartime Paris after her father had been shot; the latter had lived in a 'sense of hopelessness' with her morose father and unsympathetic stepmother. Supposed emancipation comes to both women only through marriage. For Christine, the love object is Fibich, whilst the helper-antagonist is Fibich's 'Aunt' Marie: 'helper' inasmuch as she provides an environment outside the unhappy childhood home, 'antagonist' by holding Fibich in a routine from which he is unable to escape, until his friend Hartmann explains what he must do.

Yvonne's relation to Christine may also be partly analogous to that between Fibich and Hartmann: like the latter, she has virtually no helper, whilst – with her sexual indifference and total self-absorption – one might wonder if she had any love object either, beyond that provided by her own narcissism.

*A Misalliance* and *A Friend from England* illustrate other displace-ments of the recurrent pattern. The latter, according to Brookner, deals with the important subject of female friendship: a curious remark, since (focalized predominantly through Rachel) the nar-rative could equally be read as an account of female antagonism and rivalry. Or alternatively, Heather and Rachel – like Fibich and Hartmann – may represent another case of a single split identity. Rachel is the parentless child, whilst Heather is the victim of an unsatisfactory upbringing. The fusion of identities is also suggested by Rachel's later assumption of the daughter's role – she visits Heather's mother in hospital – as well as by her indignation at Heather usurping her own time and independence.

Oscar and Dorrie Livingstone are generous and loving parents, who – like Louise and Vadim – are merely incapable rather than negligent. Marriage, for the less academic Brookner heroine, is again the only form of so-called emancipation, and Heather attempts it twice. In the first instance, Colonel Sandburg is the all-too-willing helper in his keenness to settle his unsuitable son.

The marriage is understandably a failure, and the homosexual Michael is ultimately more antagonist than helper, driving Heather into the arms of Marco. The interdependence, if not the symbiosis, of the two women is also strongly suggested by the final scenes in Venice, where Rachel – 'blocked by water' - watches her 'friend' or *alter ego*, Heather, disappear down the Calle de la Vida.

In *A Misalliance*, Blanche Vernon – middle-aged divorcée by the beginning of her narrative – makes few references to childhood; from scattered remarks, however, this was obviously unhappy. Of the father, there is no mention; her mother, on the other hand, was calculating and importunate, and years later, Blanche dreams of having to row her to the Isle of Wight.

Emancipation comes ostensibly through marriage, although there is a passing reference to another narrative, as the older Blanche (in what is perhaps a Brookner in-joke) momentarily considers finishing her 'thesis on Mme de Staël'. But if the heroine's child-hood, parentage and academic talents are in fact fairly remote configurations, it is because the whole matrix has been displaced onto another subject: the infant Elinor.

Elinor is another 'virtual' orphan: her biological mother is dead, her father absent, and her stepmother negligent or resentful. Helper-antagonist figures are plentiful, including the child's grandmother, the hospital doctor, and even Blanche's cleaner, Mrs Elphinstone. Blanche might also be numbered amongst them, if she were not more obviously a self-imposed love object for Elinor.

The commonplace theme of unfulfilled maternal instincts is largely eclipsed in *A Misalliance* by Blanche's intimate identity with the child: she and Elinor are explicitly presented as counterparts to the 'pagan nymph' Sally and Bertie's lover, 'Mousie'; Blanche feels that 'Some people are lonely children all their lives' (169) and – during her traumatic visit to the Demuths at the Dorchester Hotel – literally becomes 'wordless' like the mute child.

The most problematic, if also the most challenging, of the five identifiable processes is that of emancipation: in *A Misalliance*, this seems to transcend mere artistic or academic ability, to embrace the child's acquisition of language itself. Elinor's story recalls the episode of the small girl in *Hotel du Lac*, threatened by a crippling speech defect, and – as I have argued elsewhere – emblematically re-enacting the female child's resistance to assumption into the symbolic mode of (phallocentric) language.

Finally, *Hotel du Lac* – the most justly celebrated of all of Brookner's novels – predictably offers greatest resistance to the recovery of an underlying narrative structure. Edith admittedly lost her father early, and was brought up by a 'harsh, embittered' mother, but the orphan motif is again transformed into a broader sense of cultural alienation. How much Edith's talents as a writer of popular novel-ettes contributed to her emancipation from the childhood home is not clarified; and the engagement to Geoffrey Long ('love object') under the aegis of Penelope ('helper-protagonist') may be read as parody romance, rather than the merely foredoomed romance typical of other novels.

Almost simultaneously, however, Edith conducts her clandestine affair with David; here, it might be argued, Penelope is again helper, since it is at one of her parties that Edith and David are introduced. In contrast to the situation with Geoffrey, however, Edith meets David fortuitously, and Penelope remains unaware of their relationship. Perhaps, like Hartmann – another of Brookner's more resolute and self-contained protagonists – Edith literally 'helps herself'. The heroine's references to her own childhood are triggered by the sight of the Puseys. Edith's relationship to Jennifer is a complicated one, with its intricate compound of displacement and projection, polarity and complementarity, without however excluding a genuine sense of identity.

*Hotel du Lac*, therefore, would thus seem to repeat a familiar bifurcation of the female protagonist: now Mrs Pusey keeps her biological daughter, Jennifer, in a state of prolonged adolescent dependence, even as she tries to manipulate her adoptive daughter, Edith, with advice on clothes and general behaviour. The great distinction lies in Mrs Pusey's reactions towards her 'daughters'' relationships with men: a prurient complacency in the case of Edith, and hysterical outbursts with regard to Jennifer.

Jennifer does not possess the capacity to free herself from her mother; Edith, on the other hand, has already achieved economic independence, and can supplement this with the intellectual detachment provided by her writing – illustrated in her ability to 'write up' Mrs Pusey in her letters to David. Such success and failure in the process of emancipation may again illustrate Bremond's complementary notions of 'realization' and 'non-realization' in a single narrative situation.

The love object of Edith-Jennifer is Mr Neville, although it is only for Edith that Monica fulfils the role of helper- antagonist ('I reckon that if you played your cards right you could have him' 147). The second narrative cycle also, of course, also ends wretchedly for Edith – it is Jennifer (with no 'helper' besides her own natural endowments) who has been 'having' Mr Neville.

There is, then, a quite reasonable case for regarding Brookner's novels as variations or permutations of an initially established pattern. But the connections I have traced above are not primarily intended as a contribution to any more general theory of plots and plotting. In this respect, even the plot of my own story – Brookner's novels of the eighties – is bound to remain inadequate. My immediate concern, rather, is to draw attention to far more specific plot structures, those underlying the author's own autobiographical narrative.

## AUTOBIOGRAPHICAL STRICTURES

There is a curious interlude in *Providence* when Kitty Maule pays her second visit to the Bentley country home in Gloucestershire; the narrative momentarily abandons focalization through the heroine, as Pauline and her mother go off together to a country fête. One motive for this episode may be a desire to present Kitty as she is seen by two other characters. Although the picture is an ironic one, and an indirect satire of the Bentleys' quintessential Englishness, the reader has a strong sense of of reading a barely disguised self-portrait. Such a unique example in Brookner of a 'portrait of the artist' is therefore worth quoting at length, if only to anticipate fuller discussion of autobiographical impulses:

> ' . . . Tell me, Pauline, what does she look like?'
> Pauline thought. 'She looks very pretty when she is animated and rather plain when she is not.'
> Mrs Bentley nodded. '*Journalière*, that used to be called. What else?'
> 'She is very well-dressed, almost too well-dressed. Oh, I suppose she is quite attractive. They think highly of her in the Department.'
> 'She has such a pretty voice,' said Mrs Bentley. 'Such very precise English. You rarely hear such good enunciation these days. It comes from her being a foreigner, of course.'
> 'Oh, really, Mother. She was born in London. Although I agree that she gives the impression of someone not quite at home here. Trying to learn the rules as it were.'
> 'I should call her well-bred, and that says it all. The natives, after all, don't have to bother.'

> (155)

The reader always suspects, and the interviews tend to confirm, that Brookner's novels contain a substantial autobiographical element. It will therefore be necessary to provide as balanced and objective a view as possible of the links between the author's fiction and her own life.

The attempt inevitably raises general theoretical questions of the relation between fiction and autobiography: for even the fictional narrative commonly regarded as most genuinely autobiographical (*A Start in Life*) is not a 'literal transcription' of the author's own existence; the novels are less interesting, moreover, for superficial and easily demonstrable parallels, than for various transformations of autobiographical material. Brookner's suffering heroines (and later, heroes) belong to narratives marked by the compulsive

repetition-with-variation of certain structures and motifs. The process of understanding these metamorphoses demands more than
simple collation of novels and interviews: it also draws the critic
into general discussion of the dynamics of psycho-biography.

But even this approach begs several important questions; for if
no fictional narrative is a 'literal transcription' of life, neither –
according to much recent theorizing – is any autobiographical
text.[2] And if traditionally assumed rhetorical distinctions between
fictional and autobiographical discourse are subverted, the separate
ontological status of each mode is also inevitably called into question. Discussion of psycho-biography should therefore be preceded
by some account of actual rhetoric of representation, at least as
exemplified by Brookner.

And yet complex notions of psycho-biography and referentiality
are still only examples of premature anticipation within a third kind
of narrative, that of critical discourse. Brookner is a creative writer
rather than a literary theorist of post-structuralist tendencies, and
there is every reason to be grateful for her personal faith in the
possibility of representation: there are happily already nine novels
to confirm it. It therefore seems fitting to begin with the author's
own assumptions about which elements are autobiographical – and
which are not – in the novels she has produced to date.

In this respect, a close reading of the interviews shows Brookner's
constant concern to provide, in her fiction, the kind of moral order
that she finds so conspicuously absent in life; moral order thus
belongs explicitly to fiction rather than to personal experience:

> I felt impelled by irritation with circumstances and life, which
> seemed to me so badly plotted. The morality of novels – in which
> judgements are meted out – very much recommends itself to me.
> (Haffenden, 25)

She is sceptical about the therapeutic value of this operation ('if it
were therapy I wish it had worked'), but the scepticism may only be
directed at her own personal case. For later in the same interview,
she reiterates her theory of novel writing as a kind of controlling
mechanism:

> It's a form of editing experience – getting it out in terms of form,
> because it is form that's going to save us all, I think, and the
> sooner we realise it the better. (Haffenden, 30)

The same ideas are repeated in more personal terms in the two other interviews:

> My life seemed to be drifting in predictable channels and I wanted to know how I deserved such a fate. I thought if I could write about it I would be able to impose some structure on my experience. It gave me a feeling of being at least in control. (Guppy, 150)

> I write out of a sense of powerlessness and injustice, because I felt invisible and passive. Life is so badly plotted. The novel speaks about states of mind which forced me to do something about those states of mind. (Kenyon, 12)

Rather than suggesting simple mediation of personal experience, such remarks imply a radical transformation of these elements. The process is explicitly structural, but – as will appear later – probably not consciously rhetorical. The comments quoted are, in any case, a clear caution against a simplistic autobiographical reading.

There are other attempts by Brookner to distinguish between fictional characters, on the one hand, and close family or her own person. She thus contradicts Haffenden's assumption that she has used her parents in *A Start in Life* ('No, they were nothing like; I couldn't do that to them', 27). In the Guppy interview, she faults critics for 'identifying me with my female protagonists' (165), and offers a perhaps unintentionally revealing comment on *A Friend from England* ('about an extremely emancipated young woman – whom they will *not* be able to think is me!' 167).

Such reservations nevertheless tend to be eclipsed by examples of conscious (and, more interestingly, unconscious) identification with fictional characters. Asked if she shares any of Edith Hope's characteristics in *Hotel du Lac*, Brookner replies candidly: 'Practically all of them, I should think. But I'm not going into detail' (Kenyon, 14); to a more general question of whether her 'outwardly sophisticated' heroines are herself 'in a strict sense', she answers more guardedly: 'I think they must be, though I'm not in a position to say it' (Haffenden, 28). A comment on *Family and Friends* suggests that this novel, in addition to *A Start in Life*, has particularly strong autobiographical links ('It's my family . . . They are made into fiction, but the memory of them is mine', Kenyon, 16).

The contradictory nature of these two groups of quotations may probably be largely explained as a strategy for self-protection. Together with their apparent candour, the interviews also display understandable elements of reservation and discretion. Brookner makes the essential point here whilst discussing the difference between criticism and creative writing, and the incapacity of certain distinguished critics to write fiction: 'perhaps because in fiction you give too much away while in criticism you can hide behind another writer's personality and work' (Guppy, 168). The 'woman's writing' with which Brookner is quite happy to identify herself ('It does limit itself, but it tends to go deeper' Kenyon, 22) is almost invariably personal and self-revelatory. The judgements of critics – Brookner refers to the case of *A Misalliance* – can also be of a 'semipersonal kind' (Guppy, 166). Such criticism can only be hurtful, and never constructive: for every John Haffenden, there is a Peter Kemp, and some form of self-protection is clearly desirable.

*		*		*

Reminiscences of a more personal kind – whether by authorial design or the interviewer's editorial function – are often as self-consciously 'crafted' as her explicitly fictional narratives. Here is Brookner on the subject of Dickens, as reported in an interview with Michael Barber:

> [My father] had the brilliant idea that all would be revealed if I read Dickens. He was wrong, of course, in that as in most things. But not entirely. However, he gave me two books at Christmas and two for my birthday until I'd polished them off. I grew up thinking that the world was peopled with larger than life characters – so naturally it proved a great disappointment to me. 'Where is John Jarndyce?' I would say. 'Where are the Brothers Cheerybyle [sic]? Where is David Copperfield?' (1983, 27)

In a passage of this kind, decidedly closer to crafted literary anecdote than to unguarded personal confession, documentary accuracy is arguably not the speaker's greatest priority.

The most striking examples of identification between novelist and fictional characters are therefore probably those made unconsciously in the course of an interview. Consider, for example, the following exchange with John Haffenden on *Look at Me*:

> [Haffenden]: It's a very desolating story in which nothing really happens, other than *Frances Hinton*'s yearning to be

admitted to the ranks of the glamorous and charismatic people
. . .

> [Brookner]: It is indeed. I'm very envious of careless people.
> It's about not being able to be like them, and how the rewards
> of being that sort of person are infinitely greater . . .
>
> (my emphasis; 26)

or a comment from the discussion with Shusha Guppy:

> [Guppy]: In Hotel du Lac you say that you prefer the company
> of men to that of women. . . .
> [Brookner]: I prefer the company of men because they teach
> me things I don't know.
>
> (my emphasis; 161)

(The you responsible for this remark in Hotel du Lac was not
even the extradiegetic narrator, but Edith Hope herself [21]. The
identification is first made by Guppy, but Brookner does nothing .
to contradict it.)

Yet another example of this kind of fusion occurs in the Olga
Kenyon interview, during an exchange on the functions of writing
for a marginal person:

> [Kenyon]: What useful functions has writing had for you?
> [Brookner]: The function of writing for a marginal person is
> to reabsorb all the attention that has been wasted by too much
> listening and watching. This is a vital function for a passive
> person.
> [Kenyon]: There are variations on that in your third novel
> Look at Me.
> [Brookner]: Yes. The heroine, Frances, tells us that writing is
> 'a penance for not being lucky'. It is an attempt to reach others
> and to make them love you.
>
> (12–13)

The very fact that each of the interviews can produce similar
instances of unconscious identification argues against mere editorial
imprecision on the part of the interviewer. The presence of the latter,
however, should remind us that the interviews themselves are in
some ways quite as complex in structure as Brookner's fictional

narratives. Each of them has a specific context and, in view of the great emphasis placed on the major interviews in the present study, some brief distinction between them should be made.

John Haffenden's conversation with Brookner appeared in *The Literary Review* in September, 1984, to coincide with the publication of *Hotel du Lac*; Shusha Guppy's was published in *The Paris Review* in the autumn of 1987, after *Family and Friends* and *A Misalliance*, and in immediate anticipation of *A Friend from England* – about which the interviewer tactfully inquires; Olga Kenyon's interview, finally, formed part of an anthology entitled *Women Writers Talk* (published in 1989) – *A Friend from England* receives closer attention here, and there is even a reference to *Latecomers*. The Kenyon interview is notable for what might be most kindly described as its 'synoptic' tendencies: in addition to echoes of the earlier interviews, it also reproduces *verbatim* comments by Brookner from a television interview (*Kaleidoscope*, 18 October, 1984), after the award of the Booker Prize.

For a novelist as prolific as Brookner, a mere five years produces considerable changes in her status as a writer, thus requiring similar adjustments in critical perspective. The point may be easily illustrated by one of the author's own comments. Unaware of the critical acclaim in store for *Hotel du Lac*, she could tell Haffenden of inconclusive attempts to come to terms with her own European background in a new book:

> As a matter of fact I'm trying to write a novel about that, but I very much doubt that I shall finish it – it seems so heartless at the moment. (25)

After the successful completion of this novel (*Family and Friends*), followed by four other novels by the end of the decade, her remarks have a certain irony. If there is a strong inducement to regard Brookner's novels as one all-embracing fiction, we may remember Walter Benjamin's insight that the end of a fiction – like death itself – determines the meaning of what has gone before.[3]

All three interviews are remarkably similar in their accounts of Brookner's early life, her sense of alienation, her close ties with nineteenth century literature and morality, her admiration for certain French and English writers. There are nevertheless significant differences. Thus Haffenden, with whom Brookner emerged as a particularly vulnerable and unhappy person, clearly regards his subject as an autobiographical novelist, and probes kindly for the requisite parallels in the four books he knows; at a date, moreover, when four substantial studies in art history (in addition to regular review essays) could still sometimes overshadow four slim novels, Haffenden also pays detailed attention to Brookner's academic career.

Guppy extends the discussion of Brookner's relations to other writers, and concentrates on thematic patterns in the novels. She questions Brookner on her relation to contemporary feminist issues – and, more specifically, on the situation of a female novelist writing from the point of view of male characters. In the tradition of *Paris Review* interviews, moreover, she expresses special interest in the writer's actual working methods.

Kenyon's interview, finally, has a clear ideological interest: together with the other pieces collected in *Women Writers Talk*, it provides a companion volume to Kenyon's critical study, *Women Novelists Today* (1988), where Brookner is presented as a 'post-feminist writer' (13). For this reason, Brookner's willingness to be identified with 'women's writing', and her view of what this implies, give the interview an important new dimension.

But interviewers may unfortunately make more dubious contributions to shifting critical perspectives. There is thus an interesting exchange between Brookner and television interviewer, Richard Mayne, immediately after the announcement of the Booker award:

> *Mayne*: . . . did you have to write [*Hotel du Lac*] many times, or did you find that it flowed?
> *Brookner*: No, I just wrote it once. I was lucky. It came out right.
> *Mayne*: Is it the book of which you are most pleased?
> *Brookner*: No, I think the one I've finished is better.

Whatever the value of this judgement on *Family and Friends*, Brookner's admirers will be happy that the novelist's moral rectitude does not preclude a little healthy self-advertisement. More curious, however, is the fact that when the last two lines are incorporated *verbatim* into Kenyon's interview five years later (15–16), they can now only be read as a reference to *Latecomers*!

In addition to their autobiographical links, therefore, the interviews may also be analogous to the novels even in terms of relativity and reliability. When the novelist characteristically focalizes events through one or more protagonists, balancing this technique with the extensive use of extradiegetic narration, both agents are engaged in recreating, through discourse, a particular story, the hypothetical 'first narrative' of structuralist theory.

In the interviews, however, the 'story' is an author's life, in which the novels themselves may be regarded – for the moment – as a simple series of embedded narrative acts, subordinate to the pattern of autobiographical discourse. The interviewer acquires a dual function: in the original, presumably oral, interview situation, (s)he exists as a character within the narrative, but in the final printed version of the interview, the editorial role is more equivalent to that of the extradiegetic narrator in the novels. And whether or not fictional discourse infers the kind of 'basic story' implicit in autobiographical discourse, the likelihood of unreliability must be omnipresent in both forms of narrative. If, then, the structural distinctions between the interviews and novels are so attenuated, it is reasonable to ask whether ontological distinctions are not also suspect.

I should like to pursue this argument by referring to another English author about whom I have elsewhere posed similar questions: Philip Larkin.[4] I hasten to disclaim any intention of seeking literary 'influences', conscious or unconscious – in either direction – between Brookner and Larkin; although there are tantalising echoes of Brookner in Larkin's references to awkward, remote parents or a 'childhood unspent', in his lonely single existence, his determinism, his general reticence and elusiveness, or simply in his profound sense of personal loss. The real relevance of Larkin, however, lies in the interesting relation between poetic and autobiographical discourse; the primary source for the latter is *Required Writing*, a collection of the poet's miscellaneous prose writings (including interviews) from 1955 to 1982.

Although Larkin criticism is generally wary of the direct autobiographical approach – preferring to speak more cautiously of poetic *personae* – the poet himself often links poems quite casually with his own personal opinions and experiences. In a 1982 Paris Review interview, for example, he confided 'Yes, I've remained single by choice, and shouldn't have liked anything else' (*Required Writing*, 65); whilst in another conversation in the *Observer*, three years earlier, he anticipated this comment by quoting *verbatim* two verses of a then uncollected poem:

> Who can be satisfied
> Putting someone else first,
> So that you come off worst?
>
> My life is for me:
> As well deny gravity.

Here then, the interesting point is less the sentiment itself than Larkin's readiness to quote a poem as *unmediated* opinion.

Similarly, the semi-articulate voice in 'A Study in Reading Habits' (*The Whitsun Weddings* 31) remembers adolescence:

> When getting my nose in a book
> Cured most things short of school . . . .

But he uses terms uncannily similar to an autobiographical recollection of 'reading at the rate of a book a day, even despite the tiresome interruptions of morning and afternoon school' (Brownjohn, 4)

These kinds of parallels are not difficult to find in Brookner's fictional and autobiographical discourse, respectively; treated with tact and caution – and with due reference to context and narrative voice – they can provide the basis for a psycho-biographical study.

> *               *               *

Even the conventionally 'autobiographical' *A Start in Life* is not simply a strategic redeployment of personal history; and in later novels, such as *Latecomers* and *Lewis Percy*, there is a clear fragmentation and dispersal of autobiographical impulses; these may be shared between two or more characters, male or female. The process of splitting the autobiographical subject has obvious analogues in Larkin's dyadic – poetic and autobiographical – discourse.

Thus Larkin's 'Mr Bleaney' (from the *Whitsun Weddings* collection of 1971) depicts a bleak existence in an upstairs bedsitter, where the anonymous poetic 'voice' speculates on the life of the previous lodger:

> . . . I lie
> Where Mr Bleaney lay, and stub my fags
> On the same saucer

Larkin tells us that the poem was written at Hull in 1955–56 (*Required Writing* 56), whilst a prose piece a few years later depicts the poet himself leading a Bleaney-like existence ('I know his habits – what time he came down') when living in Leicester:

> The room was at the top of the house (a familiar situation to me: I have lived most of my working life in rooms at the top of houses – I am in one now) . . . . (*Required Writing*, 36)

The same process may be seen in variants of another familiar Larkin *topos*, the evocation of the pampered writer: here, autobiography is transformed into pure rhetorical play. Thus, in the humorous detachment of an *Observer* interview, Larkin records – in explicitly autobiographical discourse – his naive preconceptions of worldly success:

> I'd have visions of myself writing 500 words a day for six months, shoving the result off to the printer and going to live on the Cote D'Azur, uninterrupted except for the correction of proofs. (*Required Words*, 49)

In another example of poetic discourse, however, character collapses through caricature to cliché, while irony is reduced to hyperbole and mere alliterative rhetoric:

> So the shit in the shuttered chateau
> Who does his five hundred words
> Then parts out the rest of the day
> Between bathing and booze and birds . . .
>        ('The Life with a Hole in it': *Collected Poems*, 1987)

What was an 'I' in autobiographical discourse is, in poetic discourse, ironically transformed into a series of alliterative tropes. (Larkin incidentally used the same rhetorical device to reduce all his modernist antipathies to Pound, Parker and Picasso). (*Required Writing*, 292).

In Brookner, too, there are analogous passages – from both autobiographical and fictional discourse – where pure 'rhetoricity' tends to upstage mere matters of 'representation'. One recalls the amusing lunch-time discussion in *Hotel du Lac* between Edith Hope and her agent. The latter refers hesitantly to what he discerns as new trends in popular fiction ('It's sex for the young woman executive now, the *Cosmopolitan* reader, the girl with the executive briefcase', 26), whilst Edith emphatically rejects such ideas:

> You see, Harold, my readers are essentially virtuous. And as far as they are concerned – as far as *I* am concerned – those multi-orgasmic girls with the executive briefcases can go elsewhere. They will be adequately catered for. There are hucksters in every market place. (28)

Edith's outburst might be read as impressive indexing of an autonomous fictional character, but for the existence of a strikingly similar protest in the Guppy interview:

> What I can't understand is the radical inauthenticity of some women's novels which are written to a formula: from the peatbogs of Killarney to the penthouses of Manhattan, orgasms all the way! Pornography for ladies. It is not only impure artistically, it is untrue and unfeminine. (161)

The coincidence of Edith's views with those of the author is quite unexceptionable, but it is the common rhetorical structure of the two passages that is more revealing: for in each case, the counterposition is reductively presented through a form of ironic hyperbole – identical even to the multi-orgasm *topos*. Allied with general scepticism about the recuperability of 'basic stories' in any narrative mode, the demonstration of a common rhetorical base to Brookner's fictional and autobiographical discourse invites us to question conventional ontological distinctions between them.

The conflation of fiction and autobiography, with their ironies and reversals, their fragmentation and dispersal of the self points towards a well-known and influential model of autobiography: the deconstructive labyrinth of Paul de Man.

In *Allegories of Reading* de Man suggests that

> the recuperation of selfhood would be accomplished by the rigor with which the discourse deconstructs the very notion of the self . . . . (173)

De Man went on to affirm that 'the action proper to autobiography is not historical but rhetorical'; I have argued that such a claim is particularly valid in the case of Larkin, although it now seems equally applicable to Brookner. De Man also suggested that all autobiographical discourse is tropological and drew the radical conclusion:

> We assume that life produces the autobiography as an act produces its consequences, but can we not suggest, with equal justice, that the autobiographical project may itself produce and determine the life and whatever the writer does is in fact governed by the technical demands of self-portaiture . . . .
> ('Autobiography as Defacement', 1979, 992)

One may in fact cite numerous instances in Brookner's interviews where what the writer did in the past is 'governed by technical demands of self-portaiture' – in fact, by *rhetoric*.

Some apology may be necessary for any banality in the examples chosen; but rhetorical strategies are probably more transparent at such basic levels. Furthermore, although there is no question of Brookner's existential urgency and deep personal investment in the novels, she is presumably unconscious of such rhetorical manipulations of autobiographical material. It is fortunate, in fact, that she is *not* inhibited by certain theoretical implications of rhetoric or tropology; for de Man and his disciples have not written many novels.

The best example for my argument is provided by the various tributes to Dickens in Brookner's interviews. Her very Polish father 'thought that the best thing he could do for me was to unveil the mysteries of English life which could be found in the novels of Dickens' (Haffenden, 28); or, alternatively, he 'thought Dickens gave a true picture of England, where right always triumphed' (Guppy, 149); or even took the novels of Dickens to be 'true pictures of English life' (Kenyon, 9). In each case, Brookner began reading Dickens at the age of seven and has been reading him ever since.

The very similarity of the three accounts might be convincing evidence of 'authenticity', except for one final detail. In 1987, Brookner told Shusha Guppy: 'I still read a Dickens novel every year and I am still looking for a Nicholas Nickleby!' (149). Two years later she told Olga Kenyon: 'I still re-read a Dickens novel every year. I am still looking for Nicholas Nickleby' (9). The explanation might of course be as trite a matter as 'recycling' by the second interviewer; but it would be strange if an author living in London, with contacts in the literary and publishing world, had been unable – over the course of two years – to obtain a copy of an English classic never out of print. The inevitable conclusion, then, is that the reference to *Nicholas Nickleby* is as much a 'fictional' indexing of the trait, 'love of Dickens', as a genuine 'autobiographical' detail.

Other examples of this process may be quoted more briefly: Commenting on her retirement from teaching activity, Brookner remarked: '. . . I have taught for twenty-five years and the thought of having to go through the syllabus for the twenty-sixth year was more than I could take' (Guppy, 168). It seems unlikely that Brookner would stop at the thought of the twenty-sixth year, any more than she might for the twenty-fifth or twenty-seventh.

One might be similarly reductive towards Brookner's twice recorded longing for a large family: 'I only ever wanted children: six sons' (Haffenden, 26); 'If I were happy, married with six children, I wouldn't be writing' (Guppy, 151).

It is not the intention of the present argument to 'dismiss' as pure fiction Brookner's autobiographical discourse, any more than it is to follow the reviewers who have emphasized autobiographical elements in the fiction. One cannot suggest that the interviews are deceitful or misleading, or that the novels lack imagination and originality. The proven similarities in the rhetoric of representation simply undermine distinctions between 'fact' and 'fiction', and serve to conflate the two narrative modes.

The structural analysis completed in the previous section, together with the generic synthesis attempted above, suggests that all of Brookner's novels may in some sense be regarded as continuations or variations of a single narrative. In addition to the impressive internal evidence for this view – apparent from the readings of the novels offered in this study – Brookner herself makes an extremely revealing comment to John Haffenden:

> I would just think of the novels as transcripts from a random passage through life, and a rather unsuccessful passage. (28)

It should, however, be remembered that when this interview was completed, Brookner had only produced four novels, the putatively autobiographical first trilogy, and *Hotel du Lac*.

Certainly, however, when these four novels are juxtaposed to the three interviews, one becomes increasingly aware of a whole *matrix* of motifs, further emphasized by striking textual similarities, which tends to conflate all seven narratives. Brookner stresses the sense of alienation she shared with her Polish-Jewish parents:

> I think my parents' lives were blighted – and in some sense mine is too – largely by this fact of being outside the natural order, being strangers in England . . . I've never been at home here. (Haffenden, 25)
>
> As for the 'displaced person' aspect, perhaps it is because although I was born and raised here I have never been at home, completely. (Guppy, 150)

This entire dimension seems to have been transferred to the existences of Kitty Maule and her grandparents in *Providence*. An 'expression of pity' passes over Vadim's face as he realizes that his granddaughter has been 'affected by an alien and sentimental culture' (16); Louise, however, will say with a glint in her eye: 'come, *ma fille*, tell me about England' (17).

Kitty is also the archetypal Brookner orphan (cf. *Providence* 26), reared by grandparents affectionate but remote and 'baffled', like Brookner's biological parents. Frances Hinton of *Look at Me* is another orphan (now without benefit of kindly grandparents), who lives with her mother's old maid, Nancy. The orphan state is, to some extent, raised to a figural level – Nick calls her jokingly 'Little Orphan Fanny' (34), Frances regards herself as 'the beggar at the feast' (51); and in this rhetorical mode, the motif is inevitably reminiscent of an occasion when Brookner described herself as 'this grown-up orphan with what you call success' (Haffenden, 26).

Even in the writing process, it is difficult to distinguish Brookner from her two protagonists who are novelists in their own right: the opening words of the novelist's first major interview characterize novel-writing as a penetential activity which gives her a headache (Haffenden, 25). Frances Hinton tells us that writing is 'a penance for not being lucky' (*Providence*, 53), whilst Edith Hope, finishing the account of her wedding day, feels her head aching after 'the follies and perils of prolonged reminiscence' (*Hotel du Lac*, 135).

There is a striking verbal similarity in interviews five years apart in Brookner's references to looking after her parents: 'I nursed my parents until they died: it's a dreary, Victorian story' (Haffenden, 25); 'Mine was a dreary Victorian story: I nursed my parents till they died' (Kenyon, 12). In Brookner's 'fictional' world, the duty is merely transferred to the maid Nancy, who nurses Frances's dying mother in *Providence*.

A final example of fiction and autobiography conflated is provided by references to a sense of anachronism, found both in the early Brookner heroines and in the novelist herself. To a question on the moral rectitude of her characters, Brookner makes another unconscious identification with them by referring to:

> . . . a grounding in nineteenth-century novels and nineteenth-century behaviour. My family was very rigorous in that respect; I've never unlearned these lessons, and I promise you I regret it. I would love to be extremely plausible, flattering and dishonest: there are useful dishonesties. (Haffenden, 27)

Questioning Brookner on the same subject, Guppy perhaps remembered the phrase 'moral rectitude' from Haffenden. It is unlikely, however, that Brookner had been memorizing her previous interview, and the verbal similarities of her answer are therefore all the more remarkable:

> In my case it comes from a grounding in the nineteenth century novel and because my own family were very strict in that respect. I have never unlearnt the lesson. I would love to be more plausible, flattering, frivolous, but I am handicapped by my expectations. Isn't it sad? (Guppy, 168)

It can only suggest, on the author's part, a consistent and omnipresent awareness of certain attitudes. It is of course the same repressive morality and sense of information withheld that characterizes all three of the early Brookner protagonists. The novelist herself discusses the predicament of her 'solitary heroines':

> Yes, they obey all nineteenth-century rules of morality and duty and seriousness, dedication and devotion without realising that these are important but anachronistic qualities. They come to this realisation too late. (Kenyon, 20)

This sense of frustration is strongest in the Haffenden interview, where Brookner admits: 'My characters exasperate me. I find myself deeply exasperating, and so do other people: you can't gainsay that'

(29). The heroines are '[p]oor little things'; they are 'idiots'; there is no other word for them. And Brookner does not 'know any more than they do' (30).

*        *        *

The theoretical tendency of this final chapter has been to erode clearcut distinctions between fictional and autobiographical discourse. After so many examples of analogy and cross-reference, however, the first three novels – and, to a certain extent, *Hotel du Lac* – might still be regarded as frequently motivated by some form of 'autobiographical recollection'.[5] But such recollections, as they occur in the interviews, take on the appearance of fictional modes. In their parallel rhetoricity as much as in their common subject matter, however, autobiographical recollection and fictional representation begin, for Brookner, to conflate in a single narrative form.

There certainly remain details in all of Brookner's novels where the impression of personally lived (and suffered) experience is overwhelming: the scent of lemon peel in Kitty Maule's nostrils after her mother's death seems one such example of barely mediated *image-repertoire*.[6] The pathology of water, or the barely repressed trauma of an earlier erotic experience suggest a similar intimacy. But it should be clear from my previous arguments that the pursuit of sensational correspondences between the 'fiction' and the 'autobiography', in the case of Brookner at least, is ultimately meaningless.

One may conclude, however, by spelling out a circular pattern of generic and ideological affinities implicit in the present chapter. All three serious studies of Brookner to date – those of Samarth, Kenyon and Waugh – have emphasized the existential, rather than the 'autobiographical' dimension of the fiction. The existence in question is inescapably female, and Brookner herself – generally scathing on the subject of feminism – has on the other hand readily accepted the designation of 'woman's novelist'. But James Olney's influential essay, 'Autobiography and the Cultural Moment' (1980), emphasized the fundamental relevance of autobiography to Women's Studies programmes in the academy; whilst his claim, in turn, only recalls Waugh's argument that contemporary feminism is attempting to construct a subject. In this process, Anita Brookner – whether regarded as *pre-* or *post*-feminist (or even pre- or post-modernist) plays a not inconsiderable part.

# Notes

## CHAPTER 1:  INTRODUCTION

1. I am grateful to Hanna Kirsten Brugmans of Bruges for providing me with reviews of Brookner novels from the French and Dutch press; and for Lidia de Michaelis of the University of Milan for similar help with Italian sources. Like their French counterparts, several Italian critics find analogies between Brookner and Woolf; none of them snipe at her connections with the French *conte*.
2. I would like to thank Tiziana Arcangeli of the University of Florence for a collection of Brookner's articles in *The Times Literary Supplement*.
3. The neologisms are from Gerard Genette's *Narrative Discourse* (English trans. 1980). For *intradiegetic* and *extradiegetic*, see ch. 5 'Voice'; and for *focalization*, see ch. 4 (161–211), 'Mood'. Genette's terminology is used widely in a number of later English-language syntheses of narrative poetics. See especially Seymour Chatman (*Story and Discourse*, 1978), Shlomith Rimmon-Kenan (*Narrative Fiction: Contemporary Poetics*, 1983), and Mieke Bal (*Narratology*, 1985).
4. Cohn's study is divided between 'Consciousness in Third-Person Context' and 'Consciousness in Third-Person Texts'. Particularly useful in the former area is Cohn's term *psycho-narration*, with its concepts of *dissonance* and *consonance* to denote the degree of sympathy felt by the narrator towards the subject.

## CHAPTER 2:  THE FRENCH CONNECTION

1. See Barbara Hardy's classic essay on this subject, 'Food and Ceremony in *Great Expectations*', incorporated in *The Moral Art of Dickens* (London: Athlone Press, 1970), 351–63.
2. Long before Iser's *The Act of Reading*, the ambivalent quality of Cervantes's parody was argued forcefully in the introductory chapter (9–19) of Dorothy Van Ghent's influential *The English Novel: Form and Function* (New York: Harper Torchbooks, 1961).
3. The classic modern discussion of *mimesis* and *diegesis* (a distinction originally made by Aristotle) occurs in Genette's *Narrative Discourse* (162–70).
4. Quotations from *Eugenie Grandet* are from the Penguin Classics translation by Ayton Crawford (1985), references to which are incorporated in the body of the text.
5. Subtitled *The Teachings of Twentieth-Century Art Forms*, Linda

Hutcheon's scope thus transcends the purely literary. See especially ch. 2 (30–49), 'Defining parody'.

6.  Extremely suggestive in this context is Franco Moretti's *The Way of the World. The Bildungsroman in European Culture* (London: Verso, 1987). In Moretti's study, the nineteenth century English tradition – with its idyllic tendencies – compares badly with the models of Goethe or Stendhal. Brookner's particular form of determinism ensures that the patterns of her own fiction lie closer to *Le Rouge et Le Noir* and *Madame Bovary* than to *Nicholas Nickleby* and *David Copperfield*.

7.  Two of the author's own comments are particularly relevant here. Objecting to John Haffenden's suggestion that her novel writing was 'a function of maladaptation', Brookner replied, 'No. I'm not going to let you get away with that. It's a form of editing experience – getting it out in terms of form, because it is form that's going to save us all, I think, and the sooner we realise it the better' (Haffenden, 30). To Shusha Guppy, she added, 'I do think that respect for form is absolutely necesary in any art form – painting, writing, anything' (Guppy, 163).

8.  Quotations from *Adolphe* are taken from the Penguin Classics edition translated by Leonard Tancock (1964), references to which are incorporated in the body of the text.

9.  See above (*Introduction*, n. 3) for the *intradiegetic* narrator. For an excellent review of contemporary theories, see also Wallace Martin, *Recent Theories of Narrative* (1986). I am also indebted to the classic American discussion of point of view and the 'self-conscious' narrator, Wayne Booth's *Rhetoric of Fiction* (revised edn 1983).

10. See the more extended comparison of narrative technique in Brookner and Austen with reference to *A Friend from England* (ch. 3).

11. There is a celebrated exchange between Seymour Chatman/Nelson Goodman and Barbara Herrnstein Smith in *On Narrative* (ed. W. J. T. Mitchell). Smith's essay ('Narrative Versions, Narrative Theories' 209–32), denying Genette's concept of 'first narrative', is a sustained and informed critique of certain basic tenets of structuralist narratology. Although Smith would seem to have the better of this exchange – in spite of the right of reply allowed to Chatman and Goodman in this volume – I have still tentatively used this central concept of narratology. For further discussion, see the introduction to my *Tell-Tale Theories* (1989), 11–22.

12. For the simplest account of the hierarchical structure of narrative, see Rimmon-Kenan (1983), ch. 7: 'Narration: levels and voices'.

## CHAPTER 3:  NOVEL DEPARTURES

1.  The terminology is based on categories proposed by Dorrit Cohn (see *Introduction* n. 4).

2.  If *Hotel du Lac* has interesting thematic parallels with *The Mill on the*

*Floss, A Friend from England* has an equally striking analogue with Eliot's novel, in its extensive use of water metaphors (see ch. 3). For more detailed treatment of this motif in *The Mill on the Floss*, see W. C. Knoepflmacher, 'Of Time, Rivers and Tragedy: George Eliot and Matthew Arnold', *Victorian Newsletter*(33), 1–5; Jerome Thale, 'Image and Theme: *The Mill on the Floss*.' *University of Kansas City Review* (23), 227–34.

3.  I am thinking of a classic structural analysis of *Wuthering Heights* by Dorothy Van Ghent in her *Form and Function in the English Novel* (1966).

4.  The unsuitability of this term, with its strong extra-literary associations, is discussed by Dorrit Cohn in the introduction to *Transparent Minds* (4f).

5.  On the problems of focalization in the latter, compared with those encountered in *Hotel du Lac*, see my *Tell-Tale Theories* (1989), ch. 3, 'The Limits of Narratology: Ford Maddox Ford's *The Good Soldier*'.

6.  Walter Ong's argument is developed in the opening chapters of *Orality and Literacy* (1982).

7.  See Belsey's *Critical Practice*, esp. ch. 6 (125–46), 'Towards a Productive Critical Practice'.

8.  The term 'character-indicator' is borrowed from Rimmon-Kenan (1983), see ch.5, 'Text: characterization' (59–67).

9.  See Barthes's *S/Z*, and the author's withering comments on the cultural codes underlying *Sarrasine* (Divagation LXXXVII 'The Voice of Science', 205f).

10. For a comprehensive and highly suggestive application of Jakobson's distinction between *metonym* and *metaphor*, see David Lodge's *The modes of modern writing: metaphor, metonymy, and the typology of modern literature* (London: Edward Arnold, 1979).

11. Brookner presumably owes her highly-developed iconographic techniques as much to her own professional background as to an intimacy with the novels of James.

## CHAPTER 4:  CREATIVE RETURNS

1.  See for example Brookner's references to a 'grounding in nineteenth-century novels and nineteenth-century behaviour' (Haffenden, 27) or her 'grounding in the nineteenth-century novel' (Guppy, 158).

2.  Barthes's essay 'The reality effect' – concentrating on Flaubert – may be most conveniently found in Todorov's *French Literary Theory Today* (1982), 11–17.

3.  The distinction between 'story' and 'discourse' is the conventional one of structuralist narratology, and actually provides the title of Chatman's own synthesis of Russian formalist and French structuralist theory.

4.  On the orphan motif in Dickens, see, for example, Nina Auerbach, 'Incarnations of the Orphan', *ELH*42 (Fall 1975), 395–419.

5. See the note on Barbara Hardy's study of *Great Expectations* with reference to *A Start in Life* (ch. 1, n. 1).
6. See D. W. Harding, 'Regulated Hatred: An Aspect of the Work of Jane Austen' (1940), published in William Heath (ed.), *Discussions of Jane Austen* (Boston: Heath, 1961); Marvin Mudrick, *Irony as Defense and Discovery*(Princeton: Princeton University Press, 1953); John Halperin, *The Life of Jane Austen* (Baltimore: The Johns Hopkins University Press, 1984).
7. See especially the chapter 'Symbolic Imagery' (123–38) in Austen Warren's *Rage for Order* (Ann Arbor: University of Michigan Press, 1959).
8. See Susan Sontag, *Illness as Metaphor* [published with *AIDS and its Metaphors*] (New York: Anchor Books, 1990) .
9. For water metaphors in Eliot's *The Mill on the Floss*, see ch. 2, n. 2.
10. There is another interesting analogue here with James. One remembers E. M. Forster's witty account of everything that had to be left out before James could 'do us a novel' (*Aspects of the Novel*, 161).
11. See Jim Phelan's recent new study of character (*Reading People and Reading Plots*), discussed in the introduction to this study. Rimmon-Kenan's mediation between *mimetic* and *semiotic* theories (*Narrative Fiction*, 31–34) is also extremely helpful: 'In the text characters are nodes in the verbal design; in the story they are – by definition – non (or pre-) verbal abstractions, constructs' (33).
12. This kind of 'bifurcation' in Dickens is related to the 'fairy-tale' dimension of his fiction; in this context, see Michael Kotzin, *Dickens and the Fairy Tale* (Bowling Green, Ohio: Bowling Green University Press, 1972); Fred Kaplan, *Dickens and Mesmerism. The Hidden Springs of Fiction* (Princeton: Princeton University Press, 1975).
13. Dorrit Cohn offers a simple test for distinguishing between psycho-narrative and narrated monologue: in the latter case, a character's thoughts only require minor changes at the deictic level in order to be converted to hypothetical direct speech.
14. Cohn discusses this distinction for third person narratives in ch. 1, 'Psycho-Narration' (26–32), and for first person narratives in ch. 4, 'Retrospective Techniques' (143–60). I have elsewhere applied Cohn's methods to modes of consciousness in *The Great Gatsby* (*Tell-Tale Theories*, 115–34).

## CHAPTER 5:   FICTIONS OF THE SELF

1. See especially A-J. Greimas's *Structural Semantics; an attempt at a method* (Lincoln, Nebraska: Nebraska University Press, 1983).
2. See James Olney's collection, *Autobiography: Essays Critical and theoretical* and Avrom Fleishman's *Figures of Autobiography* (Berkeley: University of California Press, 1983), especially part (iii). 'The Fiction of Autobiographical Fiction'. Note also the striking *mise en abyme* in Fleishman's introduction: 'As this book declined and swelled over the years, I have come to think of it as *my* autobiography' (xiii).

3. Walter Benjamin, 'The Storyteller' in *Illuminations* (trans. Harry Zohn, 1969), quoted and discussed by Peter Brooks (*Reading for the Plot* 22, 28).
4. See my essay, 'Philip Larkin by Philip Larkin', *Ariel* (January 1989), 77–95).
5. The phrase is used by Paul-Gabriel Boucé in his excellent study *The Novels of Tobias Smollett* (English trans. 1976). Smollett is another author dogged by fairly crude critical speculation on the autobiographical element in his fiction. Boucé therefore develops a useful distinction between 'explicit autobiography' and a more implicit 'self-portraiture' (ch. 2, 40–67).
6. The phrase is borrowed from Barthes's 'anti-biography' *Roland Barthes par Roland Barthes*.

# Bibliography

Alter, Robert. *Partial Magic. The Novel as a Self-conscious Genre*. Berkeley: University of California Press, 1975.

Auerbach, Nina. 'Incarnations of the Orphan.' *ELH* 42 (Fall 1975), 395–419.

Austen, Jane. *Mansfield Park*, ed. Tony Tanner. Harmondsworth: Penguin, 1966.

Bal, Mieke. *Narratology. Introduction to the Theory of Narrative*. Toronto: University of Toronto Press, 1985.

Balzac, Honoré de. *Eugénie Grandet*. trans. Marion Ayton Crawford. Harmondsworth: Penguin, 1985.

Barber, Michael. Interview with Anita Brookner, *Books and Bookmen* (March 1983), 26–7.

Barthes, Roland. *Roland Barthes by Roland Barthes*. trans. Richard Howard. New York: Hill & Wang, 1977.

——, *S/Z*. trans. Richard Miller. New York: Hill & Wang, 1974.

——, 'The reality effect', in Tzvetan Todorov, ed., *French Literary Theory Today*. Cambridge: Cambridge University Press, 1982. 11–17.

Belsey, Catherine. *Critical Practice*. London: Methuen, 1980.

Benjamin, Walter. 'The Storyteller', in *Illuminations*, trans. Harry Zohn. New York: Schocken Books, 1969.

Boucé, Paul-Gabriel. *The Novels of Tobias Smollett*. London: Longman, 1976.

Bremond, Claude. *Logique du récit*. Paris: Seuil, 1973.

Brookner, Anita. *Kaleidoscope*, 18 October 1984 (radio interview with Richard Mayne).

Brooks, Peter. *Reading for the Plot. Design and Intention in Narrative*. Oxford: Clarendon Press, 1984.

Burgess, Anthony. *Horizon*, 9 November 1989 (radio discussion with Gore Vidal).

Caws, Mary Ann. *Reading Frames in Modern Fiction*. Princeton: Princeton University Press, 1985.

Chatman, Seymour. *Story and Discourse*. Ithaca, N.Y.: Cornell University Press, 1978.

Cohn, Dorrit. *Transparent Minds. Narrative Modes for Presenting Consciousness in Fiction*. Princeton: Princeton University Press, 1978.

Conrad, Joseph. *Heart of Darkness*. Harmondsworth: Penguin, 1983.

Daley, Mary. *Gyn/Ecology: The Metaethics of Radical Feminism*. Boston: Beacon Press, 1979.

Constant, Benjamin. *Adolphe*.trans. Leonard Tancock. Harmondsworth: Penguin, 1964.

De Man, Paul. 'Autobiography as Defacement', *Modern Language Notes* 94 (1979), 919–30.

——, *Allegories of Reading. Figural Language in Rousseau, Nietzsche, Rilke and Proust*. London: Yale University Press, 1981.

——, *Blindness and Insight. Essays in the Rhetoric of Contemporary Criticism.* Minneapolis: University of Minnesota Press, 1983.

Dickens, Charles. *Great Expectations,* ed. Angus Calder. Harmondsworth: Penguin, 1965.

Eberstadt, Fernanda. Review of *A Misalliance, New York Times Book Review* (29 March 1987), 10.

Felman, Shoshana. 'Psychoanalysis and Education: Teaching Terminable and Interminable', *Yale French Studies* 63 (1981), 21–44.

Fleishman, Avrom. *Figures of Autobiography.* Berkeley: University of California Press, 1983.

Ford, Ford Madox. *The Good Soldier.* Harmondsworth: Penguin, 1972.

Genette, Gérard. *Narrative Discourse.* trans. Jane E. Lewin. Oxford: Basil Blackwell, 1980.

Gide, André. *The Counterfeiters [Les Faux-Monnayeurs].* trans. Dorothy Bussy. Harmondsworth: Penguin, 1966.

Greimas, Algirdas. *Du Sens.* Paris: Seuil, 1970.

——, *Structural Semantics: an attempt at a method.* trans. Daniele McDowall, Ronald Schleifer and Alan Velie. Lincoln, Nebraska: Nebraska University Press, 1983.

Guppy, Shusha. Interview with Anita Brookner. *The Paris Review* (Fall 1987), 147–69.

Haffenden, John. 'Playing Straight'. Interview with Anita Brookner, *The Literary Review* (September 1984), 25–31.

Halperin, John. *The Life of Jane Austen.* Brighton: The Harvester Press, 1984.

Harding, D. W. 'Regulated Hatred in Jane Austen' (1940) in William Heath (ed.), *Discussion of Jane Austen.* Boston: Heath, 1961.

Hardy, Barbara. *The Moral Art of Dickens.* London: Athlone Press, 1970.

Hopkins, Viola. 'Visual Art Devices and Parallels in the Fiction of Henry James'. *PMLA* 76 (1961), 561–74.

Hutcheon, Linda. *A Theory of Parody.* London: Methuen, 1985.

Iser, Wolfgang. *The Act of Reading.* Baltimore: The Johns Hopkins University Press, 1978.

James, Henry. *Daisy Miller,* ed. Geoffrey More. Harmondsworth: Penguin, 1986.

——, *Washington Square.*ed. Brian Lee. Harmondsworth: Penguin, 1984.

Jones, Robert. Review of *Hotel du Lac, Commonweal* (20 September 1985), 502–3.

Kaplan, Fred. *Dickens and Mesmerism. The Hidden Springs of Fiction.* Princeton: Princeton University Press, 1975.

Kemp, Peter. 'The mouse that whinged'. Review of *Lewis Percy, Sunday Times* (27 August 1989), G6.

Kenyon, Olga. *Women Novelists Today.* Brighton: The Harvester Press, 1988.

——, Olga. *Women Writers Talk.* Oxford: Lennard Publishing, 1989.

Knoepflmacher, U. C. 'Of Time, Rivers and Tragedy: George Eliot and Matthew Arnold.' *Victorian Newsletter* (33), 1–5.

Kotzin, Michael. *Dickens and the Fairy Tale.* Bowling Green, Ohio: Bowling Green University Press, 1972.

Larkin, Philip. *Collected Poems*. ed. Anthony Thwaite. London: Faber & Faber, 1988.

Leavitt, David. Review of *Latecomers, New York Times Book Review* (2 April 1989), 94.3.

Lejeune, Philippe. *On Autobiography*. trans. Katherine Leary. Minneapolis: University of Minnesota Press, 1989.

Lessing, Wendy. Review of *Providence, Hudson Review* 37, 478–9.

Lodge, David. *The modes of modern writing*. London: Edward Arnold, 1979.

Macherey, Pierre. *A Theory of Literary Production*. trans. Geoffrey Wall. London: Routledge & Kegan Paul, 1978.

Mars-Jones, Adam. Review of *Hotel du Lac, New York Review of Books* (31 January 1985), 17–18.

Mitchell, W. J. T. (ed.), *On Narrative*. Chicago: University of Chicago Press, 1981.

Moretti, Franco. *The Way of the World. The Bildungsroman in European Culture* London: Verso, 1987.

Mudrick, Marvin. 'Character and Event in Fiction', *Yale Review* 50 (1961), 202–18.

Morrisette, Bruce. *Novel and Film. Essays in Two Genres*. Chicago: University of Chicago Press, 1985.

Olney, James (ed.), *Autobiography. Essays Theoretical and Critical*. Princeton: Princeton University Press, 1980.

Ong, Walter. S. J. *Orality and Literacy*. London: Methuen, 1982.

Phelan, James. *Reading People, Reading Plots*. Chicago: University of Chicago Press, 1989.

Propp, Vladimir. *Morphology of the Folktale*. Austin: University of Texas Press, 1968 (orig. publ. 1928).

Rimmon-Kenan, Shlomith. *Narrative Fiction: Contemporary Poetics*. London: Methuen, 1983.

Samarth, Manini. 'The Internalized Narrative: A Study of Lyricism and Irony in the Novels of Anita Desai and Anita Brookner' (unpublished dissertation, Purdue University), 1988.

Skinner, John. *Philip Larkin by Philip Larkin*. *ARIEL* 20,1 (January 1989), 77–95.

——, *Tell-Tale Theories: Essays in Narrative Poetics*. Turku: Annales Universitatis Turkuensis, 1989.

Smith, Barbara Herrnstein. *On the Margins of Discourse. The Relation of Literature to Language*. Chicago: University of Chicago Press, 1978.

——, 'Narrative Versions, Narrative Theories', in Mitchell (1981), 209–32.

Smith, Stevie. *Collected Poems*. ed. James NacGibbon. London: Faber & Faber, 1985.

Sontag, Susan. *Illness as Metaphor*. New York: Doubleday, 1989.

Spender, Dale. *Man Made Language*. London: Routledge & Kegan Paul, 1980.

Taliafero, Frances. Review of *Providence, Harper's Magazine*, (February 1984), 268: 75–6.

Thale, Jerome. 'Image and Theme: *The Mill on the Floss*.' University of Kansas City Review (23), 227–34.

Tyler, Ann. Review of *Hotel du Lac, New York Times Book Review* (3 February 1985), 1, 31.

Updike, John. Review of *Latecomers. New Yorker* (1 May, 1989), 111–13.

Van Ghent, Dorothy. *The English Novel: Form and Function,* New York: Harper Torchbooks, 1966.

Warren, Austen. *Rage for Order.* Ann Arbor: University of Michigan Press, 1959.

Waugh, Patricia. *Feminine Fictions: revisiting the postmodern.* London: Routledge, 1989.

Weinstein, Arnold. *Fictions of the Self: 1550–1800.* Princeton: Princeton University Press, 1981.

Wharton, Edith. *The Age of Innocence.* London: Virago, 1988.

# Index

```
823.914    Skinner, John,
SKI          1945-

           The fiction of Anita
           Brookner.

                                    33716
$35.00
```

| DATE | | | |
|---|---|---|---|
| | | | |
| | | | |
| | | | |
| | | | |
| | | | |
| | | | |
| | | | |
| | | | |
| | | | |
| | | | |
| | | | |
| | | | |
| | | | |